CONTENTS

COOK, EAT, REPEAT: these words, the day-in, day-out, never-endingness of it all, no doubt sum up the Sisyphean drudgery of cooking for those who resent time spent at the stove. For those who, like me, find structure, meaning and an intense aliveness in the rhythms of the kitchen, they represent an essential liberating truth.

Cooking is not something you do, and then it's finished with. It is a thread woven through our lives, encompassing memory, desire and sustenance, both physical and emotional. It can never be an end in itself. We return to dishes we love, not just because they mean something particular to us, but also because our hands feel comfortable preparing food that is familiar. Life is full of challenges – not a bad thing in itself, of course – and although there seems to be an ever-increasing amount of pressure to rise to the occasion of cooking something new and complex and unfamiliar (also, assuredly, not a bad thing), it becomes *our* food only when it eases its way into our repertoire, that list of dishes we return to and repeat, a list that grows and changes, to be sure, just as we grow and change.

But what seems essential to me, as a home cook, is that however many times we cook a recipe, and perhaps especially when we cook it so many times it ceases to feel like a recipe at all, we never exactly replicate it. In winter, pans will be colder than in summer, so cooking times will be different. That is, perhaps, a plodding example. But ingredients vary all the time, as do our moods, and if we'd expect the former to make a difference, I have found over the years that it is no less true of the latter. When I test recipes – and this is even the case with baking, where the precision required would seem to guarantee some degree of uniformity – I am freshly astonished how each time there will be some small variation in either cooking process or outcome. I find freedom in this, and feel grateful that we who cook in our homes, as distinct from those who cook professionally in restaurants, do not have to be shackled by the creativity-draining need for consistency. Quite apart from the variables I have no control over – a lesson in itself – cooking at home in the normal run of things simply allows for less freighted experimentation.

But if my defence of repetition seems at odds with my championing of a less confining or conformist approach, I can assure you that it is this dynamic relationship – between reliance on familiarity and curiosity about the as-yet-untried – that underpins, perhaps even defines, what cooking is all about. For cooking, like life, in order to be manageable, enjoyable even, relies on both structure and spontaneity. We all need a framework, but we also have to know when to break free and just go with the flow. And this is something you learn as you go along.

If repetition sounds boring to you, rest assured I don't mean cooking the same recipes week in week out (although under the many pressures of everyday life, it is easy to fall into such a rut), but that cooking relies on many repeated actions that, added up, teach us ease in the kitchen, and help us acquire that instinct which too many perceive as being some innate gift.

It is precisely in those many mindless, mundane, repeated actions that cooking consists of, that allows it to be a means of decompression for so many of us. I have tried to meditate many times, and not always successfully; cooking might well be the nearest I can get to a meditative act. The routine busyness of all the peeling and chopping and stirring can be a balm for the buzzing brain. So many of the kitchen activities we might dread not because they are difficult but because they are monotonous – peeling two kilos of potatoes, say – are exactly what free us up, allowing us to relax or at least wind down a little. Of course, peeling a potato is not exactly mindless, but unless one has never peeled potatoes before, it is not something that requires hyper-vigilance. It's quietly absorbing. And as someone who is terminally fidgety, I am gratefully soothed by the many necessary low-level kitchen rituals that constitute cooking. Just enough focus is required to silence that chattering monkey-mind. Because one is doing something so familiar, so unthinkingly rehearsed, one isn't on high alert, but can let the senses – touch, smell, sight, sound – take over from intellect. Indeed, in all cooking one has to learn to let the senses take over: onions caramelising in a pan start sounding different as they cook; a cake in the oven smells suddenly more of itself when it's ready. It takes practice to trust your senses, but essentially that's what cooking is: a practice, like doing yoga is a practice, and not a performance. I'm not saying that the kitchen is always necessarily a zen place to be, but it can be a safe space for the frenetic soul.

Novice cooks shouldn't be daunted by my emphasis on the lessons taught by experience; we all have to start somewhere, and even if you're starting at the beginning, you soon learn how those small tasks and processes that you are obliged to do to get dinner on the table are transferable to the next, new recipes, as yet untried. For me, it is the essential repetitiveness of cooking that takes the pressure off. It's not now-or-never: every day, every meal, is another opportunity. And herein lies the particular joy of leftovers, when ingredients are repeated, reworked, to make something new and different. This is very much the province of the home cook, and it gives me pleasure, with many of these recipes, to suggest how they might be repurposed on another day or in different circumstances.

Food, for me, is a constant pleasure: I like to think greedily about it, reflect deeply on it, learn from it; it provides comfort, inspiration, meaning and beauty as well as sustenance and structure. More than just a mantra, 'cook, eat, repeat' is the story of my life.

Mackerel Plaki

Crème Brûlée
1 Pint cream add 1 oz Sugar
                    Stick
                    and
               old then
               & well
               egg yolks the
               whip
               cream
               dish
               water in
               let it
               over
               of caster
               under

Paprika Worcester sauce
of is salter   Cream god
        dish.

the
ENGL
COOK
BOO

Edilen

Lucy
Nic

INGRE
these days
of fat, eac
with the
are no ris
Raising F
actual co
single bat
These co
to get th

Evening Standard.

Song and the

WHAT IS A RECIPE?

In writing recipes, I have had to learn another language. Indeed, my initial interest in writing about food was a linguistic one: how could I use language to convey a realm that lay so far beyond it? Simile and metaphor can often evoke the flavours of a dish, the textures the cook must aim for, so much more directly than the most rigorously precise description. A recipe has to take root in the reader's imagination. I learned this long before I started writing about food, at a time when I never considered it a possibility, or even knew to consider it a possibility. When I was in my teens and obsessed with Aldous Huxley, I was struck by an account of a young man's first taste of champagne in *Time Must Have a Stop*, a book I haven't read for over forty years, in case I find my youthful fervour be replaced with irritation. It tasted, the young man thought like 'an apple peeled with a steel knife'. This is not a scientifically accurate description, but it speaks truly to the senses. It lets you feel that sharp effervescence, taste that sherbetty tang, and conveys the wincing abruptness of that first, unexpected sip.

Of course, a recipe cannot rest on evocative language at the cost of precision. However imaginatively written, a recipe is worthless if it is not reliable. It's not a prose poem, after all: it has to convey information, and clearly. But clarity and precision are not quite the same thing. For precision has a way of tripping us up, and this is as true for the person writing a recipe as for the person following it. I struggle, as many food writers do, with just how precise to be, and my books reflect how I feel at any given time about what is helpful and what is confining. In some books, I have decided that stipulating 'a large onion' is advice enough; in others, I give an approximate weight, say 150g; sometimes, I have just called for an onion. And sometimes, I can vary the urgency of my commands within a single book. The truth is, the weight of an onion, or the size of it, is not always critical; perhaps – within normal parameters – rarely so. When I give weights and measurements for onions, carrots or leeks in a stew, it is because I feel it might be helpful to give an indication of what I tend to use, but in truth this is in itself a false accuracy, and is really mere happenstance. That's to say, it may be based on nothing more than the onions, carrots or leeks I pulled out of the vegetable drawer. There is a part of me that feels it is only fair to record faithfully what I have done, but if that is then read as an absolute instruction, then I am misleading my readers; the word 'approx.' can often ease the anxious recipe-writer's heart.

But nothing gives me more disproportionate angst than the question of serving sizes. I live in fear of not providing enough to eat or, conversely, inviting waste. And yet it is impossible to know exactly how many people any recipe definitively feeds. There are simply too many variables: the age and appetite of the eaters; what other food is served alongside the recipe in question; how much each person has had to eat previously; what time of day the meal is; even – as I've said before – the size of the plates and serving dishes. It all makes an unknowable, constantly shifting difference. And so I gently remind myself, and you, that the recipe-writer's role is to be a guide in the kitchen, not its ruling monarch.

Now I know I said in my introduction that however many times one cooks any particular dish, it is never replicated exactly; I also know that when writing a recipe (or following one, at least for the first time) I need to believe this is possible. Recipe writing can be a dangerous job for the control freak: I get inordinately exercised over every little detail, wanting to bring the reader with me into my kitchen, at the same time as my being in theirs as they cook. This kind of approach is no friend of minimalism or brevity: every instruction begs a yet-unanswered question, and I – perhaps foolishly – want to pre-empt every possible query. I see my job as part enthusiast, part troubleshooter. It is perhaps not the best recipe for serenity, but it's the only way I know to make sure the recipe really works. Besides, the general assumption that a long recipe indicates a complicated dish is a misguided one. A short recipe that fits neatly onto one page of a book may indeed satisfactorily reflect that it is a simple one, but often it just means that details which could help the cook have been jettisoned. A case in point: I try to remember to give the diameter of any saucepan I am using for any particular recipe. I know, of course, that you have the saucepans you have, and will use them; I'm not expecting you to go out and buy a saucepan of the selfsame dimensions, but it may help you to know what my timings are based on. We are all cooking under different conditions, with different implements, on different stoves, after all. And further to that, timings alone will not always suffice: you need to know what you're looking for. Sometimes this can be explained, but I admit, too, that in many cases a cooking process owes more to habit than anything else.

When I began writing about food, I defined a recipe as essentially an account of how I'd cooked something once. I saw it as a framework, to a certain degree a starting point. Some of this I still hold true. A recipe can indeed be, for any number of people who read it, no more than an encouraging suggestion of something good to eat. But before I'd even finished my first book, I realised that no recipe – or none that I wanted to write – could be an account of a dish I'd cooked just once. Recipe testing, while pleasurable, is arduous. Even one that comes out right the first time cannot be filed away as completed. It is only by cooking any recipe a number of times that I see how it could be simplified or improved. And it is not even enough that a recipe works: it needs to demand its way into my repertoire. If I don't want to keep cooking it, I don't want to waste your time with it. Along the way, many friends are given not-yet-recipes to cook in their kitchens. This isn't because I distrust my own instincts, but I need to know they have been convincingly conveyed. Not that I have any time for the focus-group approach: while I always want to know how my food fares in other people's kitchens, a recipe can reflect only one person's palate. And here, much as I enjoy creative collaboration, I am an absolute dictator. But given this, it is to me something short of a miracle that a recipe can have such widespread currency: we all have different tastes, come from varied cultures, have our own particular prejudices and predilections. I sometimes feel that a successful recipe – by which I mean one that takes root in many kitchens, many lives – is not just a unit of shared enthusiasm so much as a magical undertaking, anchored in practicality, that is entered into with abandon. It is, thus, a hopeful act of communality.

A recipe can be many things: a practical document; a piece of social history; an anthropological record; a family legacy; an autobiographical statement; even a literary exercise. You don't have to take your pick: the glory of food is that, beyond sustenance, it comprises a little of everything – aesthetics and manual labour, thrown in.

There is a particular immediacy about a recipe, in that it can never be written for posterity. Even if it endures long after its author, it is a message entirely in the present. There is often something unbearably poignant about old photographs – those hopeful faces, trapped in time, not knowing anything of the depredations of the future. Old recipes can seem similarly guileless, similarly vulnerable. It is not so much that the people for whom the recipes were written no longer exist, but that the food itself can often seem so unrecognisable, even alien, to us now: such urgent sustenance reduced to historical interest. Recipes from our recent past can seem yet more quaint: sometimes baffling; often risible. The decorative centrepiece (itself a somewhat dated concept) on both my grandmothers' summer tables, and on my mother's, too, for at least the first ten years of my life (resolutely not family food but when Entertaining-with-a-capital-E) was a whole poached salmon, covered with overlapping slices of cucumber to denote scales, laid out with ghoulish jauntiness. When I think of it now, I don't so much get waylaid by the styling, but hear so clearly my paternal grandmother, her beringed fingers with their long red nails waggling in my face, while she gave me, as she saw them, eternal and essential directions for poaching a salmon: namely that the salmon must be covered with cold water, aromatics thrown in – an airy wave at this point – brought gradually to a simmer, allowed to bubble gently for 10 minutes, then – and here she gave an abrupt twist of the hand to indicate the switching off of the flame – left to get cold.

So many recipes are remembered in this way, passed down through families, a living legacy so precious that we often mistake it for a sacred authority that – my grandmother's insistence notwithstanding – deeper scrutiny questions. My late mother-in-law, Carrie Diamond, once told me a story that she'd heard on a radio programme about how recipes are inherited. A home cook was discussing her family's pot roast recipe, which began with the instruction to cut both ends off the piece of meat. The interviewer asked why. The woman didn't know. She said she did it because her mother had always done it. They rang her mother and asked her. She, in turn, replied that she didn't know, but her mother had always done it. The grandmother then came on the line. Oh, she said, I just didn't have a casserole big enough. (Rest assured, though, this is no story about waste: it was understood that the offcuts were to be used for soup.) I smile every time I think of that, and I think of it often as I cook or write a recipe.

I fear that many times if I were asked by a reader why I do something the way I do, my answer would have to be either that it's the way my mother always did, or that I had to make the recipe work with what I had in my kitchen and saw no reason to revise my method in future tests. It doesn't mean there couldn't be another way of cooking it. And if I do, later, find myself making an old, trusted, familiar dish in a different way – with a new piece of equipment or an ingredient I hadn't cooked with before – it still doesn't invalidate my earlier instructions. I am not good at authority, even my own, and I often make my recipes with a rebellious disregard for my directives or commands. Nor do I mind if you do the same. I admit, though, that it is disconcerting when, on their first attempt, someone chooses to change everything and then actually complains that the recipe hasn't worked (a common gripe among food writers). But if you've made a recipe of mine and then want, reasonably enough, to play with it to suit yourself, or need even from the outset to make adjustments, you are right to do so. In fact, it is immensely rewarding, a real joy, to witness a monologue become a conversation. A recipe, much like a novel, is a living collaboration between writer and reader. And in both cases, it is the reader who keeps it alive.

When I started off, I assumed that readers would bring their own tastes and touches to my recipes, and was somewhat surprised by some of the questions raised by my excellent US editor when *How to Eat* was being translated into American. When I said 'fresh parsley to sprinkle over at the end', he asked, 'How much parsley do you mean?' Perhaps it is never a good idea to answer a question with a question, but my response, namely 'What business is it of mine how much parsley people sprinkle over their food?', certainly didn't settle the issue. But if guidance is helpful, I am more than happy to give it. After all, even if parsley-sprinkle levels of precision are not needed when you cook, you do need to know how much to buy before you cook a recipe. And so I have grown accustomed to being a little more specific with my stipulations. But a strange thing has happened in recipeland in the past few years: a recipe now is required to be both utterly precise and yet shape-shiftingly flexible. As soon as a recipe goes out into the world, people will clamour to know how it can be made gluten-free or vegan; someone who doesn't like chocolate (yes, those people exist) will ask how they can make my chocolate cake with something else; anchovy haters will request a substitute in a recipe for roast lamb with anchovies. I could give different answers to all these queries, with varying levels of helpfulness or politeness. To work backwards: it might seem rude to tell the haters of chocolate or anchovies to choose another recipe, and I don't think I have yet done so; but if I suggest that the offending ingredients simply be left out, it necessarily follows that they will be making another recipe, and one that won't perhaps taste as good as a recipe that wasn't intended to include them in the first place. As much as I can, I do offer alternatives when asked for them – black olives or yeast extract such as Marmite, say – but they can be only suggestions: if I haven't tested a recipe in a different incarnation, I can only guess at the result achieved, not be utterly confident in it. But cooking in real life necessarily involves compromise; a recipe has to be open to this, and to be able to bend to the needs of the cook. Those of us who write recipes know that, but many who follow them are hesitant to do so without utter obeisance, asking permission to substitute an ingredient or deviate from the sacred text.

At the time of writing, however, shopping is restricted and many ingredients are in short supply, during a lockdown that forces everyone into their kitchens if they are to feed themselves. No one has the stifling luxury of inflexibility. It is never a question of a recipe working or not with a substituted ingredient, but a matter of letting an idea find another expression. When you think about using a different ingredient from one specified in a recipe, you need to think of what that ingredient is offering. Is it sourness or fattiness? Is it crunch or sweetness? At this point, the reader has to let go of the words on the page, and think only in terms of taste and texture. I am always happy to make suggestions, give pointers, or say what I would do, and often this leads to a quite other but even more pleasing rendition. Cooking, like life, is an experimental art.

When it comes to baking – which is where the gluten-free concerns are raised – I am more hesitant to pronounce on substitutions and deviations. Baking is predicated on precision, and even a small change can alter the outcome. I take full responsibility for a recipe I've written, and therefore tested, but if I am asked by someone whether they can change the flour in a cake recipe, sometimes the only honest answer is 'there's only one way to find out…', and it's an answer I have had to give often. But the more people a recipe pleases, the happier I am, and so with each cake recipe in this book, I have offered a gluten-free version when the outcome is just as good. Interestingly, in some cases – for example the Lemon and Elderflower Drizzle Cake on p.75, I positively prefer it, and so have led with that version.

If cooking for vegan friends, sometimes changing a vegetarian recipe to a vegan one is as simple as suggesting oil in place of butter, no harm done. But if the recipe in question contains cheese, I am more hesitant to suggest vegan cheese as an alternative. No, I'd go further: I am disinclined to offer vegan cheese as an alternative, as I cannot make a recipe with vegan cheese taste the way I mean the recipe to taste. This doesn't mean I am opposed to vegans using whatever alternatives they are happy with. Indeed, I would expect them to, and have faith that they are more conversant with appropriate substitutions than I am. As for changing a meat recipe to a vegan recipe, I am not sure that can be accommodated without starting again from scratch. But I regularly cook entirely vegan meals and feel that this has added to rather than taken away from my pleasure in cooking. Vegan baking is a technical challenge that I am always interested in exploring, but it could never feel right to me to give a recipe for a cake (or indeed, for anything) if the best that could be said for it was that it was 'good for vegan'. It needs always to be an unqualified joy.

To some, these explanations may seem defensive. However, I am not trying to defend myself, but defend the recipe form itself. It is flexible, it is accommodating, and it is open to, if not infinite, then certainly multifarious interpretation. But all these possible or putative variations have to be tried in the kitchen, not posited on paper. I sense that there is a growing belief that all recipes should be able to cater for everyone, and that writing a recipe that excludes any eater is a wrong that could be righted with a little goodwill. Quite apart from the technical constraints that make this impossible, there simply could not be space or time enough to give each recipe its fullest, most universal expression, although the obsessive in me would certainly like to. I sometimes imagine writing a one-recipe book, but that one recipe expanded to a multiplicity of possibilities; I fear, though, it would be a life's work even for someone who embarked on it when half my age. I used to think that some small concession to accessibility in this direction could be made by adding 'optional' to certain ingredients where possible. In the end, frazzled, I came to the conclusion that in a recipe you could argue both that all ingredients were optional and that none was.

But then this all becomes an abstract argument, and a recipe is the very antithesis of abstract. The recipes I write come from my life, my home. They tell a story, and that story is mine; I could not tell another's. I sometimes think that the appetite for recipes, for reading and writing about food and how we cook it, says just as much about our hunger for stories – these little condensed chronicles that say so much – as about our hunger for pleasure and sustenance. In the recipe form, these hungers are fused.

Never have I felt that more, or as painfully, than in reading *In Memory's Kitchen: A Legacy from the Women of Terezín* edited by Cara de Silva. This is a compilation of recipes from the inmates of the concentration camp of Theresienstadt who, imprisoned, starving and facing extinction, shared between them the recipes they'd grown up with, the recipes, as de Silva recounts, that said who they were, what was taken from them and what they longed to return to; recipes they argued over – whose version was the better one, why it should be cooked this way and not that way – and the recipes they hungered for. These women were telling stories to sustain themselves, stories that were about their identity, the identity that had put them in that concentration camp, an identity they clung to, as a way of clinging on to themselves and to life.

What makes these recipes so particularly, unbearably poignant is that they are written simply, practically. They are recipes to be followed, recipes they hoped to cook from again; they remain a living testimony.

A recipe should not have to bear this weight, or tell this story. I am glad and grateful we can quibble over ingredients, or look forward hopefully to lunch, choose which recipe we will cook for dinner, and then again the next day do the same.

A IS FOR ANCHOVY

For cooks, and certainly – if not emphatically – for this cook, anchovies are of the essence. Few other ingredients arrive in the kitchen with such confrontational pungency, and yet manage to imbue so many dishes with transformational subtlety. The bacon of the sea (and how I wish I could claim this coinage as my own, or even remember whom to credit for it), the anchovy's initial attack lies in its fierce and uncompromising saltiness, it's true, but it packs a double punch: after that first hit of saline intensity comes richness and depth, that resounding, flavour-enhancing savouriness we have learned to call *umami*. Meat has it, Parmesan has it, as do – *inter alia* – mushrooms, tomatoes, Marmite or Vegemite. It's a good word, but can be bandied about so excitably and so often, it begins to distract rather than elucidate. For that reason, I sometimes hesitate to use it, although I do gain a shy pleasure from saying it out loud: the reverberation it makes in your jaw as you utter the word agreeably echoes the deep rumbling of the taste it denotes. But for all that umami is indeed generally understood to be the fifth taste – after salty, sweet, bitter and sour – it is more than that alone; I think of it rather as *oomph*, another word that is deliciously satisfying to pronounce.

The oomph of anchovies is undeniable. I am talking here not of fresh anchovies, the marinated *alici* of Italy or *boquerones* of Spain, silvery and soft (fine enough, but often served a little too vinegary for my taste), but rather the salted or cured version, those mink-brown strips of almost caramelly saltiness that come chiefly in tins, and such beautiful tins, too, if you get the good ones. We have come to use 'processed', in relation to food, as a byword for all manner of iniquities, shorthand for newfangled dietary debasement; the anchovy provides the ancient, eloquent case for the defence.

Not for everyone, though: the anchovy is a divisive ingredient. Much as I feel there is scarcely a savoury dish that couldn't be improved by them, I am aware that anchovies instil disgust in many. The criticism generally levelled against them is that they are too fishy, which seems to me a slightly unfair way to criticise a fish. To what estate should they – those innocent, elemental anchovies – then aspire? It's true, undeniably so, that the pungency of anchovies can alarm many people, but melt them in olive oil at the start of making a stew, and when you, hours later, eat it, neither pungency nor fishiness is the quality you'd detect. Rather, they dissolve into the dish, bringing a rounded, almost oaky saltiness. I have made the beef stew with anchovies and thyme from *How to Eat* for self-professed anchovy-phobes for over twenty years now, and – with the exception of my children, naturally – there has been no dissent. It is annoying, I know, to tell people who protest that they don't like a particular foodstuff that they're wrong. I concede that there are those whose antagonism to the anchovy is insurmountable. This chapter is not for them. Food should never be a battleground. (Though I will just say that if your idea of an anchovy is that bristly, rusting shred of corrosive supersalinity that is left to curl up and die on top of an undistinguished pizza, you have been most lamentably misled. Also: Worcestershire sauce contains anchovies. But we move on.)

There are many ways for those who love anchovies to celebrate them, and I start with the simplest: take a slice of good bread, spread it thickly with sweet, unsalted butter, and drape some excellent Spanish anchovies on top. The butter should be neither so hard that it tears the bread, nor so soft that it greases rather than tops it. And by thickly, I mean to invoke that wonderful Danish term *tandsmør*, which translated literally means 'tooth butter', and is used to describe butter spread thickly enough on a slice of bread that when you bite into it you leave tooth marks. This for me is the perfect canapé – better than the fanciest, most curlicued cocktail-party offering. When I ate this once, at the Ristorante Ratanà in Milan, it came with some sweet, roasted and skinned peppers on the side (just hold a red pepper, with tongs, over a gas hob to char the skin, which you can then rub away, until the pepper is a tender silky rag, and continue with as many peppers as you'd like – or see p.204 for the hands-free oven method). The contrast was so good, I had to close my eyes, in concentrated rapture, as I ate.

But then, peppers and anchovies have had a long-standing and successful relationship. I sometimes make the recipe on p.202, but instead of dressing them with pomegranate molasses, I warm a little extra-virgin olive oil in a small pan, melt some anchovies in it – by melting, I mean add anchovy fillets and stir them around in the warm (not hot) oil until they dissolve into it – mince or grate in a clove or two of garlic, and continue stirring for a scant minute, making sure that the garlic doesn't colour. Take the pan off the heat and add some more olive oil, and a drop of vinegar – Moscatel, red wine, sherry, whichever vinegar you prefer, or indeed lemon juice – and pour this warm dressing, murky yes, but full of flavour, over the waiting peppers.

If I feel like sprinkling capers over it all, then I might forgo vinegar or lemon juice. Or you can just pour the olive oil over the peppers, lattice with anchovies, and dot with capers. When time is short, you can do exactly the same with a jar or two of those Italian chargrilled peppers *sott'olio*.

There is a good argument, too, for crisp buttered toast with anchovies on top, but here I favour sliced white plastic bread, the butter softly melting to a yellow pool: a home-grown take on Italian bruschetta or crostini. Indeed, when I lived in Italy in my late teens, and couldn't often afford to go to restaurants, I'd go to a bar, order a Campari soda and anchovy crostini. Three to a plate, the warm lozenge-shaped toasts were wiped with garlic and topped – in ascending order of deliciousness as well as expense – either with mozzarella, burrata or dribbly stracciatella, the creaminess (more properly, milkiness in the case of mozzarella) simply and perfectly offset by the singular anchovy fillet that made a salty stripe over each one.

I thought of these as I came across, only recently, a recipe for Canapés à la Crème in *Savouries à la Mode* by Mrs de Salis, published at the end of the nineteenth century, which instructs the cook to 'cut little rounds of bread, fry them a pale colour, curl some washed and boned anchovies and place on them, and pour over either Devonshire or whipped cream'. And you know what? These are rather good. Just cut out some rounds of bread with a glass or cookie cutter and fry them in butter and, if you take my advice rather than Mrs de Salis's, transpose the order and spread with clotted cream, and top with anchovies. I fear we are going into scone territory now, and I certainly do not wish to reignite the most tiresome debate in the land, namely whether the cream comes first or last. It may well be that I have, sadly, failed to convince you that these are worth trying, though they very much are; and best savoured with a glass of dry sherry. But I quite understand if you wish to take the crème out of these canapés and stick to the simple pairing of butter and anchovy.

Still, cream and anchovies always sing wonderfully together and, inspired by a recipe of Carla Lalli Music's, I make an intense and, yes, creamy anchovy and garlic dressing which is best suited to robust or bitter leaves: the crunch of cos; the red curl of radicchio; and certainly all chicories or endive. And I love it, too, on that much maligned lettuce, the iceberg. Whichever salad leaf you use, it is essential, I feel, to add toasted walnut pieces once the dressing's been tossed through.

Chop 4 anchovy fillets. Pour 5 tablespoons – or use an American 1/3 cup – of double cream into the sort of small pan that is intended as a butter-melter, if you have one. Add the chopped anchovies and the smallest pinch of ground mace along with a fat pinch (or 1/8 teaspoon) of sweet smoked paprika, or otherwise a go-for-it generous grinding of pepper. Mince or grate in 2 cloves of garlic or 1 very fat one. Heat as gently as you can, stirring with a little wooden spoon to mix everything and break up the anchovy fillets; most will seem to melt away as you stir and press the spoon against them, and almost instantly you will have the palest buff-coloured cream, flecked with paprika or pepper and the small dark dots of anchovy that haven't quite dissolved. When the anchovies have merged with the cream, simmer for 30 seconds, still stirring, just to thicken it a little, before taking it off the heat. Cover (my pixie pan doesn't have a lid, so I put a side plate on top of it) and leave to cool. If you don't have such a teeny-tiny saucepan, move faster and stir everything together just to warm it, without giving it the half-a-minute simmer.

I often do all this hours ahead, by the way, and feel it helps the flavours to mellow. Depending on how much in advance I do this and, indeed, the time of year, I decant it once cold to a baby bowl, and stash it covered in the fridge. I have to say, I always prefer to leave food I've cooked ahead in a cool place rather than the fridge, but in high summer, even I follow the health and safety instructions I'm encouraged to give.

Anyway, make sure the cream is not too chilly once you actually want to dress your salad, first beat vigorously and then more gently as you stir in 1 teaspoon of extra-virgin olive oil and a drop of vinegar (I like Moscatel vinegar here) or lemon juice and a few tablespoons of chopped chives. These are guidelines only: I just go by taste, and your taste may differ. Sometimes, too, I add a whisper of freshly grated Parmesan.

Without the oil and vinegar this makes a wonderful sauce – my idea of absolute heaven is a solo supper of steak and sprouting broccoli with this thick cream drizzled or spooned on top. Or just luxuriate in a baked potato, with the sauce mashed into its soft flesh, with or without the addition of chopped chives. I don't reheat the anchovy and garlic cream when I eat it as a sauce, although I do as an occasional treat make what I think of as the salt version of a steak au poivre. In other words, after I've cooked a steak, and when it's resting in a tightly sealed but baggy foil parcel, I add a little butter to the pan I've cooked it in, throw in some anchovy fillets, and stir to let them melt (over low heat) into the meaty, buttery juices, before adding some minced garlic, and then double cream, turning the heat higher, so that it all bubbles up. Take off the heat immediately. Release the steak from its foil wrapping and place on a warmed plate, quickly pouring the meat juices collected in the foil into the cream sauce. Stir well, add chopped chives, pour over the waiting steak. It's that simple. But then, cooking can be when you have an ingredient that does so much work on its own.

I feel I need hardly add that lamb can be accorded the anchovy treatment with alacrity. I have spent much of my cooking life, as have many of us, daggering cavities into lamb legs and shoulders to stuff with garlic, anchovy, rosemary or thyme so they may infuse the sweet meat with that familiar, heady, mingled aroma. But I do want, anyway, to say that an anchovy sauce is perfection with lamb, whether you make it ahead or deglaze the pan after, though when deglazing the pan after cooking lamb, I'd be more likely to leave the cream out, adding red vermouth or port in its place. And if there are more than two of us eating (or if it's me and a similarly greedy person), I go straight for the Anchovy Elixir (p.26), which we'll get to, and rhapsodically, later.

But then – and thank you for humouring my culinary stream of consciousness, which meanders, indeed, through this book – there are many plain cuts of meat and fish that can be almost instantly transformed by a final hit of anchovies. Oh, and scallops: how that makes their sweetness sing! In all cases, cook plainly then deglaze the pan with some butter or olive oil, or a mixture of both, along with anchovies, garlic, lemon zest and fresh thyme (or, for a fiercer rasp, chilli flakes in place of the thyme) and a slug of liquid of your choice, which can take in water, stock, vermouth, sherry and Marsala, just to cite the usual suspects; and bottles of each clutter my worktop a handgrab away from the hob.

Vegetables can be dressed in just such a mixture, though in which case I generally leave out the liquor, adding instead a sharp spritz of lemon juice, or Seville orange when in season: this is the only way I really like boiled carrots; true, it does add a subduing murkiness to their hopeful brightness, but only to look at. Steamed new potatoes similarly doused are one of the undeniable joys of spring. In winter, the much and unfairly disparaged Brussels sprout can be thus enlivened, too. I could go on, and I do find it hard to stop, so insistent is my enthusiasm. But I will leave the world of vegetables after proposing three other appropriate applicants for anchovising: namely kale, broccoli and spinach; in particular cavolo nero, or Tuscan kale, and Tenderstem broccoli, also called Broccolini (we'll come to the spinach shortly). Once you've melted some anchovy fillets in olive oil (use a suitably capacious pan that comes with a tightly fitting lid), stir in your garlic, lemon zest and chilli flakes, then add your chosen greens, toss well, and pour in a little water, just enough to steam the vegetables. Quickly clamp on the lid, and cook until unfashionably soft, checking regularly to make sure the pan's not burning dry, and if it is, just add a little more water; here's when you might consider a *spruzzata* of lemon juice, too, or splosh of dry white wine or vermouth. Once cooked and looking drab but tasting lively, these are ready – bar a final, grandiose pour of olive oil, your best – to be eaten as a side dish, main course (with a poached egg and perhaps some fried bread-crumbs on top) or pasta sauce, in which case you might consider a sprinkle of toasted pine nuts.

Spinach can certainly be treated exactly as above, but here are the two other ways that are on repeat in my house. First, and most comparably, though reaching back for the anchovy's ally, cream, I wilt the spinach completely and press down on it gently in a colander in the sink to get rid of excess water. For two people (possibly three), I'd use around 500g spinach as a side dish; I specify this, as it's always a matter of fresh amazement to me, even though I cook spinach more than once a week, how much you need to start off with and how little it cooks down to.

Pour a couple of tablespoons of olive oil into a wok-shaped pan, and over low heat melt 4 anchovy fillets, stirring well, then mince or grate in 2 fat cloves of garlic and keep stirring. Once the air is rich with their fug, add the wilted spinach, half at a time, tossing well after each addition. Keep tossing in the warm pan until the spinach is hot, then give a good grinding of pepper and grate in some nutmeg, and finally pour in a couple or so tablespoons of double cream, and stir or toss to incorporate. Add more cream if you want, then taste for seasoning, as always; I like anyway to grate a little more nutmeg on top before serving.

Everyone needs a quick and simple lunch or supper, a regular on auto-repeat, to rely on when the mind is focused elsewhere, or the schedule squeezed, leaving little time for organisation, shopping or cooking. This is mine: everything I need for it is always in the house; obviously, there's variation, but this is the basic premise and procedure. I boil a couple of eggs somewhere between soft and hard; by which I mean I put the eggs into a small pan of cold water, bring to the boil, let boil for 1 minute, then turn off the heat, and leave the eggs to sit in the water for 9 minutes. I wilt some spinach, but not so much that the leaves cook down completely, and when it's in my chosen bowl, I pour over a dressing made simply by shaking together extra-virgin olive oil and a little harissa (though there is a rich red seam of chilli pastes or sauces that would do) in one of the many empty mustard jars that line my kitchen windowsill. Once the spinach has been tossed in it, I top with the peeled and halved eggs and a tangle of anchovy fillets before giving a final drizzle of dressing, using a spoon to scrape out the terracotta-tinted sediment at the bottom of the jar.

Eggs and anchovies are the perfect union. I am always happy to add my breakfast poached egg to toast slathered in butter and striated with anchovy fillets. But you could go one step further and whip some butter, pepper, a little lemon zest and anchovy fillets together in a small bowl, if you're feeling fierce in the morning. Spread this over hot toast (I recommend rye, or really any bread that's tangy and hearty) and top with a poached egg or a peeled and schmushed boiled one; if you softly dollop with scrambled eggs instead, you're eating that gentlemen's college-and-club favourite, Scotch Woodcock. And I should say, I am always ready to Holstein anything, by which I mean top with a fried egg criss-crossed with anchovy fillets and dotted with a jaunty sprinkle of capers.

So many anchovian adumbrations, and yet there is some breathlessly eager part of me that feels that anything less than an exhaustive account of all my enthusiasms, taking in every possibility in any permutation, is a matter for eternal, anxious regret. It's a foolish way to look at it, I know, as the whole point about cooking is that there is always another way, another idea, another enthusiasm, another pleasure to share. One book can't do it all, or even, I think, one life, let alone one small chapter.

It would still be, for me, a failure too far to proceed to the discipline of the recipes proper in this chapter without according what is due to the unfamiliar but convincing alliance between anchovy butter and roast chicken. Melt 8 anchovy fillets in 2 tablespoonfuls of unsalted butter, mince or grate in 1 fat clove of garlic and the zest of a lemon. Whisk in 100g of butter to make a scant sauce and, once melted, add lemon juice to taste. (This Anchovy Butter Sauce is also glorious with asparagus.) Or, while the chicken's resting on its board, you can make a simple anchovy gravy. Pour the chicken juices from the roasting tin into a jug, and scrape the schmaltz – the chicken fat – left at the bottom of the tin into a saucepan, add a generous amount of butter and, over low heat, melt some anchovy fillets in it. Once these have dissolved into the pan, add minced or grated garlic, lemon zest, fresh thyme and a chilli flake or two. Stir for 30 seconds then throw in a slug of dry white wine or vermouth, let it bubble up, and then add the chicken juices waiting fragrantly in your jug. Season to taste (you may want a spritz of lemon juice, too) and bring to the table in a warmed gravy boat with a fork in it, so that it can be freshly whisked by each person as they pour.

Of course, you could equally well introduce anchovies to the roast Chicken with Garlic Cream Sauce on p.164. Or, finally – and I do promise that – you can make my Anchovy and Red Vermouth Gravy, which has the advantage of being able to be made in advance. Right, so here we go: gently cook a couple of onions, sliced into fine half-moons, in about 3 tablespoons of olive oil in a heavy-based saucepan, until the onions are golden and softened, though not completely – around 20 minutes – checking regularly to see they're not burning or sticking and giving a good stir as you do so. Now add 6 anchovy fillets to the pan, stirring until they've all but dissolved into the sweet onions. (This alone is just asking to be smeared on a piece of toast.) Turn the heat up to medium and stir in 1 tablespoon of plain flour, and to this gunge add – still stirring – 75ml of red vermouth and then 350–500ml of chicken stock, depending on whether you want school gravy or something a little more fluid. Turn the heat to high to bring it all to the boil, then clamp on a lid, turn the heat immediately back to low and leave to simmer: 10 minutes if you're making this in advance; 15 if you're serving it straightaway. Taste for seasoning before pouring into a warmed gravy boat or jug and bringing joyously to the table.

Obviously, this works wonderfully with beef, too, in which case use beef stock instead. And when the beef is cold, whether you served the anchovy gravy or not, it is crying out for the Caesar Mayo which my sister Horatia brought into my life.

So, very finely chop 8 anchovy fillets, and leave them on their board for now, then drop a large room-temperature egg yolk into a bowl (and have another egg, also at room temperature, handy) and add to it ½ teaspoon of Dijon mustard and start whisking; I like a balloon whisk for this. Keep whisking as you very, very gradually add 250ml of cold-pressed rapeseed oil: whisk fast; pour slowly. If you haven't got someone else to pour the oil as you whisk and hold the bowl, you should be able to steady it by placing a wet cloth underneath it. (Of course, you could use light olive oil, but the golden and mustardy rapeseed oil is always my first choice here.) If at any time the mayonnaise splits, just start again with your spare egg yolk, gradually whisk in the split mayonnaise as if it were oil, and calm should be restored to the universe. When all the oil's absorbed and you have a thick yellow mayonnaise in front of you, whisk in 2 tablespoons of lemon juice – and watch it suddenly lighten and brighten – followed by the chopped anchovies. Mince or grate in 1 fat clove of garlic, add 5 tablespoons of freshly grated Parmesan, and taste to see if you want more lemon juice; I often add a little more. Ditto the Parmesan. You may also want a good grinding of pepper. What you absolutely have to do, I'm sorry to say, is leave this in the fridge for half a day, overnight if possible, to let the flavours develop properly. Then you are ready to dollop this on cold beef, or use it to make a potato salad, cover cold, halved, hard-boiled eggs, serve as a dip (particularly with chicory) or find any number of ways to eat this. You won't find it hard.

I promised this would be the end of my opening arguments, and so it shall be. I am not abandoning my advocacy of anchovies in these pages quite yet, though. The three recipes that follow champion the cause eloquently enough.

SPAGHETTI WITH CHARD, CHILLI AND ANCHOVIES

I first ate this at a lovely restaurant, Fitzroy, in Fowey in Cornwall last Christmas, and knew that, once home, I had to make it myself. And I pretty much haven't stopped since.

I like to use rainbow chard, chiefly, because I find myself cheered the instant I get a beautiful bunch of it in the house. It's hard to believe it can even exist, with its ridiculously bright-hued stems – red, bright pink, orange, yellow, all jumbled together – and isn't just the product of a nursery-schoolchild's imagination. If I can't get rainbow chard, I happily settle for ruby chard, the stalks almost indistinguishable from the reddest of rhubarbs. But any chard, so long as it's tender, will do. And of course, do feel free to use cavolo nero, spinach, broccoli, beet tops or whatever else you may want, in place of the chard if you can't get any.

While there is no point pretending that the anchovies aren't central to this, it does seem a bit mean to give a recipe for pasta with vegetables without at least presenting a vegan-friendly alternative. I can't quite reproduce the oomph of the anchovies, but black olives, finely chopped, are a good enough substitution so long as you can find those intense semi-dried ones in foil pouches or vacuum packed in jars or good unpitted olives in olive oil; the ones in brine are disappointingly lacking. Or increase the garlic and stir in a dab of Marmite. On top of that (to boost the elusive umami, and to replace the saltiness further provided by the Parmesan), you will need expansive recourse to nutritional yeast flakes and be prepared to salt the water the pasta cooks in with even more abandon than usual.

I cook the chard in what's sometimes called a stir-fry pan – it looks rather like a wok, but has a flat bottom and comes with a lid – though any pot or pan that will have room for the spaghetti later, and which you can toss everything together in comfortably, would do. Or just use a medium-sized saucepan and toss pasta and sauce together in a warmed bowl.

Before we get to business, I feel I must share with you a frequent, favourite solo supper, which is an anchovian take on that simple Italian classic, *olio, aglio e peperoncino*; let us call it *olio, aglio e acciughe*. For 100g of spaghetti – and yes, I am marvelling at my restraint – I warm, when the pasta's nearly ready, 2 tablespoons of extra-virgin olive oil in a pan, then add anything from 4 to 6 anchovy fillets depending on how deep my need for that rich saltiness is (I'd start with 4 if I were you; shortly, though, I may be up to 8) and stir and press down on them so that they all but melt into the oil; I like a few shreds and small pieces still visible though. I add a pinch of chilli flakes, and finely grate in the zest of a lemon, and then mince or grate in 1 fat clove of garlic. Stir

everything about in the pan for a minute or so, then remove from the heat until the spaghetti's cooked. When it is, put the anchovy and garlic pan back on the heat and, using tongs, lift the spaghetti into the pan and toss to mix, slowly adding spoonfuls of the cooking water, until the pasta is lightly covered in this now emulsified sauce. Throw in a handful of freshly chopped parsley, toss well again, then greedily tip into a bowl, using a silicon spatula to get every last bit of anchovy sauce from the pan. Sprinkle with more parsley and eat with quiet joy, along with a cold glass of Gavi di Gavi, or an even colder (though very much less Italian) IPA.

I gladly make the spaghetti with chard, chilli and anchovies just for myself as well. While I concede it makes enough to serve two generously, I'm grateful for leftovers. It tastes excellent cold – especially with a little more extra-virgin olive oil and a spritz of lemon juice – even if this does sound idiosyncratic to Italians. But I dare say I have infuriated enough of them already by suggesting you grate over Parmesan or Pecorino Romano when you serve this first time out. The sacrosanct rules in Italy forbid cheese with pasta dishes that contain either a lot of garlic or fish: this is divinely abundant in both.

SPAGHETTI WITH CHARD, CHILLI AND ANCHOVIES

SERVES 2, heartily

300g rainbow (or other) chard (and see recipe intro)

3 x 15ml tablespoons extra-virgin olive oil, plus more to pour over at the end

8 anchovy fillets (from a jar or tin)

3 fat cloves of garlic

¼ teaspoon dried chilli flakes

125ml hot water from a just-boiled kettle

200g spaghetti

2–3 x 15ml tablespoons (approx. 15–20g) freshly grated Parmesan or Pecorino Romano, plus more to serve

For make-ahead, store and/or freeze notes, see p.332

1. Put a large saucepan of water on for the pasta and put the kettle on to boil at the same time.

2. Strip the leaves from the stalks of chard. Roll them up and slice finely, then leave to one side. Cut the stalks into 1–2cm pieces, depending on their girth.

3. Into a large pan, add the olive oil and the anchovies, and warm slowly, stirring and pressing down on the anchovies until they seem to melt into the oil.

4. Take off the heat, peel and mince or grate in the garlic, add the chilli flakes, then put back on the heat, this time turned up to medium, and stir briefly before adding the chopped chard stalks.

Turn the stalks around in the chilli-flecked anchovy oil for a minute or so to soak up the flavour.

5. Pour in the hot water – I use an American ½ cup here for ease of measuring – stir again, and bring to a bubble. Put the lid on the pan and cook at a fast simmer until the stalks are tender; this will take 5–7 minutes. If you're cooking with larger stemmed, more robust chard, then you may need to go for 10 minutes.

6. When the pasta water has come to the boil, salt it – it will rise up excitedly. Once it's calmed down again, drop in your spaghetti and cook according to the packet instructions, though start checking a couple of minutes before it says.

7. Add the shredded chard leaves to the stalks in their pan, give a good stir, replace the lid, and leave them to wilt in the hot pan. This could take anything from 2–4 minutes. Once they're ready, turn the heat off under the pan, keeping the lid on, while you wait for the pasta.

8. Use a pasta fork or tongs to add the cooked spaghetti straight to the waiting pan of chard. It doesn't matter if the pasta is dripping with water, as that starchy liquid will help thicken your sauce. Turn the spaghetti well in the chard and anchovy mixture; you may need to add up to 4 tablespoons (60ml) of cooking water as you toss everything together; go slowly, and stop when the chard seems to turn into a sauce that cleaves to the strands of spaghetti.

9. Grate over about 2 tablespoons' worth of Parmesan or Pecorino Romano and toss again, then give a generous pour of olive oil, and do likewise. Taste to see if you want more cheese or oil, and proceed accordingly, then turn into a warmed bowl or bowls, and bring the cheese, a grater and the bottle of olive oil to the table with you.

CELERIAC AND ANCHOVY GRATIN

I adore celeriac, that beautiful monstrosity with its stringy skin, its whorled and bumpy exterior – rather like an albino coconut – that hides the secret of its creamy turnip-like flesh within (and you can admire its portrait on p.191). It tastes delicately of celery, but a nutty, parsley-ish celery, more herbal than aniseedy. It is a generous partner to so many ingredients (see the Soupy Rice with Celeriac and Chestnuts on p.101 and the Roast Celeriac with Olives, Chilli and Parsley on p.189) and here it lends itself perfectly to the deep umami of anchovies, their fierce rasp mellowed by the blanketing cream.

I first made this to go alongside the Beef Cheeks with Port and Chestnuts (p.112) and continue to do so, but it pairs well with any stew, and is very fine with a plain roast chicken, too. If you want to make this with half the weight of celeriac below, making up the other half with potatoes, sliced similarly, then do so by all means, in which case you will not have to remove and blitz a little of the celeriac to thicken the anchovy and garlic cream.

I have specified the size of the gratin dish I use just for guidance. It can help you choose the right size dish if you, instead of plunging the sliced celeriac straight into the lemony water, quickly arrange the slices in a dish first to see if they fit, remembering that as the celeriac cooks it will lose a little volume.

As for the slicing: I am now an obsessive mandolin user and my timings are accordingly based on having those perfectly thin slices it produces, but if your slices are thicker, it shouldn't add more than a few minutes. If you are going to use a mandolin, I must insist you get a cut-resistant glove (that's the official name; to me it's my *Game of Thrones* glove) to wear as you do so.

Depending on the dish you use, you might need more of the celeriac-cooking liquid to make the cream cover. Just add a little more as required and let the dish stand a while, so the extra water blends with the cream before you put the dish into the oven. Talking of which, I often make this up ahead of time, and leave it in a cool part of the kitchen for a few hours before it goes into the oven. It can also be left, covered, in the fridge for up to 2 days, making sure you let it get to room temperature before roasting it. Keep some of the celeriac-cooking water, too, in case it needs topping up.

I find the combination of celeriac and anchovies so persuasive that I now have to add the salty fillets to *céleri rémoulade*, that gorgeous, elegant alternative to coleslaw. For a celeriac of 600–700g, make a dressing by mixing 5 tablespoons of mayonnaise, 3 tablespoons of double cream, 1 teaspoon of Dijon mustard, 2 minced cloves of garlic and 8 finely chopped anchovy fillets. Cut and peel the celeriac, and grate or cut it into juliennes (I use the larger julienne disc on my food processor), and immediately put them into a large bowl to which you have added the juice of a lemon. Turn to coat them in the lemon juice, then add the dressing and toss well to mix. On serving, you may consider sprinkling over some chopped toasted hazelnuts or tarragon (as pictured).

SERVES 4–6

1.5 litres cold water, plus more
 as needed

2 x 15ml tablespoons lemon juice

2 teaspoons sea salt flakes (or
 1 teaspoon fine sea salt)

1kg celeriac

4 fat cloves of garlic

15g butter, plus more for greasing dish

300ml double cream

8 anchovy fillets

A good grinding of pepper

For make-ahead, store and/or freeze notes, see p.332

1. Put the cold water into a saucepan large enough to take all the celeriac comfortably. It doesn't have to be huge; I fit mine into a pan that's 22cm in diameter and 9cm deep. Add the lemon juice and salt the water. Very carefully cut the celeriac into quarters and then peel. In a processor or with a mandolin or, indeed, with the knife you used to cut and peel the celeriac, slice very thinly. (If using the slicing disc in the processor, you will probably have to cut each quarter in half.) Add to the lemony water in the saucepan, topping up with a little fresh water if the celeriac isn't just about covered.

2. Peel the cloves of garlic and drop them into the pan too, then bring to the boil over high heat. I put a lid on to make it faster, but keep an ear open so that you don't miss when it starts boiling. Cook on a rollicking boil, partially covered, for about 5 minutes until the pieces of celeriac are tender, but not so soft that they're cooked through.

3. With a large sieve over a batter jug or bowl, strain the celeriac; I do this because I keep the liquid for making stock. If you know you won't, then lower in a ladle or measuring jug to remove some of the celeriac-cooking water – get about 250ml or a cup, just in case – to add to the anchovy cream later, and just drain the celeriac in a colander in the sink, though it pains me to write those words.

4. Once the celeriac is cool enough to handle, remove 75g of it (I go for the little chips and pieces, so that I have as many of the proper slices as I can for layering up in the dish later) and put into a bowl you can use with a stick blender. Retrieve the garlic cloves and add those to your bowl, too.

5. Butter your chosen dish (the one I use has internal measurements of 26 x 18 x 5½cm) and fill with the celeriac slices.

6. Add the cream and anchovy fillets to your bowl of celeriac offcuts and garlic, along with 100ml of the celeriac-cooking water, then give a generous grinding of pepper and blitz with a stick blender. Resist the temptation to knock this back in one – or is it only me? – and pour over the celeriac in its dish (adding more of the reserved water should the cream not just cover) and leave for a couple of hours – or up to 2 days in the fridge – or blithely proceed straightaway.

7. Heat the oven to 190°C/170°C Fan. Dot the 15g of butter on top of the cream-covered celeriac and cook for 50 minutes to 1 hour, until piping hot and golden brown, with the odd scorched bit, on top. If you're making this to go with the Beef Cheeks with Port and Chestnuts, make sure the gratin is on the higher shelf.

ANCHOVY ELIXIR

In the conventional way of these things, a dip to be eaten with crudités, drink in hand, before you even sit down to dinner, should be presented as the first of these three recipes. But this extraordinary elixir is for me the very apogee of anchovydom; it demands the final place on the podium. This isn't about favouritism, but more about its essential attributes. For the anchovy lover, there can be no purer celebration of its qualities.

I say a dip, but this is equally a sauce – for steak, roast beef, lamb, whatever you feel like pouring it on or eating it with, and I could pour it over almost anything. It is no beauty, it is true. I write elsewhere about brown food (see p.93), but this takes the concept of the boldly unprepossessing one stage further: it is positively grey; actually, it is more what my mother would have called greige.

If Jim Lahey, founder of the Sullivan Street Bakery in New York, didn't already have my eternal gratitude for his no-knead bread method (p.39), this dip, this sauce – what Italians might deliciously and expressively call *un intingolo* – would be enough to earn all due devotion. He sees it as the recipe that can convert even the most anchovy-averse. And while I hesitate to disagree with someone to whom I am so indebted, I feel it is pre-eminently one for the Anchovy Appreciation Association and make it only when I have card-carrying members over. As the only anchovy-eater in my happy triangle of a family, it is thus a good prompt to sociability, when times allow.

In many ways, it is most comparable to *bagna cauda*, only without the fuss of the flame or the fear of its splitting. To make this elixir you need salt-packed anchovies, not the ones in oil, and while I have never seen them in the supermarket, they are often stocked by Spanish, Greek and Italian delis; I buy mine, in abundance, online. The directions for preparation on the packets I buy instruct you to soak and then fillet them with your fingers under a running cold tap, but there's really no need to remove the bones. Think of all that calcium! Once everything's blitzed in a bullet blender, you really wouldn't be able to tell the difference. If you don't have a bullet blender, you can make this with a stick blender though the texture may not be quite the same. What this doesn't work in, I'm afraid, is a food processor.

The crudités you choose to serve with this are of course up to you: I always provide radishes, their pink pepperiness perfectly offsetting the salty greige of the dip, and red chicory, with its bitter spears just built to scoop it up; for sweet contrast, I suggest red peppers. Beyond crudités, asparagus is an obvious contender, but I also often steam new potatoes any time I make this heavenly elixir, to ensure I have leftovers of the former to dip greedily into the

leftovers of the latter. Potato wedges are to be considered too, so long as they're not still so hot you burn the roof of your mouth. Can you tell I'm speaking from experience? I am now desperate to try dunking in some proper chips. And when I was clearing up late one night after having had a friend over for dinner, I found myself, while I was supposedly in the process of pouring what remained of the exquisitely salty sauce into a smaller bowl, dipping a hunk of Rye and Cider Bread (p.39) into it. They could have been made for one another.

But then again, it's hard to beat the combination of red rare beef and salty grey sauce. I cooked the steak you see opposite – a slice of rump 2½cm thick – for 3 minutes each side in a cast-iron frying pan, rested it in foil for 5 minutes, then sliced it thinly against the grain, flung it excitedly on a plate, dribbled the elixir over it and scattered a few finely chopped chives on top, and dolloped more sauce on my plate as I ate.

I've altered Jim Lahey's original recipe to suit my own tastes. I suggest you do too, so by all means proceed with less garlic and lemon than I have stipulated below, tasting to see if you want, like me, to go for maximum punch.

MAKES approx. 350ml

100g salt-packed anchovies
3 fat cloves of garlic, peeled
2½ x 15ml tablespoons lemon juice
175ml extra-virgin olive oil
125ml cold water

TO SERVE

A few heads of red chicory
Radishes or other raw vegetables of
   your choice

For make-ahead, store and/or freeze notes, see p.332

1. It might be wisest to follow the preparation instructions that come on the packet of your salt-packed anchovies, but what I do is soak them in a dish (about 23cm square) of cold water for 5 minutes, then throw the water out, fill up again, and leave to soak in the fresh water for a further 5. Then rinse each anchovy under the tap with the cold water running, tearing away and discarding the tails. If you want to remove the bones, too, be my guest; you will thereby gain huge respect for those who fillet anchovies for a living.

2. If using a bullet or other high-speed blender, put the soaked and drained anchovies, and all the remaining ingredients, into it, and blitz until you have a smooth, buff-grey and gloopily fluid sauce.

3. If using a stick blender, put the soaked and drained anchovies into a bowl with the garlic and lemon juice and blitz to a paste. Still blitzing, gradually pour in a third of the oil, and when that's

absorbed, a third of the water, and carry on in this vein until both are used up.

4. Decant into a small serving dish or a few mini bowls and sit, respectively, on a platter or number of plates, and arrange your crudités around them.

PLEASURES

If I could ban any phrase, it would, without doubt, be that overused, viscerally irritating, and far-from-innocent term itself, the Guilty Pleasure. I don't think I actually groan out loud when I'm asked, every time I'm interviewed, 'What are your guilty pleasures?', but from deep within the cacophonous orchestra of my mind, the woodwind section starts up a searing wail, the cellos come in with their melancholy sob, only giving way to the brass section to end with the *wah wah wah waah* of the sad trombone. I may be smiling, but I'm keening on the inside.

My answer to that question is always the same, and while I worry that I repeat it so often it might be beginning to sound glib, I have to say that I feel it profoundly. And it is this: no one should feel guilty about what they eat, or the pleasure they get from eating; the only thing to feel guilty about (and even then I don't recommend it) is the failure to be grateful for that pleasure.

I am very aware that the joy I celebrate in food is a privilege. And for me, it's vitally important not to belittle that, or to forget it. Taking pleasure in the food we eat is an act of gratitude. And truly, the world is not always rich in occasions of joy. I know I might seem soupy when I say that I see every mealtime, every mouthful, as a celebration of life, but (with lamentable exceptions) I do, or I try to. It's such a waste otherwise.

The other day, I went to see some friends of mine whose eight-month-old baby has just started eating what we so unappealingly call solids. It was feeding time when I got there and the way his little toes curled up with pleasure every time a spoonful of mush was lowered into his mouth, the way he pumped his padded, dimpled fists, as plump as overstuffed dumplings, and gurgled with almost drunken delight, was such a joy (and yes, I repeat myself, but there is no other word adequate to the purpose) to witness. And a piercing reminder of what we can so easily lose. This was pure pleasure: it occupied his whole body, his entire being. There was nothing that interfered with or diminished it in any way, except perhaps the intervals between spoonfuls.

This is the state of bliss to which we should all aspire. I agree, however, that not many mealtimes can measure against the giddy wonder of a baby eating food for the first time, or indeed offer the total immersion of its urgent nursing at the breast. We really do fall from grace as we leave infancy behind.

But I believe we can find our way back to that rhapsodic paradise, or at least gain temporary occupancy. I'm now going to say something which I know makes me sound like some sottish fool, but here goes: there are times when I eat that I am made so completely happy by what I'm eating, and so intensely aware of and alive to the deep-seeping pleasure of every mouthful. I used to start feeling anxious as I neared the end of my plate, horrified by the knowledge that this very state of bliss was soon to come to an end. I've changed my ways since I've got older; I've made myself, as perhaps we all must. I can't afford to let the dread of its looming conclusion mar my very real pleasure. (Although I've yet to view the approaching end of a book I'm reading and loving without a pang of panic, that regretful sense of pre-bereavement.)

And it's not only food proper that fills me with sudden, uplifting delight. Sometimes when I'm drinking tea, I just feel seized with glad wonder that something as glorious as tea can actually exist. This is no exaggeration or expression of cute whimsy, for all, I fear, it might sound like it. And of course, the downside is I am childishly, inconsolably disappointed by a bad meal or a too-cold or too-milky mug of tea. But I can live with that. What I refuse to live with, categorically and essentially set myself against, is the erosion of pleasure by dint of turning it into a means of self-persecution.

No one, obviously, chastises themselves for tea-drinking. When they talk of 'guilty pleasures' they mean the food they feel they shouldn't be eating or, indeed, the food that others feel they shouldn't be eating. The sad refrain from women ever since I can remember has been 'I shouldn't be eating this, but ...'; and when I had a daughter, I vowed those words would never come from my lips. But even – especially, maybe – the words we don't say out loud can run rampage in our head. It perhaps sounds improbable to be able to train yourself away from the cycle of reproachful self-indulgence and self-recrimination, but I'm living proof it can be done. I was brought up by a mother – the cook I have learned most from – whose grimly exuberant output in the kitchen was set in painfully sharp relief, and indeed fostered, by an ever-expanding pattern of self-denial and self-punishment; not an uncommon syndrome, incidentally. Diagnosed with terminal cancer two weeks before her death, she started eating – for the first time, she said giddily – without worry or guilt. How unbearably sad to allow yourself unmitigated pleasure in food only when you receive a terminal diagnosis.

And so I protect fiercely the deep enjoyment I get from food, and want so fervently for others to share it, too. Every gorgeous mouthful stills the world, and yet revels in it at the same time; eating joyfully keeps me in the pleasurable present. This doesn't mean I just carry on eating as much as I can and for as long as I can. I want to maximise my enjoyment, not just eat for the sake of it. When I eat chocolate I linger over each square, deciding which I will let melt slowly in my mouth, which I chomp on rapaciously, quickly, feeling how different the sensations are. At no time do I feel guilty, and at no time do I want to carry on once the exquisite rapture has receded, and it becomes mindless or automatic. For I am not talking, I should most vehemently emphasise, about that egregious misnomer, comfort eating. For me that conjures up an unhappy search for mind-numbing obliteration: food as narcotic; not food as a celebration of life.

The accepted notions of comfort eating and guilty pleasure, while different from one another, stem from the same Manichaean universe: a foodstuff is either good or bad; ditto the eater thereof. Thus people seek to deny themselves the tastes and textures they crave, and castigate themselves when they give in to temptation. From this comes the crippling sense of shame, which gives rise to the guilty pleasure. But truly, where is the pleasure when it provokes shame or guilt?

Of course, I understand that many people, when they designate their pleasures as guilty, simply mean to indicate rebelliousness rather more than self-loathing, a strutting refusal to obey the dietary diktats of the day. But I am not entirely convinced. There is still a sense of 'I shouldn't, but ...' This doesn't surprise me: criticism is easily internalised; and a pre-emptive strike, even against ourselves, can seem, in our embarrassed defensiveness, the easiest way to deflect it.

And it is self-defeating. Not least because if you cling to the idea that pleasure is to be found only in those foods you are not apparently supposed to eat, you thereby limit the amount of pleasure you actually could be allowing yourself. Yes, a bar of chocolate is a true joy. But so is a plate of garlicky spinach or a lemony salad. I once posted a picture of my lunch on Instagram, comprising a bowl of sesame-sprinkled broccoli and prawns, and was told in the comments that I was just being 'good' and obviously would prefer to be having cake. I really wasn't, and I really wouldn't have. I ate what I wanted, what my body felt like, and I exult in that at all times. That can make me tiresome in restaurants as I focus on the menu, using what I call my Stanislavski ordering method, which entails going through each dish, in turn, in my head as I imagine myself eating it, calibrating the amount of happiness each one might bring, until I settle on the one that most instinctively matches my needs and desires. It can be a slow process, but for me a necessary one. And even though it is in my mind that I conjure up these projections of what I might be eating, it is with my body that I respond; I trust its intuition. This is not a special gift, I assure you. But it can't survive a diet of denial.

Of course, there's a lot of snobbery bound up in the guilty pleasure, too. Perhaps you fear it doesn't show you in the best light, or you feel that you'll be judged for it, and so you get in first, as if amused by your own poor taste, a self-conscious shrug of the shoulders. Now, maybe there really are those who gain some extra thrill from thinking they are enjoying something they perceive to be illicit, but I am not persuaded that can purely – or impurely – be the case. No, you name something your guilty pleasure if you feel that were you not to jump in with the word 'guilty', others might feel you seriously thought Mills & Boon novels high literature, or a processed cheese triangle the cate of the connoisseur. But it is truly impossible to enjoy the taste of something ironically; it is just a shame-induced distancing stance.

I have as little time for purists who disdain the lowly tastes of others as I do for the puritans who shudder at our bodily appetites. Nor do I wish to ally myself with the defensive mockery of inverted snobs, who feel that those who love any sort of food they themselves find fancy are simply pretentious frauds. Eating is such a huge and elemental pleasure: what a strangely puny act to want to police it. But perhaps it is because it is so personal and fundamental that we genuinely cannot conceive of feeling differently, and so distrust or dismiss those who do. I must admit that I have had to train myself out of forcing forkfuls of food – 'just try it!' – into the mouths of those I'm eating with, even after numerous polite refusals; and I am somewhat abashed to say that I don't mean my children here. I can't say that I have learned to temper my enthusiasm – and nor would I wish to – but I try to keep my sorrow at not being able to share it quietly to myself.

I can't help but feel, you see, that to share a pleasure is to increase it. I relish eating alone and cooking for myself and, on those occasions, frankly never miss a fellow diner; indeed, I positively and luxuriantly revel in this solo ceremony of the senses. But once I'm around others, I am greedy for them to find the happiness in food that I do.

For me, too, it is not enough to eat food: I need to wallow in the whole process; stretch out the pleasure I get from it. Cooking is not just part of that process, it is full-body immersion: the rich contemplation of the beauty of the food; the feel of it in my hands; the sounds as it splutters or bubbles in the pan; the smell of it all. The more absorbed I am, the greater the rewards. Perhaps there is a particular innocence, a particular purity, about cooking just for oneself, in that it wrests cooking away from being an act of service; for all that we'd like to think otherwise, the kitchen is still a much more freighted arena for women. The joy to be got from feeding others is not to be minimised, but – perhaps counter-intuitively – there is less ego involved in cooking for oneself, and that is enormously liberating. It is for this reason that I often tell people who are nervous about cooking that the best way to learn confidence in the kitchen is to cook just for themselves. When you cook for yourself, the burden of feeling you have to perform or impress is taken away, and you can, in your own time, find a way of being in the kitchen that makes sense to you. You're cooking to please yourself, no one else, and you neither have to second-guess your guests' tastes nor apologise for your own. Indeed, you can develop and expand your own, take risks and give yourself the freedom to make mistakes, without which we learn so much less. When your focus is on the food rather than on the reception it will be met with – in other words, when you yourself do not feel you're being judged – cooking itself will become so much easier, so much more enjoyable.

I had thought of confining the recipes to illustrate my many guilt-free pleasures to food for one, but the truth is, when I cook just for myself, I'm not really thinking about recipes. Quite often I have no idea when I start what I'm going to end up with. I'm just feeling my way. Or, as the phrase has it, following my bliss. Cooking for myself can lead to new combinations or reawaken old enthusiasms, both of which reanimate my cooking when I have others to feed.

I must, however, own up to one area of potential guilt in the kitchen. I have said before – many times, no doubt – that while I am undoubtedly often extravagant when it comes to food, I am never wasteful. For me, food waste would always be a legitimate cause for guilt. It is not entirely rational. In order to avoid wasting food, I often act in ways that could be construed as profligate: rather than throw away a couple of limp, blackened bananas, for example, I blithely make banana bread, which relies on eggs, sugar, chocolate, ground almonds and so forth, and therefore, you could well argue, uses more than it saves. Perhaps because I was brought up by a mother who was a child during the war, who herself grew up with rationing, and had a quaking horror of throwing anything away, I cannot throw food away myself. Nothing makes me feel happier in cooking than making a meal out of repurposed scraps.

So I feel quite delighted now that I have found a use for the banana skins that would otherwise end up in the bin after I've made yet another banana bread. Yes, you can eat the skins, and they form the basis of my Banana Skin and Cauliflower Curry, which you can see on p.36. The cooked cut-up banana peels look rather like aubergine skins; I can't honestly say they have a pronounced taste, though if you concentrate, you can detect a light floral and mineral flavour. Chiefly, they have a wonderful velvety texture and soak up the spices and seasoning of the curry sauce. To make this, you'll need first to have trimmed and soaked the skins you have left over from the Gluten-Free Banana Bread with Chocolate and Walnuts on p.78 or either of the recipes for Chocolate, Tahini and Banana Two Ways on p.80. I make this curry the same way even though the amount of banana skin yielded differs from one to the

other. Cut off the tough stalks and bottom ends from each skin and put them, thus trimmed, in a large-ish heatproof bowl, and fill up with a kettleful of just-boiled water, add ½ teaspoon each of turmeric and salt, give a little stir and leave until the water is cold. Boil or steam both florets and tender leaves from a smallish cauliflower, then set them aside in a colander in the sink while you make a curry paste, using the ingredients and method I give from step 2 until the end of step 6 for the Short Rib Stew For Two on p.106; the only difference is, you leave the seeds in the chilli, dispense with the cardamom, replace the beef dripping with vegetable oil, fry everything not in a small casserole, but in a wok or wide pan, and cook the paste for 7 minutes rather than 5. To this bubbling pan, stir in 2 tablespoons of tomato purée, and cook for a further 3 minutes. Now add a 400ml can of coconut milk (full-fat, not light please), 1½ teaspoons of sugar, 2½ tablespoons of lemon juice and 2 teaspoons of sea salt flakes (or 1 teaspoon of fine sea salt). Cook, uncovered, letting it bubble, reduce and thicken a little for 5 minutes.

Drain the banana skins, squeezing out any excess liquid, and either chop them into slightly smaller than bite-sized pieces or take a fork and, with the interior of the banana skins facing you, press the tines into the top and push all the way down so that you have long thin strips. I enjoy doing this, but it does make them look a bit spooky; I feel I'm eating that Klingon delicacy, Gagh.

Anyway, whichever way you want to prepare them, add the skins to the pan, and simmer for a further 10 minutes, or until the sauce has thickened and the banana skins are soft. Tip in the cauliflower florets and leaves and continue to cook until they're hot all the way through. Taste to see if you want any more salt, then chop the coriander leaves left over from the stalks in the curry paste, and scatter over the curry. This should feed two hungry people most pleasingly.

On the whole, I prefer to use up everything in the fridge as I go, rather than allow the freezer to serve as a bin in virtuous guise, but I must also admit that there are more bags of breadcrumbs in my deep freeze than I could probably ever get through. And yet I still can't throw them away. This doesn't mean the freezer isn't genuinely helpful. I've written before about my bone collection, the chicken carcasses I stash away until I have enough to make stock; I also keep vegetable peelings and scraps in freezer bags, slowly amassing them, until I have enough to add them to the stockpot, too.

My fridge is full of little cups of bacon fat, beef dripping and schmaltz (chicken fat, and a golden joy) that I've rescued from frying pans and roasting dishes. My mother always had a pot near the stove, which she poured any fat into – mixing them up without concern – as she cooked.

I find it hard to throw away either potato- or pasta-cooking water, keeping it to use (when cold) for making bread, as it gives a wonderful rise, and helps the baked loaves stay fresher for longer (see p.39 for the bread recipe). And I also salvage spoilt milk for bread dough, as you will see on p.43. As for potato peelings, you can certainly make crisps out of them. I've always just deep-fried mine, but my friend Alex Andreou makes his, and now hundreds of others do following his example, by heating some oil on a lipped baking sheet in a 200°C/180°C Fan oven, then tossing in the washed and dried potato peelings, sprinkling them evenly with salt and paprika, and roasting them for around 15–25 minutes (depending on their thickness), checking on them and turning them regularly. But I prefer, in the main, to use them to make up potato water for bread-baking. So, if I have the peelings from 500g of potatoes, I put them into a pan with 500ml of water, bring them to the boil, let bubble for about 15 minutes, then leave them to cool in the water, removing them only when cold, every bit of their starchiness left behind in the now cloudy water.

You can use the potato water (and any water you've boiled vegetables in) for making soup or gravy, too, as indeed has been common practice in kitchens through the ages. If I had my way – and if there were the space for it – I'd nudge you in this direction every time. Thriftiness is the habit of cooks, however extravagant: I could no more throw a butter wrapper away before using it to grease cake tins than I could allow chicken bones to go in the bin. And if this sounds to many like drab, penitential asceticism, I have to tell you that these old ways give me as much joy in the kitchen as the heady, luxuriant flourishes of newfound enthusiasms.

NO-KNEAD BREAD

In considering the elemental enjoyment of eating, I have to start with bread: in life, there can be no pleasure without *pain*.

It also demonstrates something very important in my cooking life, namely my gratitude to other food writers, as I hope all my books express. It may surprise you to know that you cannot copyright a recipe; anyone is free, from a legal point of view, to take someone's recipe and claim it, with a few minor changes, as their own. And many do. It has always been important to me to try, however much I adapt a recipe, however substantially it runs freely away from its original iteration, to give a fair account of its provenance. I haven't, in fact, changed much of Jim Lahey's recipe for No-Knead Bread, but certainly it has provided a starting point for a number of variations of my own.

I enjoy kneading bread dough, but have willingly given it up for this loaf – not out of laziness, but because of the bread this method produces. While it isn't actually sourdough, its slow cold rise in which it begins to ferment, gives it that same desirable tang; baking it inside a casserole in a hot oven yields a crumb and crust you could normally only dream of. For now, this robust, chewy loaf is an everyday miracle I can't get over, and don't want to. I bless Jim Lahey's name every time I make or eat this bread.

I have given ingredients for a white loaf here, as I think it makes sense to master the basic recipe before branching out. And while you can adapt this using other flours, in various ratios, I advise you – whichever flour combination you go for – to make sure at least 50%, i.e. 200g, of the flour is strong white bread flour, though you may find it better to start your experiments with 300g of strong white bread flour and 100g of other flour; the only exception to this is if you use regular plain flour instead, which works well by itself, though makes for a slightly less robust crumb. I have made this successfully using a huge variety of flours, with the sole, lamentable exception – sadly – of gluten-free flour. My favourite deviation, as it were, and a loaf I make just as often as this original version, uses 200g of strong white bread flour, 200g of dark rye flour, with yeast and salt as below, but approx. 350ml of dry or medium-dry cider in place of the water; rye flour needs a little more liquid to form a dough. If you don't want to use the cider, increase the yeast to ½ teaspoon and add 1 tablespoon of lemon juice to the water. Indeed, I often add 1 tablespoonful of lemon juice to the cold tap water for the white loaf. It seems to help the rise. But you can do this, too, by replacing the tap water with the water you've cooked potatoes or pasta in, left to get cold, in which case you may need to reduce or omit the salt when you mix up the bread. And sorry to sully the purity of this recipe, but if I don't have any of this desirably starchy water to hand, I often just add 2 tablespoons of instant mashed potato powder to the flour, and proceed with tap water, though omitting the lemon juice.

　　　　While this is just about effortless to make, I should warn from the outset that you have to mix up the dough the day before you want to eat the bread; you also need to factor in the second proof on the day you bake it.

MAKES 1 modest-sized loaf

400g strong white bread flour

1¼ teaspoons (8g) fine sea salt

¼ teaspoon (1g, but it's hard to get it to register on the scales) fast-action dried yeast

300ml cold tap water (or cooled pasta- or potato-cooking water, see recipe intro), plus more as needed

1 x 15ml tablespoon lemon juice (omit if using potato- or pasta-cooking water, or instant mashed potato powder)

Polenta or additional flour, for dusting

NO-KNEAD BREAD

For make-ahead, store and/or freeze notes, see p.332

For make-ahead, store and/or freeze notes, see p.332

1. In a medium-sized bowl, stir together the flour, salt and yeast. Measure the water into a jug, stir in the lemon juice if using water from the tap, rather than water you've cooked potatoes or pasta in. Pour into the flour and, using your hand, a wooden spoon or a Danish dough whisk, mix it together until you have a wet, sticky dough; this will take under 30 seconds. Add more water if you feel it needs it, but just a tablespoon at a time – you don't want to make it too liquid. This is something you will feel surer about once you've made this a couple of times.

2. Cover the bowl with food wrap or a shower cap and sit at room temperature out of direct sunlight until the surface is dotted with bubbles and the dough almost doubled. This will take 16–18 hours. (This is the case for the white bread; other flours show a less dramatic increase in size.)

3. Once your dough has reached this point, dust a work surface or board generously with flour. Use a dough-scraper, for ease, to scrape out the dough onto your floured surface in one piece. It will be quite stringy and feel loose and sticky. Bring the edges of the dough up and over, into the middle, to form a low-slung round of dough.

4. Dust one half of a cotton or linen tea towel (not a waffle or terry cloth one) liberally with polenta or flour, and then transfer your rounded dough onto the dusted side of the tea towel, tuck marks down. Now sprinkle the top of the dough lightly with a little more

polenta or flour before folding the tea towel over to cover it. Leave in a warm, draught-free spot for 1–2 hours for its second rise. I don't find it rises up much in this time but rather it expands outwards. I tend to leave it for 2 hours in winter, but find otherwise 1 hour is best for the white loaf or it spreads too much.

5. About 45 minutes before this second rise is up, put a cast-iron, ceramic or heat-resistant glass casserole with its lid on into the oven and heat to 250°C/230°C Fan. While Jim Lahey stipulates the casserole be 4.5–6.5 litres capacity, I find this works best for me in a Pyrex casserole of 3.5 litres capacity.

6. When the dough's had its second rise, take the heated pot out of the oven, and take off the lid. Uncover the dough under the tea towel and then quickly and carefully invert it into the pot. And yes, you will get polenta or flour all over the place; I rather feel a handheld vacuum cleaner or dustpan and brush should be listed in the ingredients. After you've made this a few times, you may feel confident enough to lift it up from the cloth and invert with your hands.

7. Bake for 30 minutes, then remove the lid and cook for a further 15–30 minutes until the bread is a deep golden brown and bronzed in parts. When I'm baking my Rye and Cider Bread (see recipe intro), I give it 45 minutes with the lid on, and 15 with it off. If you rap the bottom of the loaf, it should sound hollow when it's cooked, but don't burn yourself doing this. Once it's ready, slip the bread out of its casserole and onto a wire rack to cool thoroughly before eating, I'm sorry to say. This, perhaps, is a counsel of perfection, but if you cut or tear into it while it's still warm, it will stale immediately (unless you eat it all at that first sitting, of course). To keep the loaf fresh for as long as possible, store in a bread bin. The next best method is to wrap it in a tea towel.

OLD-FASHIONED SANDWICH LOAF

While the everyday bread on my table is always the round, crackle-crusted no-knead loaf that precedes this recipe, there are times when I just want a slice of old-school bread, deeply unfashionable in these sourdough-days, but oh-so-comforting to eat. I mean, I love sourdough, but I don't want to make a fish finger sandwich with it. And a fish finger sandwich – the food that most often sustains me as I write – made with this bread has led me to recant utterly my long-held view that it could be made only with shop-bought sliced white. Two pieces of this Old-Fashioned Sandwich Loaf, both spread with squirty Japanese mayo and my Fermented Hot Sauce (p.300), the crunch of iceberg lettuce and fish fingers between them, is my idea of heaven when I'm harried, hungry, and have no time to cook.

But I'm getting ahead of myself. The first slice I cut from this life-enhancing loaf I eat spread only with butter (cultured salted butter for choice, but most often it's just regular unsalted, with sea salt flakes sprinkled on top). This bread makes superb toast, too. And I favour the two-stage approach when it comes to buttering: I slather it quickly in butter when it first comes out of the toaster so that it sinks in, giving the toast an almost crumpetty bite; then I leave it just a little before adding a bit more butter that, now the toast's no longer piping hot, will stay unmelted and golden on the surface. My fussy strictures notwithstanding, hot buttered toast – just slightly charred at the edges – has to be the quintessential simple pleasure, and a profound one.

Dan Lepard came to my aid in person for the No-Knead Black Bread on p.305, and he came to my rescue through the pages of his invaluable baking book, *Short & Sweet*, for this. I cannot bear to throw anything away, even spoilt milk, and was looking for a way to use some up; I found it in the form of his Sour Cream Sandwich Bread recipe. I tried it out, using my spoilt milk and adding butter (the amount guessed at, rather than scientifically worked out) to make up for the loss of the cream's fat content. It worked beautifully, and continues to however much I play around with it, depending on what I have to hand. If my milk-management has been spectacularly poor, and I have more than the 125ml required, I replace the 150ml of cold water in the recipe with spoilt milk, too, adding only 2 tablespoons (30g) of butter in that case. I have also made it with full-fat Greek yogurt, when I reduce the salt to 1 teaspoon, and add 2 tablespoons of butter. And I discovered it is glorious when veganised, too. I had some almond-soy yogurt left over from the Vegan Lemon Polenta Cake on p.257, added 3 tablespoons (45g) of vegetable shortening and reduced both the salt and sugar to 1 teaspoon each. It was a triumph! But then, this is the most easy-going recipe.

It is also very, very simple to make. If it sounded odd earlier when I said that when too busy to cook I make a sandwich with this loaf, it's because I find it very relaxing to make when I'm in the middle of a long bout of work. Indeed, I have a loaf rising in its tin as I write.

The most stringent demand on you, in the course of making this bread, is that you knead it 3 times for 10 seconds at 10-minute intervals. It's a great loaf to make with small children – a science lesson in the kitchen, as the yeast kicks into action, making the bread grow between each short knead, and you can feel the dough getting smoother and bouncier under your fingers – and older children could make it by themselves. And as with all bread, if it helps your schedule, you could leave it to rise, not for an hour out in the kitchen, but in the fridge overnight, though be sure to let it come to room temperature before proceeding further.

Finally, a small suggestion for what to do with any leftover bread – an absurd concept, I know, especially as this loaf seems to stay soft and fresh for ages. Still, should you miraculously not finish it before it stales, I propose this rum-spiked French toast. So, cut two thinnish slices of bread (and if not stale, leave them out for a couple of hours first) and cut these in half to make triangles. In a dish – I use one of 25 x 20cm in which they fit perfectly – whisk 1 large egg with 2 tablespoons of full-fat milk and 1 tablespoon each of soft dark sugar and rum. Let the bread triangles steep for 2 minutes a side, or until they've drunk all the rum-spiked, sugary milk, then fry them in butter for 3½–4 minutes a side or until cooked through, and crisp and golden and browned in places on the surface; I use a 28cm non-stick frying pan, and a generous amount of butter, but if you use a smaller pan, you'll need to fry them in two batches. I stir up a syrup by mixing 2 tablespoons of golden syrup and 1 teaspoon each of maple syrup and rum. And, though this may sound odd, I like to pour the syrup over mine, then leave the French toast to get cold before eating it. But it makes a rather jaunty weekend breakfast for two, eaten hot with some cubes of mango or slices of banana tumbled on top.

OLD-FASHIONED
SANDWICH LOAF

MAKES 1 beautiful loaf

500g strong white bread flour, plus
  more for dusting

2½ teaspoons (7g) or 1 sachet fast-
  action dried yeast

2 teaspoons (8g) caster sugar

2 teaspoons (12g) fine sea salt

125ml spoilt milk (or sour cream),
  straight from the fridge

150ml cold water

100ml hot water from a just-boiled
  kettle

3 x 15ml tablespoons (45g) soft
  unsalted butter (omit if using sour
  cream, plus more for greasing tin

Vegetable oil, for kneading

For make-ahead, store and/or freeze notes, see p.332

1. Mix the flour, yeast, sugar and salt in a large bowl.

2. Pour the spoilt milk (or sour cream) into a measuring jug, add
the cold water (which will take you to the 275ml mark) then the
boiling water (and I'm presuming you don't need me to say that it
should now read 375ml). Stir the soft butter into the jug; it won't
melt entirely, but that's fine.

3. Pour the jug of wet ingredients into the bowl of dry ingredients, stirring as you go, either with a wooden spoon, a Danish dough whisk or – and these are my tools of choice here – hands. Stir until all the flour – apart from a little that's clinging to the sides of the bowl – is absorbed into the dough; if this takes a minute I'd be surprised. Form into a rough ball, cover the bowl with food wrap or a shower cap, and leave for 10 minutes.

4. Pour a little oil onto the kitchen counter and spread it with your hand to give a light sheen to an area big enough to knead on. Take the dough out of its bowl and duly knead it for 10 seconds. How you knead is very personal: we all have our different styles; I push the dough away with the heel of my hand and bring it back with my fingers. Form the dough back into a ball, return it to its bowl, cover it again, and leave for 10 minutes. Repeat this process twice, and after the third 10-second knead, form the dough into a ball again, put it back in the bowl, cover, and leave for an hour.

5. Line the bottom of a 2lb (900g) loaf tin and very lightly grease the sides; I use an old butter wrapper for this. Take the plumptiously risen dough out of its bowl, and pat it out on your oiled surface so that you have a soft, puffy mattress about 2cm thick, with one edge about 4cm shorter than the length of your tin. Starting with this edge, and using both hands, tightly roll the dough into a scroll – or swiss roll, if that helps you visualise it better – and tenderly place it seam side down in your prepared tin; you may have to press the short sides gently to fit it in, as the scroll can get longer as you roll. Leave to rise for 1–1½ hours, until it's peeking out just above the top of the tin. Turn the oven on when it looks like it's nearly there.

6. So, heat the oven to 200°C/180°C Fan. Dust the top of the dough with flour and bake for 45 minutes, by which time the bread will be risen, with a rounded and deep biscuity-gold top. Unless your oven is misfiring, it will definitely be done. Armed with oven gloves, quickly take the bread out of the tin, and place it on a wire rack to cool before slicing into it. To keep the loaf fresh for as long as possible, store in a bread bin. The next best method is to wrap it in a tea towel.

PASTA WITH CLAMS AND BOTTARGA

A year or so back, I had lunch with my publisher to discuss this very book, when it was still fumbling its way into being. We went to a small Sardinian seafood restaurant called Olivomare, where I ordered the *lorighittas con vongole*. It seemed only right to include a recipe for it here, as I've been making it ever since. Besides, it is to me inextricably linked to the very conception of *Cook, Eat, Repeat*. It's not easy to come by lorighittas, I know – it's a braided round pasta shape, like a hair-tie or a child's bracelet – but you could certainly use linguine in their stead.

Pasta with clams has always been a true love of mine, and I would concede that it doesn't in itself need any embellishment. But the addition of bottarga – the grey mullet roe also known as Sardinian caviar – is a truly inspired one. It is smokily strong, saltily pungent: a grating of it over pasta seems to bring with it all the deep and briny mysteries of the sea.

And a favourite supper of mine is just that: I put 100g of spaghetti or linguine on; warm quite a lot of extra-virgin olive oil in a pan, and stir in 2 minced cloves of garlic and the finely grated zest of a lemon for a minute or so; when the pasta's cooked, I tong it into the garlicky pan, add a good squirt of lemon, and some of the pasta-cooking water; then off the heat, I add a couple of tablespoons of finely grated bottarga, toss it well, and once it's in my bowl, I grate more over greedily. A little bit of chopped parsley could be considered, too. For a double dose of ocean-evoking pungency and a bit of high-impact visual drama, make this with squid ink spaghetti or linguine (see p.51). And once you have your bottarga open and in the fridge, it lasts a long time, always cheeringly on hand for a very special standby supper. You mustn't think it's only pasta you can grate it over: it's glorious sprinkled over a poached egg, or a bowl of broccoli, or buttered new potatoes; were I minded to make steak tartare at home, I would most definitely finish it with a flourish of golden, grated bottarga. I love it, too, very very thinly sliced on buttered toast. It turns everything it's added to into a sumptuous treat. The important thing is that you never actually cook it; always add it off the heat.

I have written a recipe for pasta with clams before, I know, but I cannot apologise for repeating myself, here of all places. I trust you will understand. You certainly will once you've eaten it. Besides, this is not a retread, but a rewarding new step.

A final note: while cooking clams in olive oil is traditional and proper, I hope I won't offend Sardinians by my suggestion that you might also consider adding just *un pochino* – a little, little bit – of unsalted butter as a perfect finishing touch.

SERVES 1, as a special treat

250g small clams

Bottarga, enough to give 3 x 15ml
 tablespoons when grated (never buy
 pre-grated bottarga)

1 fat clove of garlic

100g lorighittas or linguine

2 x 15ml tablespoons extra-virgin
 olive oil

1 lemon

¼ teaspoon dried chilli flakes

3 x 15ml tablespoons dry white
 vermouth or wine

1 teaspoon unsalted butter

TO SERVE (OPTIONAL)

Fresh parsley

Bread, to soak up the juices

It is not advisable to make ahead, store or freeze.

1. Put the clams into a bowl of cold water, and leave them for
15 minutes. Put the water on for the pasta, and assemble and measure
out all your other ingredients. First, peel back the pellicle (or covering)
of the bottarga to leave about 1½cm uncovered, and grate it finely into
a bowl, until you have 2 tablespoons' worth, leaving a bit more to grate
straight over the pasta if you want more as you eat. Peel the garlic,
ready to be minced or grated shortly.

2. When the water is boiling, add salt and wait for it to fizz up, calm
down and then come back to the boil again before adding the pasta,
and cook according to directions, but be prepared for it to be ready
earlier, so start checking in good time.

3. Drain the clams, discarding any that are open.

4. When the pasta has about 4 minutes more to go, get out a heavy-
based pan that comes with a lid and that will fit both clams and pasta
in later (this is a solo portion, so it hardly needs to be big) and gently
warm the olive oil in it. Take the pan off the heat and finely grate in the
zest of the lemon, then mince or grate in the garlic, add the dried chilli
flakes, and stir well for a scant minute back on lowish heat.

5. Turn the heat up and add the clams, followed by the vermouth or
wine, and quickly clamp on the lid so the clams steam open; this should
take a couple of minutes. Discard any clams that remain closed.

6. When the pasta's ready, but on the al dente side, use a spider to ferry
it from its pot to the clam pan (but if you're cooking linguine, tongs or a
pasta fork would be better), add the teaspoon of butter, put the lid back
on and give everything a good shake. Leave to stand with the heat off
for 2 minutes.

7. Uncover, add most of your grated bottarga, and a little chopped
parsley if wished, and give a gentle stir. Turn out into a shallow bowl,

and sprinkle over the rest of the grated bottarga, grating in even more as you eat if that makes you happy. It makes me happy. As does dunking some chewy bread into the briny juices left in the bottom of the bowl.

CRAB MAC 'N' CHEESE

After holding out for years against the insidious encroachment of the American appellation of mac 'n' cheese over here, insisting primly and pointedly on macaroni cheese, I have now officially given up. I know when I'm beaten. Besides, after a while, harrumphing over a change that's already happened becomes more than a little embarrassing; I was in danger of boring even myself. I can't stop calling it macaroni cheese when I mean the nursery staple I was brought up on, but otherwise I'm not going to quibble. Saying mac 'n' cheese still feels awkward to me, but I'll get over it. And, in all fairness, this crab mac 'n' cheese is really my take on that American menu favourite of recent years, the winkingly opulent, defiantly rich, deluxe-special, lobster mac 'n' cheese.

It is perhaps inelegant of me to claim my version to be better, so let me just say I very much prefer it; it also happens to be a good deal more affordable. Crab offers the briny sweetness of lobster, but without its almost perfumed intensity, which can be quite heady enough even without a cheese sauce and pasta to accompany it. And, for some reason, while the tender delicacy of lobster meat can be reduced to challenging richness when blanketed with cheeses, crabmeat subtly holds its own in this paprika-spiked cheese sauce, giving it an almost honeyed depth, beguiling at first, compelling to the finish. All this rests, however, on your using equal quantities of the brown meat – like a ready-made seafood pâté – and the tender sweet-soft strands of white meat. I fear I must insist upon it. I get excellent crabmeat, in a 50/50 mix, in tubs of exactly the size specified below. I hope you will find these as easy to come by. And certainly a good fishmonger, should you be lucky enough to have one near you, will be able to give you exactly what you need.

After I'd made this a few times, I knew what I had to go on to do: turn it into a sauce for nachos. How right I was. And if you feel like doing this, too, then bump the milk in the recipe up to 300ml and, once the crab's gone in at the end, if you still think it needs thinning out, simply stir in more milk as wished. Tip good unsalted tortilla chips out on a platter, and warm in a low oven (around 150°C/130°C Fan) while you make the sauce. Drape the chips with it, then put them back into the oven while you chop a red chilli into rings, and finely slice some radishes; I like to use a mandolin for the radishes to get them almost transparently thin. But if you prefer the idea of finely sliced spring onions, go with that, in which case a knife is all you need. Sprinkle gaily over the warmed nachos, and watch them disappear almost immediately. Obviously, you can scatter over whatever you want, although I'd guard against adding avocado or anything that will increase rather than offset the richness of the sauce. And I have an inkling that it could be quite glorious as a warm,

queso-like dip, chips on the side rather than underneath, though you would need to boost quantities to fill a bowl.

As mac 'n' cheese, I like this just as it is: no need to add cheese or buttery breadcrumbs on top and then blitz it under the grill; indeed, I advise against it. I find a freckling of Aleppo pepper more than makes up for the familiar heat-scorched finish.

And while I use a mixture of Aleppo pepper and sweet smoked paprika to provide both bright and musky heat, you can use whatever chilli powder or paprika you have to hand; just be sure to add small amounts first, and taste as you go.

I recommend warming the bowls before you start, even if you do no more than fill them with hot water from the tap and leave them in the sink while you cook. All you need with or after this is a crisp green salad. And perhaps a very chilled flinty white wine, or light – and colour-coordinated – Provençal rosé, alongside.

SERVES 2, although I fear I could eat all of it without too much trouble

100g Gruyère

2 x 15ml tablespoons (approx. 15g) freshly grated Parmesan

1½ x 15ml tablespoons (15g) plain flour

¼ teaspoon ground mace

¼ teaspoon sweet smoked paprika

⅛ teaspoon Aleppo pepper, or hot smoked paprika, plus more to sprinkle at the end

250ml full-fat milk

1 x 15ml tablespoon tomato purée

2 x 15ml tablespoons (30g) unsalted butter

1 fat clove of garlic

½ teaspoon Worcestershire sauce

200g conchiglie rigate pasta

100g mixed white and brown crabmeat (50/50)

For make-ahead, store and/or freeze notes, see p.332

1. Grate the Gruyère into a bowl and add the 2 tablespoons of grated Parmesan. Mix the flour with the spices in a small cup. Pour the milk into a measuring jug and stir in the tablespoon of tomato purée. Put a pan of water on to boil for the pasta.

2. Find a smallish heavy-based saucepan; I use one of 18cm diameter. Over lowish heat, melt the butter, then peel and mince or grate in the garlic and stir it around in the pan quickly. Turn the heat up to medium and add the flour and spices. Whisk over the heat until it all coheres into an orange, fragrant, loose paste; this will take no longer than a minute. It soon looks like tangerine-tinted foaming honeycomb. Take off the heat and very gradually whisk in the tomatoey milk, until it's completely smooth.

Use a spatula to scrape down any sauce that's stuck to the sides of the pan.

3. Put back on the heat, turn up to medium and cook, stirring, until it has thickened and lost any taste of flouriness; this will take anything from 3 to 5 minutes. Stir in the Worcestershire sauce.

4. Take the pan off the heat and stir in the grated cheeses. It'll look rather fabulously like Velveeta now. Put a lid on the saucepan, or cover tightly with foil, and leave on the hob, but with the heat off, while you get on with the pasta. If you have an electric or ceramic hob it may be better to take the pan off completely.

5. So, add salt to the boiling water in the pasta pan, then add the pasta and cook according to the packet instructions, though start checking it a couple of minutes earlier.

6. When the pasta is just about al dente, add the crabmeat to the smoky cheese sauce, then once you're happy that the pasta shells are ready, use a spider to lift them into the sauce or drain them, reserving some pasta-cooking liquid first, and drop the shells in. Stir over lowish heat until the crabmeat is hot. If you want to make the sauce any more fluid, as indeed you might, add as much of the pasta-cooking water as you need. Taste to see if you want to add salt – the crab meat you get in tubs tends to be quite salty already, but if you've got yours from your fishmonger, it might need it.

7. Divide between two small shallow bowls and sprinkle with Aleppo pepper or hot smoked paprika.

WIDE NOODLES WITH LAMB SHANK
IN AROMATIC BROTH

While I could never have a recipe in any book I wrote that I didn't love inordinately, this is just one of those special ones that fill me with a sense of glad-hearted awe. It's not too much to claim for it: it's almost ridiculously easy to make – I relish the quiet ceremony of its slow-cooking preparation – and is both comforting and enlivening to eat. I don't know how it came to me, but I think that a visit to Master Wei in London, with its glorious bowls of punchily spiced aromatic broth and handmade biang biang noodles, might have had something to do with it, even if not entirely consciously. I didn't set out to replicate what I'd eaten there, but I was hungering for something to deliver up exactly that combination of chilli-hot intensity and shoulder-lowering serenity. And while I haven't been cooking it for long, my children already ask me for it regularly when we're planning an evening together. It's bowlfood at its best.

You do need to plan for it, as the gorgeous broth has to be made a day in advance (longer if you want), but it's a very straightforward procedure once you've got the key ingredients in stock. And gochujang, that fermented Korean red chilli paste that provides rich, rounded depth as well as heat, is the magic ingredient here. While it may not be a new enthusiasm, it is an enduring one. I recommend you get it for adding both oomph and umami to chilli, shepherd's pie, mayonnaise, soups and stews. Here, however, it simply makes for a broth of such complexity, you'd think a thousand and one exactingly calibrated spices went into it.

If you can't get hold of gochujang, I dare say a teaspoon of dried chilli flakes would serve as a stand-in; it certainly would bring the heat (stir miso into the broth before eating). But if you can get it – and it's easy enough to find online – you need to know as well about one of my favourite, low-effort, solo suppers, and one that provided me with a lot of comfort during my solitary Covisolation, my Gochujang Pork Noodles. So, put water on for the noodles. I use 75g of Thai sen lek, which are rice noodles with a similar thickness to linguine, though ramen could work very well here (as would linguine or spaghetti). Heat a wok, or a wok-like stir-fry pan, and add a very little vegetable oil. When hot, crumble in 125g of pork mince (I keep mince in bags in the freezer, ready-portioned for this) and cook for 2 minutes, stirring it around in the pan with a fork to break it up, so that it dries a little. Add a tablespoon of gochujang and stir it into the crumbled meat, then let it cook, stirring every now and again, for 5 minutes, by which time it will be almost caramelised. Throw in 100ml of water and, still over high heat, give a good stir until most of it is evaporated (this will happen very quickly) and the crumbly pork is sitting in a scant orange sauce. Turn off the flame, and put on a lid so that it keeps warm while you cook the noodles. Once they're cooked, use tongs to ferry them from their pan to the pork's and mix well. If you wanted, you could add a drop of toasted sesame oil here. Turn them into a bowl, top with chopped coriander, and – for old times' sake – apply to face.

But back to the matter at hand. While I use one lamb shank to feed two, if you're making this just for yourself you can easily freeze half the meat and broth once both are cooked and cooled. However, it would be no hardship to have an entire lamb shank oneself. Indeed, I gave this recipe in an early stage to a friend with three teenage sons and they all insisted on a shank each. Should you need to feed more, then bulk up as needed; though while I often double the amount of lamb shanks if all three of us are home and also double the liquid, gochujang, and most other of the ingredients, I just add one and a half times the spices.

I keep meaning to try this recipe with oxtail, but it's hard to make myself change a thing when it gratifies so exquisitely as it is. Having said that, it is certainly wonderful with short ribs; I use two, measuring about 11cm long each (so they fit in my pan) and weighing about 600g in total. And you could always throw in some dried shiitake mushrooms and miso, dispensing with the lamb shank, for a vegan version.

As for the noodles, until I make my own, I use durum wheat pappardelle; I find egg pappardelle too tender but if they're the only ones you can find, I'd advise you to cook them and the cabbage in separate saucepans as the delicate egg noodles can overcook easily.

And while I'm not saying you absolutely must get a jar of Chilli Crisp oil (the Chinese condiment of condiments) to eat with it, I wouldn't want to proceed without. It also comes into play in the Fried Chicken Sandwich on p.67, and so often in my life. Truly, it becomes hard not to add this crispy chilli oil to everything.

WIDE NOODLES
WITH LAMB SHANK
IN AROMATIC BROTH

SERVES 2 lucky people

1 litre cold water

1 x 15ml tablespoon gochujang paste

2 teaspoons sea salt flakes (or
   1 teaspoon fine sea salt)

1 teaspoon allspice berries

1 teaspoon cumin seeds

1 star anise

1 lamb shank

25g fresh ginger

1 carrot (approx. 125g)

2 fat cloves of garlic

70g banana shallots (2 smallish or
   1 large) or ½ an onion

200g Savoy cabbage

175g pappardelle (not egg
   pappardelle) or other wide noodles

TO SERVE

Chilli Crisp oil

For make-ahead, store and/or freeze notes, see p.332

1. Heat the oven to 150°C/130°C Fan. Pour the litre of water into a small casserole with a tightly fitting lid (I use one of 20cm diameter) and stir in the gochujang paste until dissolved, then add the salt, allspice, cumin seeds and star anise. Now add the lamb shank to the pot, and put over medium heat.

2. Cut the ginger into coins and add to the pot as well, along with the carrot, peeled (if you want) and cut into four, the garlic cloves, bruised with the flat of a wide-bladed knife, and the shallots, cut in half, though there is no need to peel them. In fact, I don't bother to peel anything. Once everything's in the pan, the lamb shank should be just covered. If it isn't, add some more water.

3. Once it's come to the boil, clamp on the lid and cook in the oven for 2–2½ hours, by which time the meat should be very tender indeed, and ready to fall off the bone.

4. Using tongs, transfer the lamb shank to a large-ish bowl, then strain the liquid over it. Leave to cool, then refrigerate overnight.

5. The next day, remove the solidified fat, and shred the meat – not too finely, you don't want stringiness – into a small saucepan, pouring over the liquid, and in another pan, large enough to take the pasta and cabbage, bring water to the boil.

6. Shred the cabbage. When the water's come to the boil, add salt, and turn the heat on very low under the pan of lamb and its broth so that it warms gently, though you do want it to be piping hot by the time the pasta and cabbage are cooked.

7. Add the pappardelle to the boiling salted water and when it's 3 minutes away from its full cooking time (check the packet for instructions) add the cabbage and stir well. When both cabbage and pasta are cooked, drain, then divide between two noodle bowls.

8. Using a slotted spoon, lift out the hot lamb and share between the two bowls, then ladle the broth on top. If you have any of the crispy chilli oil add 1 teaspoon or so to each bowl, and take both bowls to the table, making sure you come back for the Chilli Crisp oil, so you can add more as you eat.

FISH FINGER BHORTA

I am so grateful to the political journalist Ash Sarkar for this new love in my life. I have to say I had never heard of it before I saw a tweet of hers in April 2019, which read:

> Nostalgia in a dish: cooked fish fingers, mashed with onion, fresh ginger, and green chilli that's all fried in mustard oil, stirred through with a bit of English mustard and finished with lemon and coriander. Bird's Eye bhorta is to me what a tea-dipped madeleine was to Proust.

Up until now, I had thought the fish finger found its greatest expression in a fish finger sandwich, which for all my expounding on the subject on p.43, I don't consider the stuff of recipes; the fish finger bhorta is a different matter entirely. I have to say I became obsessed after reading Sarkar's tweet and, using her brief description, had a play in my own kitchen, until coming up with this version here. I did feel a little anxious about it at first, I'll admit. I worried about my changes, was concerned that I might be traducing what was an obviously emotionally resonant dish, and so tweeted Sarkar about it, explaining what I'd done. Her answer couldn't have been more soothing: 'As long as you're eating it at 3am straight out of the Tupperware,' she wrote, 'it's authentic.' And this is exactly what you'll want to do. If there is anything better waiting for you all boxed up in the fridge after you come back late from somewhere, the morning's hangover already in position and waiting to drop, I've yet to find it. Still, my drinking days and late nights are mostly behind me, I'm glad to say, and I'm happy to make this at any time when the need for vibrant sustenance and delicious comfort hits.

This dish says something so fundamental about what cooking is, about how we adapt to ingredients that are new to us, and make them part of our lives. Authenticity is a much overused, indeed much misused, word in cooking; in life generally, come to think of it. Honest borrowing is the natural province of the cook, and recipes are living, evolving entities.

The pink-pickled onions which I bring to the party, are not mandatory, but an addition I would be unwilling to do without. However, for all that they're quick, they're not instant. You can simply steep the onions in red wine vinegar (not the expensive kind) a couple of hours ahead, but longer is better. I plan to do this 6 hours ahead, or the day before, although I try anyway to keep a rolling stock of them in the house.

FISH FINGER
BHORTA

SERVES 2, with essential leftovers

FOR THE PINK-PICKLED ONIONS

½ red onion

Red wine vinegar or lime juice
  to cover

FOR THE BHORTA

2 regular onions (approx. 300g)

2 red chillies

2 fat cloves of garlic

1 x 15ml tablespoon finely grated
  fresh ginger (approx. 50g chunk)

12 fish fingers

3 x 15ml tablespoons cold-pressed
  rapeseed or vegetable oil

2 x 15ml tablespoons English
  mustard (from a jar)

2 teaspoons sea salt flakes (or
  1 teaspoon fine sea salt)

125g young spinach

1 lime

3 x 15ml tablespoons roughly
  chopped coriander, plus more
  to serve

For make-ahead, store and/or freeze notes, see p.332

1. Make your pink-pickled onions as far in advance as you can: at least 2 hours, and up to 24. Cut your red onion half – or use a whole onion if you prefer, as you will easily find yourself adding them to much else – into fine half-moons. Put these into a jar with a lid, or simply into a bowl that you can cover. Pour over red wine vinegar (or lime juice), pressing down on the onions until they are all just immersed. Put the lid on the jar or cover your bowl, and leave the onions to steep.

2. When you're ready to make and eat the bhorta, heat the oven to 220°C/200°C Fan. While you're waiting, peel and slice your 2 regular onions into fine half-moons, deseed the chillies (or not if you prefer) and slice them finely, and peel the garlic. If the skin is tough, peel the ginger (using the tip of a teaspoon) then grate it finely to give 1 tablespoonful.

3. When the oven's hot, and your ingredients are assembled and ready, put the fish fingers on a baking sheet and cook for approx. 20–25 minutes, which may be slightly longer than the packet directs, but will ensure the breadcrumb coating is really crisp.

4. Meanwhile, warm the oil in a large frying pan (I use a wok-shaped stir-fry pan), and cook the onions over medium-low for 20 minutes, stirring regularly, by which time they will be pale gold and soft.

5. Add the sliced chillies, stirring all the while, for 3 minutes, then stir in the grated ginger, mince or grate in the garlic, and cook, still stirring, for another 2 minutes. Spoon in the mustard and salt, stirring to combine, then add the spinach leaves and let them wilt in the pan for 2–3 minutes, stirring regularly, then squeeze in the juice of the lime.

6. Take the pan off the heat while you get the fish fingers. Break them up a bit with a spatula then add them to the wok or frying pan. Toss everything together, breaking them up further, and sprinkle over the coriander.

7. Serve topped with the pink-pickled onions, adding extra chopped coriander if wished.

SMOKY SQUID AND BEANS

I wouldn't like to say how often this is my supper and, indeed, lunch the next day when I eat it cold with a sprinkling of capers. For, although it does indeed serve two, I love it too much to keep it for company. It is, frankly, absurd how quick and easy it is to make. And yet it has such depth and complexity of flavour: the squid brings with it the briny kiss of the sea; the smokiness of the paprika, the heat of the chilli and the hit of the garlic give it a gutsiness that marries so well with the smooth, creamy beans. I adore the Spanish *judión* beans, which are soft, thin-skinned, extra-large butter beans, though you can, of course, use regular tinned butter beans, or soak and cook dried butter beans yourself.

Indeed, feel free to use whichever beans you want; this is a dish, anyway, that lends itself to easy variation. You could make it with prawns in place of the squid, or if you leave out the seafood element altogether, you have yourself the most elegant, upmarket and uplifting take on baked beans you could imagine.

Finally, without wanting to take your focus away from the particular pleasure of this simple but sublime supper just as it is, it's only fair to tell you that you can make another quickfire, killer meal, by replacing the jar of *judión* beans with a jar of chickpeas, and the squid with 600g of clams or mussels. Prepare the clams or mussels following the instructions on p.50 and, once the beans are cooked, proceed as if for the squid, but add the sherry (I wouldn't substitute with lemon juice here) to the hot pan along with the soaked and drained shellfish, and clamp on the lid.

SMOKY SQUID AND BEANS

SERVES 2

250–300g squid (cleaned weight)

2 x 15ml tablespoons Amontillado or other dry sherry (or use 2 tablespoons of juice from the lemon, below)

1 x 700g jar of Spanish *judión* beans or 2 x 400g tins of butter beans

3 x 15ml tablespoons plus 2 x 15ml tablespoons extra-virgin olive oil, and more to serve

1 lemon

4 fat cloves of garlic

½ teaspoon plus ¼ teaspoon dried chilli flakes

½ teaspoon sweet smoked paprika, plus more for dusting

2 teaspoons tomato purée

¼ teaspoon sea salt flakes or ⅛ teaspoon fine sea salt

For make-ahead, store and/or freeze notes, see p.332

1. Slice the tubes of squid to open them out, and then cut into bite-sized pieces. If the tentacles are in large clumps, halve them. Transfer the squid to a small dish, spoon over the sherry, and mix well. If you don't want to use sherry, then by all means substitute with lemon juice, but zest the lemon first with a fine grater held over a small plate. Leave the squid while you get on with the beans.

2. Empty the contents of your jar or tins of beans into a colander, rinse thoroughly with cold water from the tap, then drain (it doesn't matter if there's still some water clinging to them) and tip into a serving dish or shallow bowl big enough to fit them and the squid in later, and bring over to the hob.

3. Pour the 3 tablespoons of extra-virgin olive oil into a wok-like pan (or wide, shallow casserole) that comes with a lid and, if you haven't already zested the lemon, finely grate in the zest now, and peel then mince or grate in the garlic. Add the ½ teaspoon each of

chilli flakes and sweet smoked paprika, and warm over gentle heat, stirring most of the time, for about a minute or until the oil starts sizzling aromatically.

4. Spoon in the tomato purée and cook, stirring, for another minute and then tip in the beans (along with a couple of tablespoons of the water that's collected in the dish) and stir them into the pan, turning them in the fiery red oil very, very gently. If you have drained your beans too efficiently, you may need to get your couple of tablespoons of water from the tap. Sprinkle in the salt, give a final gentle stir (the beans out of the jar are divinely soft, and you don't want to squish them). Turn the heat up just a smidgeon, clamp on the lid, and leave to cook for 3 minutes, by which time they should be warmed through.

5. Once the beans are hot, tip them back into the serving dish, and let them wait there by the hob, ready to be united with the squid.

6. Pour the remaining 2 tablespoons of extra-virgin olive oil into the pan, add the ¼ teaspoon chilli flakes, and turn the heat to high. Squeeze the squid pieces in your hands over the dish they're in, then drop them into the hot chillified oil and cook, stirring pretty much most of the time, for 3 minutes or until they are just cooked through and opaque. Don't cook them beyond this point or they'll get tough. Pour in the sherry (or lemon) and squid juices from the dish, not worrying about the slight grey tinge they might have; even if the squid has been cleaned, you often get a little inkiness.

7. Once this has bubbled up, turn the heat back down to medium-low and scrape the beans out of their bowl into the pan on top of the squid. Stir together gently, and taste to see if it needs any lemon. If you've used lemon juice to macerate the squid, I'm sure it won't, but if you have steeped the squid in sherry you might like to add a tablespoonful at the end. Add more salt if needed, too.

8. Return to the serving dish, drizzle or douse – as you see fit – with extra-virgin olive oil, sprinkle over some sweet smoked paprika and serve immediately.

FRIED CHICKEN SANDWICH

'Fried', 'Chicken' and 'Sandwich': three alluring enough words on their own; together, they promise pure, unbridled pleasure. And, frankly, that's the only kind of pleasure I'm interested in. For this reason, I rarely feel the urge to eat this out. Or perhaps, it's truer to say, it's an urge I am unlikely to act upon. I'm not saying I never would, or never have, but I am increasingly squeamish about the kind of chicken I'm going to get, and am so much happier, so very much happier, making my own at home when I can have a quiet – or rather, noisily crunchy – dinner alone.

And it's simple enough to do. I concede the idea of deep-frying can make one hesitate, but frying one single chicken thigh is a very much less hot and bothersome activity than you might imagine. I use my 22cm heavy-based pan for this but do use a wok if you prefer.

It's hardly a takeaway-at-home impulse dinner, however, as the chicken ideally needs to marinate for quite a few hours (although, in extremis, you can leave it out on the kitchen counter for 20 minutes instead). But I like working my way up to this very special solo supper, and I plan it lovingly, making sure I get the chicken thigh fillet in its sharp, spicy marinade a good day before I'm going to be eating it. And while I have stipulated in the ingredients list what else you'll need for your sandwich, I am merely reporting on how I like to eat it. You may choose to ignore my suggestions entirely: there is no more personal food than a sandwich and I expect you to have your own strongly held views as to what to put in yours.

Chinese Chilli Crisp oil (mentioned earlier in this chapter) is a staple in my kitchen but really, any chilli component works along with the mayonnaise; if using a sweeter sauce though omit the honey. For me, shredded iceberg is pretty well non-negotiable, but I'll use cos (which you may know as romaine) uncomplainingly in its stead. And while I used to consider pickles essential, I increasingly want some sour-sharp kimchi in their place. If I don't have any, then I swap in some coarsely grated carrot and a fierily generous splodge of the Fermented Hot Sauce from p.300, which is just perfect with the crisp-coated, juicy-fleshed chicken. And it would be so very wrong of me not to tell you that the Caesar Mayo (p.16) makes this into a rich and sumptuous surf 'n' turf feast.

I always have kefir in the house, since I make it daily, but do use buttermilk or plain yogurt in its place. As for the bread you will be using for your sandwich, a burger bun might seem the obvious choice, but I am not always happy about the burger buns you can buy. If you strike lucky, go for it. Otherwise, I think regular soft white bread, whether out of a packet, or cut from a loaf, is the way to go. The Old-Fashioned Sandwich Loaf on p.43 is just made for this and, incidentally, there's no reason, I suppose, that you couldn't use the dough to make burger buns.

During lockdown, when I was running down my supplies before shopping again, I made this once with duck fat and once with schmaltz, that's to say, chicken fat (which I got out of a jar, rather than rendering down the fat from the skins from hundreds of chickens) and it was sensational with both. But then, it is when fried in oil, too.

FRIED CHICKEN SANDWICH

SERVES 1, ecstatically

75ml kefir, buttermilk or plain yogurt

½ teaspoon hot smoked paprika, plus ¼ teaspoon for flour, below

½ teaspoon fine sea salt, plus ¼ teaspoon for flour, below

1 teaspoon lemon juice

½ teaspoon Dijon mustard

½ teaspoon maple syrup

1 fat clove of garlic

1 small chicken thigh fillet

4–5 tablespoons (50g) plain flour

Sunflower oil for frying, approx. 1.5 litres for a 22cm pan, more for a wok

FOR ASSEMBLING

4 x 15ml tablespoons (60ml) garlic mayonnaise

1 teaspoon Chilli Crisp oil or other chilli sauce

¼ teaspoon honey

1 burger bun or 2 slices of white bread

A few leaves of iceberg lettuce, shredded

Kimchi or pickles of your choice

Pink-pickled onions (p.61)

For make-ahead, store and/or freeze notes, see p.332

1. Pour the kefir, or buttermilk, or yogurt into a small dish and stir in the ½ teaspoon of hot smoked paprika, ½ teaspoon of salt, lemon juice, Dijon mustard and maple syrup. Peel the garlic and mince or grate it in, too. Give a good stir, then add the chicken thigh fillet and turn it in the marinade to make sure it's well coated. Cover the dish, then leave for at least 4 hours or up to 2 days in the fridge. (If you simply cannot wait that long, leave the chicken in its marinade out on the kitchen counter for 20–40 minutes.)

2. Take the chicken, in its marinade, out of the fridge in good time to get to room temperature before you start to cook it.

3. Mix the flour with the remaining ¼ teaspoon each of hot smoked paprika and salt in a shallow dish. Lift the chicken out of the marinade, but don't try and shake it off. Dredge both sides of the chicken in the seasoned flour, then dip briefly back into the marinade and dredge again. This double-dredging is essential to get a thick, shaggy coating. You can leave the coated chicken in the flour dish until you fry.

4. Mix the garlic mayonnaise with the Chilli Crisp oil and honey, and spread both pieces of a split burger bun (or a couple of slices of bread) with it. Put a plate lined with kitchen paper by (but not dangerously near) the hob, if you want to get rid of any excess fat once the chicken's cooked.

5. Pour enough oil into your chosen pan to come about 3½cm up the sides. Heat until a small piece of bread becomes golden and crisp almost instantly; if you want to be precise, and have a food thermometer, then you want the fat to be at 190°C when the chicken goes in (and about 180°C as it cooks).

6. Using tongs, gently lower the chicken thigh into the hot oil, and cook for 3–4 minutes on each side, by which time the coating should be deep gold and very crisp and the chicken completely cooked through. Remove to the waiting paper-lined plate, remembering to take the pan of oil off the heat, and leave to stand for a couple of minutes while you shred some iceberg lettuce and get out your pickles. Put a handful of shredded lettuce on top on the mayo on the bottom slice, top with the fried chicken, add kimchi, pink-pickled onions and any other pickles you want. Scatter with a bit more lettuce and squidge on the top of the bun or second slice of bread. Go in cautiously: I have more than once burned my mouth.

MARZIPAN LOAF CAKE

I love a plain cake. There is something uniquely soothing about the simple, sweet comfort it offers. And there's a modesty about a plain cake, too: it doesn't draw attention to itself, or seek to impress with razzle-dazzle. It's there to be sliced as needed, always delivering more than it promises.

I've used marzipan in a cake before, so I knew it would work, but I'm still surprised every time I make it – and once you start, it's hard to stop – by just how easy it is. You throw everything into a processor (though I have, too, given alternative directions, so don't worry if you don't have one) and blitz together to create a fragrant, grainy batter which in turn makes a tender-crumbed, sweet-scented and buttery loaf cake, to be eaten at breakfast or throughout the day, indeed any time you want to sit down with a slice and a cup of tea.

It also serves as a proper pudding. Just arrange slices of the cake on a non-stick baking sheet, and warm up in a 200°C/180°C Fan oven for 3–4 minutes a side, until caramelised and golden. Arrange a couple of slices on each person's plate, add some fresh raspberries and a splodge of crème fraîche (and take more of each out to the table); the sharpness of the berries and tang of the cream are perfect with the toasty cake, which, when hot, tastes like a rich, almondy brioche. It's also wonderful with a bowl of roast rhubarb; and luckily, there's a recipe for that on p.127.

While marzipan and almond paste are not always interchangeable, I have made the cake with both, and am just as delighted with either. Because almond paste is softer, it will be easier for you to use that if you're not using a processor. But in any case, whether you're using marzipan or almond paste, please make sure neither has ever seen the inside of your fridge. And during cold weather, keep the marzipan or paste somewhere warm before whipping it into cake.

Perhaps I should tell you that I hesitated before calling this Marzipan Loaf Cake, if only because I know from experience that there are vociferous marzipan haters out there who nonetheless, and to their gratified surprise, adore this cake.

If you want this loaf to be gluten-free, replace the plain flour with rice flour or gluten-free plain flour and check that all other ingredients are labelled gluten-free, as brands vary.

GIVES 8–10 slices

150g marzipan (white or yellow) or almond paste, at room temperature

125g soft unsalted butter

1 teaspoon vanilla paste (or extract)

50g caster sugar

75g plain flour (or gluten-free plain flour)

¼ teaspoon fine sea salt

1 teaspoon baking powder (gluten-free if necessary)

1½ teaspoons ground cardamom

3 large eggs, at room temperature

For make-ahead, store and/or freeze notes, see p.332

1. Heat the oven to 170°C/150°C Fan and drop a loaf-tin liner into a 1lb (450g) loaf tin, or line the bottom with parchment and butter the sides.

2. The easiest way to make this is to put everything (tearing the marzipan into lumps first) into the processor and blitz until smooth, stopping to scrape down the sides a couple of times.

3. If you don't have a processor, then I advise you to use almond paste rather than marzipan and beat it together with the butter and vanilla until thoroughly combined, then beat in the sugar. Stir the flour, salt, baking powder (though if you're not making this in a processor, use just ¾ teaspoon) and cardamom together. Beat the eggs into the butter mixture, one at a time, adding a third of the dried ingredients after each egg. Carry on beating when everything's in, to make sure you have a coherent batter with no lumps of almond paste visible.

4. Pour and scrape into the prepared tin and bake for 40 minutes (adding a loose covering of foil after 30 to stop it browning any further) or until the cake is beginning to come away from the sides and a cake tester comes out clean. It runckles a little on top as it cools.

LEMON AND ELDERFLOWER DRIZZLE CAKE

This is another plain cake that fills me with quiet but profound joy. I've been making lemon drizzle cake the same way for decades, and up until now had never felt any urge to alter one single little thing. (Actually, I tried for some time to come up with a grapefruit drizzle cake, but I found it an unworthy alternative to the original lemon version.) But life changes, as do we, and I began to wonder whether a lemon and elderflower variation would be interesting. I'm glad to report that it is a delight: that necessary stinging sharpness is undimmed, but the elderflower adds a subtle sweet floral note that seems to give it a tender delicacy.

Rather than using a loaf tin, I go for a 20cm square tin (though a 20cm springform will also do), as this way the cake itself is shallower, and more of it can soak up the fragrant and tangy drizzle. Where possible, I test all cakes with gluten-free flour (and rice flour is the gluten-free flour I prefer, though you could also use gluten-free plain flour here) so that I can provide an alternative for those who need it. In this case, I found I preferred the cake made with rice flour – it gives just a little hint of resistance – so have given plain flour as the alternative here. But there is not a huge amount in it, and if you have no need of a gluten-free cake it makes sense to use the flour you have to hand.

Although I think of this predominantly as the sort of cake you have with a mug of tea mid-afternoon, I must tell you that with very little alteration, it makes one of the best Sunday-lunch puddings you will ever eat. (And the Warm Lemon and Elderflower Pudding is photographed on p.77.) Just add 50g or 4 tablespoons of full-fat Greek yogurt to the batter, and bake it at 180°C/160°C Fan in a buttered ovenproof dish (mine measures 26 x 17 x 5cm, though any ovenproof dish of the same depth, with a 1.5 litre capacity would be fine) for 25 minutes, covering loosely with foil at 20 if the top is browning too much. When out of the oven, prick the sponge and drizzle with the elderflower lemon syrup, but don't sprinkle with granulated sugar. Eat warm with double cream. You should be able to feed four to six lucky people out of this, but if there are fewer of you, leftovers microwave most satisfactorily.

And as another variant on the lemon and elderflower theme, may I introduce you to a cocktail – let us call it a Lemon Blossom – of my own devising. To make one, pour 30ml (2 tablespoons) of limoncello, 30ml (2 tablespoons) of vodka, 30ml (2 tablespoons) of undiluted elderflower cordial and 2 teaspoons of lemon juice into a cocktail shaker. Add a generous amount of ice cubes and shake vigorously. Strain into a chilled martini glass.

GIVES 9 squares

FOR THE CAKE

175g soft unsalted butter

150g caster sugar

100g rice flour (or plain flour if you don't need this to be gluten-free)

75g ground almonds

A pinch of fine sea salt

1½ teaspoons baking powder (gluten-free if necessary)

3 large eggs, at room temperature

1 large lemon

2 x 15ml tablespoons undiluted elderflower cordial

FOR THE DRIZZLE

3 x 15ml tablespoons of juice from the lemon, above

100ml undiluted elderflower cordial

1 x 15ml tablespoon (15g) granulated sugar

For make-ahead, store and/or freeze notes, see p.332

1. Heat the oven to 180°C/160°C Fan. Line the bottom and sides of a 20cm square (or round) cake tin with baking parchment, making sure the paper comes up the sides. If you're using a spring-form cake tin, just line the bottom and butter the sides.

2. Put the butter, sugar, rice flour, ground almonds, salt, baking powder and eggs into a processor. Finely grate over the zest of the lemon and blitz until you have a thick batter. Pour the 2 tablespoons of elderflower cordial through the funnel of the processor, with the motor still going, until combined.

3. If you don't have a processor, cream the butter, sugar and lemon zest together until smooth, light and aerated. Mix the flour, ground almonds and salt together, add just 1 teaspoon of baking powder; you don't need as much for the non-processor variant, as you're whipping more air into the batter. Beat 1 egg into the butter mixture, and when that's combined, beat in a third of your dry ingredients, and carry on in like manner until eggs and dry ingredients are used up. Finally, beat in the 2 tablespoons of elderflower cordial.

4. Pour and scrape this fragrant, slightly nubbly and quite delicious batter into your prepared tin and bake for approx. 25 minutes, by which time the top of the cake should have turned a deep golden brown, and the edges – themselves a darker bronze by this stage – will have started coming away from the sides of the tin and a cake tester should come out clean. Check on it at around 20 minutes and loosely cover with foil if it's getting too dark. I didn't do this, as you can see from the photo on p.74.

5. While the cake is in the oven, prepare the drizzle. Mix 3 tablespoons of juice from the zested lemon and 100ml of elderflower cordial in a jug. Ignore the granulated sugar for now.

6. When the cake is cooked, put it in its tin on a wire rack and prick all over with your cake tester, though a stick of spaghetti would do (it's a wonderful stand-in cake tester as it is), and then very gradually pour the syrup over the cake so that it sinks in slowly and doesn't pool.

7. Once the syrup is soaked in, sprinkle over the tablespoon of granulated sugar in an even layer on top of the cake, and leave to cool completely. When cold, either lift the cake out of the tin using the paper, or just unspring if you're using a springform tin.

GLUTEN-FREE BANANA BREAD
WITH CHOCOLATE AND WALNUTS

Since I am clearly incapable of throwing away even the blackest banana, I have spent much of my life making banana bread, and am always happy to find an excuse to come up with another one. A friend of mine had been begging me for ages for a gluten-free version, and this is it. The crumb is tender and light – the Greek yogurt helps here, and also counters the sweetness of the banana with its tang – and the nubbliness of the walnuts and rich goo of the chopped chocolate make it a gorgeous treat. I can't stop eating it.

I've said to chop both walnuts and chocolate roughly: although you will of course get some shards and rubble, I keep most pieces chunky enough to make their presence proudly felt in each sumptuous bite.

You can halve quantities to fill a 1lb (450g) loaf tin; I don't find it takes appreciably less time to cook.

GIVES 10–12 slices

175g rice flour (or gluten-free plain flour)

100g ground almonds

2 teaspoons gluten-free baking powder

½ teaspoon bicarbonate of soda

¼ teaspoon fine sea salt

500g (approx. 3 large) very ripe or overripe bananas (skin-on weight)

2 teaspoons vanilla extract

100g full-fat Greek yogurt, at room temperature

2 large eggs, at room temperature

125ml vegetable oil

125g soft light brown sugar

150g dark chocolate, roughly chopped

100g walnuts, roughly chopped

For make-ahead, store and/or freeze notes, see p.332

1. Heat the oven to 170°C/150°C Fan and drop a paper liner into a 2lb (900g) loaf tin or line the base with baking parchment.

2. Mix the rice flour (or gluten-free plain flour), ground almonds, baking powder, bicarb and salt in a bowl. Set aside for now.

3. Peel the bananas (don't throw the skins away, though, but use them to make the Banana Skin and Cauliflower Curry on p.35) and, in a large bowl, big enough to take all the ingredients later, mash the peeled bananas thoroughly. Beat in the vanilla, then the yogurt and, one by one, the eggs, followed by the oil and sugar.

4. When everything's combined, gradually beat in the flour mixture. Scrape down the sides of the bowl to make sure all is combined, and then fold in the chopped chocolate and walnuts.

5. Pour and scrape the batter into the lined loaf tin – it will come close to the top – then bake in the oven for 50–55 minutes until shrinking from the sides of the tin, and a cake tester (if you manage to avoid the gooey chocolate) comes out cleanish but with a few damp crumbs sticking to it. Sit the tin on a wire rack, and allow the cake to cool completely before removing from the tin.

CHOCOLATE, TAHINI AND BANANA TWO WAYS

I have been making a banana bread with chocolate and tahini on repeat for a while now, and every time I've eaten it over the last year or so, I couldn't help thinking that the particular combination of intense chocolatiness, sweet, texture-softening banana and the rich earthiness of tahini would make the perfect warm pudding. Finally, I tried it out. And much as I adore the elegant subtlety of the banana bread, I was enraptured by it in pudding form. A warm, soft and squidgy cake, it is both embracingly cosy and almost regally sumptuous. You could serve it just with crème fraîche, a little bit of tang to offset the pudding-cake's richness, but I stir 4 teaspoons of tahini into 250ml of double cream and whisk gently by hand and for not very long, until it's softly whipped. And I don't stop there: after I've dolloped the tahini cream onto my pud, I drizzle over some (shop-bought, not homemade) date molasses, which is like sticky toffee pudding in syrup form.

Whether you're making the delectable banana bread or the pudding-cake (and, for that matter, any recipe in this book that has tahini in it) do try and get proper Middle Eastern tahini, which is smokier and more fluid, with a full-bodied velvetiness, than the more widely available Mediterranean one on which I have bent more spoons than Uri Geller.

You can easily double the quantities below to fill a 2lb (900g) loaf tin or 23cm round pie dish, depending on whether you're making bread or pud; in either case, I don't find it makes an appreciable difference to the cooking time. You can make a vegan version of both, omitting the egg, and upping the bananas to 350g and the tahini to 75g. For the pudding, you will need to add 50g of plant-based yogurt, too; I used the same almond-soy variety as I do for the Vegan Lemon Polenta Cake (p.257). Neither the pudding nor the bread will rise a lot without the egg, but the taste is still magnificent. Dark chocolate chips should be dairy-free, but do check the packet.

GIVES approx. 10 slices of banana bread or makes a pudding for 2–3

250g (approx. 2 medium) very ripe or overripe bananas (skin-on weight)

60ml olive or vegetable oil

50g tahini, at room temperature (and see recipe intro)

50g full-fat Greek yogurt, at room temperature (but only for the pud)

1 large egg, at room temperature

50g caster sugar

50g soft dark brown sugar for the pud; 35g for the bread

1 teaspoon vanilla extract

60g plain flour (or gluten-free plain flour)

25g cocoa

½ teaspoon bicarbonate of soda

¼ teaspoon fine sea salt

100g dark chocolate chips

1½ teaspoons sesame seeds, to sprinkle on top (only for the bread)

For make-ahead, store and/or freeze notes, see p.332

1. Heat the oven to 170°C/150°C Fan if you're making banana bread, or 180°C/160°C Fan for the pudding. Put a paper liner into a 1lb (450g) loaf tin or, for the pudding, get out an ovenproof dish with a capacity of about 750ml; mine is 18cm in diameter and 5cm deep.

2. Peel the bananas (don't throw the skins away, though, but use them to make the Banana Skin and Cauliflower Curry on p.35) and, either by hand or using an electric mixer, mash the bananas, then beat in the oil. I use an American ¼ cup (60ml) measure to do this, and then fill it up with tahini (conveniently, 60ml of tahini weighs 50g) and beat that in. If you're making the pudding, beat in the yogurt (you can also fill the ¼ cup measure with it to get 50g). Whether you're making the pudding or the bread, now's the time to beat in the egg, then the sugars and vanilla.

3. Whisk or fork together the flour, cocoa, bicarb and salt and slowly beat into the batter and when you can no longer see any specks of white, fold in the chocolate chips with a bendy spatula, which you will need to scrape the runny batter into either loaf tin or ovenproof dish. If it's banana bread you're making, sprinkle over the sesame seeds.

4. First, instructions for the bread: cook for 45–50 minutes until risen and firm to the touch, or until a cake tester comes out almost clean; some chocolate chips will make it a little sticky in parts. And don't worry about the cracks on the top; that is part of its deal, as it is for the pudding. Let it cool completely in its tin on a wire rack and – if you can bear to wait – once it's cold, slip it out of the tin and wrap it in baking parchment, then foil, and leave it for a day before slicing and eating. I understand if this is too much to ask; I confess I don't always manage to wait.

5. And now for the pudding-cake: cook for 40–45 minutes, depending on whether you want it to have a gooily molten centre or not. Once it's out of the oven, let it stand for 5–10 minutes before diving in for that first squidgy spoonful.

MINE-ALL-MINE SWEET AND SALTY CHOCOLATE COOKIES

The lone-dweller, in need of the balm that only a freshly baked biscuit can provide, is faced with a most unsatisfactory choice: do without or make a batch big enough to keep a huge hungry household happy. I had to put that right, and not just out of altruism, you understand.

To this end, I have created a cookie recipe that answers my every requirement: deeply chocolatey, sweet but not too sweet, and sprinkled with sea salt flakes. They are the work of an easy moment, requiring no more than a couple of bowls, a wooden spoon and a spot of stirring. And while I urge you to eat one – if such urging is even necessary – when it's still warm, so that it's crisp around the edges, its centre tender and shortbready and gloriously gooey with nuggets of molten chocolate, you can for a contrasting kind of eating enjoyment leave the other until the next day (but no longer), when it will be slightly sandy and softly chewy. But these are big old biscuits so, if you find yourself in company – and a generous mood – you can graciously offer one of them without feeling short-changed.

Since there is no egg involved, it is a simple enough matter to veganise these: just replace the butter with the kind of margarine that comes not in a tub, but in a block, manufactured specifically for baking. I've tried making them with coconut oil, which would be a more wholesome substitute, but I'm afraid it just doesn't work. Dark chocolate should always be dairy-free, but do check the packet of chocolate chips to make sure. While you can make these gluten-free, you will have to let them get cold before eating them (or they won't hold together) thus forgoing the goo, but enjoying them rather as tender chocolate shortbread.

MAKES 2 large cookies

50g plain flour (or gluten-free plain flour)

10g cocoa

⅛ teaspoon baking powder (gluten-free if necessary)

⅛ teaspoon bicarbonate of soda

⅛ teaspoon fine sea salt

50g soft unsalted butter (or dairy-free baking block if you want these to be vegan)

25g caster sugar

15g soft dark brown sugar

¼ teaspoon vanilla extract

25g dark chocolate chips

¼ teaspoon sea salt flakes

For make-ahead, store and/or freeze notes, see p.332

1. Heat the oven to 180°C/160°C Fan, and get out a – preferably light-coloured – baking sheet. You don't need to line it if it's non-stick; otherwise, lie a sheet of baking parchment on it.

2. Stir the flour, cocoa, baking powder, bicarbonate of soda and fine sea salt together in a small bowl just to combine them.

3. In a slightly larger bowl – I use a pudding basin that I now can't look at without thinking of these cookies – vigorously beat the butter, both the sugars and the vanilla with a small wooden spoon until you have a buff-coloured and creamy mixture. If you aren't a messy person, you could use a cereal bowl for this.

4. Add a generous spoonful of the dry ingredients to the creamed butter and sugar and beat it in gently with your wooden spoon. Then – still gently, unless you want cocoa and flour all over the place – beat in the rest of your dry ingredients, in about three batches. Once the dry ingredients are absorbed, you can beat vigorously until you have a sticky, rich-brown dough, that clumps together, at which point you can stir in the chocolate chips.

5. It's not often I demand this level of precision, but I now weigh this mixture, and divide it in two; you don't need to be fanatical about this, a few grams here or there won't make the difference. Squidge each half in your hands to form two fat patties about 7cm in diameter and place them on your baking sheet, at least 10cm apart, as they spread while cooking.

6. Sprinkle ⅛ teaspoon of sea salt flakes over each cookie, and bake in the oven for about 12 minutes, until the top of each biscuit is riven with cracks. At 10 minutes – which is when I start checking – they will be utterly smooth, but in the next 2 minutes they seem to transform themselves. I crouch by the oven, staring through the cloudy glass door feeling like, as the old Joan Rivers joke has it (and forgive me if you've heard me tell this before), Elizabeth Taylor shouting 'Hurry!' at the microwave.

7. Once the surface is cracked, and the cookies have spread, they are ready. They will, however, feel very soft – even uncooked – to the touch, and you will doubt me. But I will forgive you, as long as you obey me. So whip out the baking sheet, leaving the cookies in place for 5 minutes. Only then may you slip a metal spatula under the cookies and tenderly transfer them to a wire rack. For optimal eating pleasure, leave for another 10 minutes before biting into one. I often succumb after 5, which is perfectly permissible, I feel, though I should warn you that the biscuit is unlikely to hold its shape by then. But in times of urgent need, such matters of form scarcely matter.

CRÈME CARAMEL FOR ONE

It's not quite true to say I had forgotten about crème caramel but, until very recently, this once luscious treat, the pudding I always chose from the dessert trolley at the restaurants my paternal grandparents took me to, and which, as I child, I thought the pinnacle of sophistication, had utterly receded from my consciousness. But this joy has now been restored to me and, by pleasing coincidence, I have my grandmother to thank for it.

There is no need to start shifting uncomfortably on your seat. I'm not going to tell you of messages from The Other Side. No, I had decided to attack my clutter, and started on a box under the bed, crammed with paper and packages, in one of which was a collection of my grandmother's handwritten recipe books. Naturally, I abandoned my project and sat down with a mug of tea to read these instead. And, after leafing through Biscuit Torte, Italian Lemon Pie and something called Uncooked Sweet, I came upon her Caramel Custard. As it happened, I had been trying to think of a way to use up the two egg yolks I had left over from the Blood Orange and Passionfruit Pavlova on p.243, and thus it was decided.

I didn't pay the strictest attention to her stipulations. In fact, I rather ignored them, and only later noticed that her version didn't use the caramel as contrast to the custard of eggs and milk, but was stirred into them before baking. Nevertheless, it set me on track, and the crème caramel re-entered my life. And I can't think of a better solitary treat: making something that needs unmoulding is nerve-wracking when you have to do it in front of people; alone, it gives a rather delicious frisson, and the bestowing of a hushed and hallowed moment. Crème caramel is just such a ridiculous thing to be making for oneself; therein lies the gift of it. And then there's the dreamy softness of the mild custard, the scorched syrup that counters it: eating it is a transporting experience.

I know it's customary to use both cream and milk in a crème caramel but to me it's the delicacy, the lack of richness, of the custard that gives it its teasing elegance. And, it's true, I used just yolks for it, rather than the more usual combination of whole egg and extra yolk, because that's what I needed to use up, but I would never toughen the texture of a crème caramel with an egg white again: this version is so exquisitely tender, its set so soft, it's like a whisper on the lips. That ethereal quality is partly, too, due to the way it's cooked. The water bath is routine enough, but covering it for the first 30 minutes it's in the oven helps it cook more gently still, as it protects the top from even the low heat it bakes at; it does need to be uncovered for the last 20 minutes, though, or else it won't hold its form when unmoulded later.

Actually, were my grandmother to come back and haunt me through the medium of desserts, it is far more likely she'd be urging me to make her Crème Brûlée, of which she was inordinately proud, and the recipe for which you can see peeking out of one of her notebooks opposite page one. I've adapted her recipe to make it a solo portion as well, and provide another use for the two yolks left over from the pav, as before. Having said that, this is a much richer confection and you could well share it with an intimate other.

To make my Granny Lawson's Crème Brûlée, warm 150ml of double cream with a third of a cinnamon stick (or one of those short cinnamon sticks from a jar) and a few long strips of zest pared from a lemon with a vegetable peeler, and bring nearly, but not quite, to the boil. Turn off the heat, cover the pan, and leave to infuse for 15 minutes. With a small silicon spatula, mix 2 egg yolks with 2 teaspoons of caster sugar in a measuring jug, and keep stirring while you pour in the infused cream. Make sure everything's combined, scraping up any yellow bits of yolk from the bottom of the jug. Strain into a crème brûlée dish – mine is wide and shallow, 12cm in diameter and 3cm deep – and, with a teaspoon, remove any froth or bubbles, then cook in a 95°C/75°C Fan oven for 50 minutes, until just set but still quivering.

If you don't have such a dish, then you can use a ramekin or similar, but it must have a capacity of 200ml, and you would have to cook as you do the Crème Caramel: that's to say, in a water bath and at 140°C/120°C Fan, though don't cover it at all; you want it to firm up a little on top, to provide a surface for the sugar later. And, unlike a crème caramel which needs to go into the fridge to set, I think a crème brûlée (when it's in an individual dish like this) is ruined by refrigeration; it will become too solid. So make this a couple of hours before you want to eat it, let it get cold, then sprinkle over 2½ teaspoons of demerara sugar, and set to with a blow torch, making sure the dish is nowhere near anything you could set fire to. Don't have the flame too high (an instruction I all too often fail to follow) or you'll burn the sugar in patches before all of it has turned from crunchy grains to smooth, tortoise-shellacked carapace.

I can see that the relatively instant gratification of the crème brûlée has its advantages, but I have grown to relish the anticipation of the crème caramel as I wait for it to set in the fridge, and regard it as part of the ceremony, and its subtle charm.

SERVES 1, blissfully

FOR THE CARAMEL

2 x 15ml tablespoons (25g) caster
  sugar

2 teaspoons cold water

FOR THE CRÈME

2 large egg yolks, at room
  temperature

2 teaspoons caster sugar

¼ teaspoon vanilla extract

150ml full-fat milk

For make-ahead, store and/or freeze notes, see p.333

1. Heat the oven to 140°C/120°C Fan, put the kettle on, tear off a piece of foil and cut out a square that's 1½–2cm bigger than the diameter of the top of the dish or mould you're using. When I first rushed to make this, I used a sweet little 200ml ceramic pudding basin that I must have bought once in a fit of cute, and found in the back of a messy cupboard. Fortune smiled: it was just right for the job. Otherwise, I favour preserving jars, drinking glasses or ceramic or glass ramekins; they all need to have a 200ml capacity and be heatproof.

2. Put your chosen mould very near the hob, and spoon the sugar into a very small saucepan with a light-coloured interior – I use my pixie-pan, more properly known as a butter melter, with a 9cm diameter, but a milk pan of about 14cm is just as good – and add the 2 teaspoons of water. Swirl the pan a little, then put over medium-low heat to melt the sugar and bring it to the boil, lifting the pan up and giving it a swirl every now and again. Don't even think of stirring it. Once the now-clear melted sugar starts bubbling away, you can turn the heat up a little, and then wait for it to turn first gold, then amber, then watch until it's somewhere between maple syrup and chestnut; I like the caramel to be as dark and smoky as it can be without actually burning. Be patient, lift up and swirl the pan often and monitor it closely; as Tammy almost sang, Stand By Your Pan. Immediately it's turned the requisite deep amber, pour the caramel into the bottom of your mould, and now give this a swirl, just so the caramel goes a little up the sides. Place the mould in a small tin or ovenproof dish.

3. In a Pyrex jug or similar, briskly stir the egg yolks with the sugar and vanilla extract, just until combined. I use a small silicon spatula for this, as a whisk would get too much air into the mixture.

4. Warm the milk – I give it 40 seconds in the microwave – and then pour it over the eggs and sugar, stirring and scraping with your little spatula, making sure there are no visible yellow bits of

egg left at the bottom. Strain this – you must not think of dispensing with this step – over your caramel-lined mould and then, with a teaspoon, carefully remove any bubbles or froth. Cover the mould with your square of foil, making sure it doesn't touch the custard mixture, and seal it well all around the edges.

5. Pour hot water from the just-boiled kettle into the tin or dish to come about a third of the way up the mould, and slowly and steadily put it in the oven. Bake for 30 minutes, then lean in and very carefully remove the foil, and leave in the oven to cook for a further 20 minutes by which time it will be just set, with a little bit of a quiver.

6. Remove the tin from the oven and very carefully lift the crème caramel mould out of the water, and leave it on the kitchen counter until completely cold. Cover with food wrap and place in the fridge overnight, or for at least 6 hours.

7. Take the crème caramel out of the fridge 30 minutes before you want to eat it. Uncover, and with a very small palette knife, try very gently to pull the top of the soft-set cooked custard away from the sides of the mould. Fill a dish about 3cm deep with water from a just-boiled kettle, or very hot water from the tap, and stand or dip the crème caramel mould in the water for the count of 5. Now for the fun part: sit a saucer or small lipped plate on top of the mould, turn it swiftly and firmly the right way up and give the smallest of shakes to help dislodge it. You will hear a muffled squelch as the crème caramel begins to slide out of the mould and onto its saucer. Gently remove the mould, and gaze at this tender, bulging, copper-topped beauty for a moment, before you plunge in your teaspoon, and become suffused, as you eat, by sweet serenity.

A LOVING DEFENCE OF BROWN FOOD

Food provides many pleasures, not least of them aesthetic. The taut purple-black gleam of aubergines; the perfect Fibonacci fractal of Romanesco; the speckled Tuscan tones of a pile of dried borlotti beans; the tiger-striped iridescence of mackerel: cooking is full of such sudden snatches of beauty. No one sense can operate satisfactorily without the willing cooperation of the others: without smell, you cannot taste; how food looks can alter our perception of it before we've even had our first mouthful.

There's a reason why I once named a recipe that called on yellow courgettes, turmeric and lemon Happiness Soup; just as another, made with sweetcorn, yellow and orange peppers, was Sunshine Soup. We have an immediate, primitive response to colour. Recently, a study found that eating yellow food made people feel happier. But long before colour psychologists were around, as Claudia Roden wrote, some Middle Eastern cultures believed that eating yellow foods would result in 'laughter and happiness'. Emma Mitchell, author of *The Wild Remedy*, told me that pink, too – salmon, red mullet, strawberry ice cream (and I'd add rhubarb, of course) – has been demonstrated to lower anxiety levels. And, quite anecdotally, we all know that there is a definite connection between colour and emotion. I'm not convinced that we are dealing in absolutes here; the associations we make are culturally informed as well as, so often, deeply personal. But there is, on the emotional level, scant distinction to be made between what is true and what we feel to be true. I indeed feel immeasurably brightened by the sight of my orange butternut draped with its bright beetroot sauce (p.224), of a tumble of red-cheeked radishes mounded in a bowl, or the jewel-like (if clichéd) scattering of pomegranate seeds on anything. It's childishly unsophisticated, this delight in colour, and yet pleasure, however simple, should always be celebrated so I can't apologise for it.

But what, then, of brown food, those stews that encounter instant disapprobation when posted on Instagram, the medium that has probably done most for the rampant championing of the colourful over the drab? Must it always be apologised for, or defended with smug superiority? As someone who posts a lot of what I eat, I am idiotically always surprised afresh when an instant response comes to an undeniably brown study of a stew to the effect that it looks disgusting. I now pre-emptively caption it with the words 'This is a stew. Stews are brown.' I understand that Instagram is a visual medium, and so often pictures of food are rated according to what they look like, not what they might taste like. It makes sense, even if it has led to a proliferation of images that veer from the practically inedible – those towering, ten-tiered cakes with seamlessly graduated ombré icing that I have yet to work out how anyone could slice or, indeed, eat – to the actively deadly, in the guise of perfectly styled plates of food decorated with flowers, some of which (as botanists have had to point out) are actually poisonous.

The defensive stance most succinctly summed up by the insistence that 'brown food is the best food' is – for all that I have wielded it myself – flawed in two important respects. For one, allowing oneself ever to get roped into that game of rating food, or pitting one type against another, is both reductive and pleasure-draining. And it implies – and sometimes is explicitly argued – that while a stew might be unappealing to look at, it must be borne in mind that the ugliest food can have the most beautiful taste. But I have to say, I do not find stews ugly. They can certainly be, in the wrong hands, unphotogenic, which is why a picture I take of my Oxtail Bourguignon struggles to make its appeal clear, and yet the same dish photographed by Jonathan Lovekin on p.117 shows it in all its comforting, deep-flavoured glory.

To the naked eye, brown food is beautiful: rich, warm, and full of depth and subtle variegation. None of this can be easily caught on camera; all that richness, all that warmth, all that promise of deep flavour from long, slow cooking is flattened by the inexpert lens, which turns the stew's meaty liquid distortingly to cold glassiness.

Crucially, it is not the brownness of the food, or not in itself, that actually dismays people, I believe – no one, after all, finds a bar of chocolate a rebarbative sight – but the fact that so many of the foods that come into this category challenge with their texture. It seems to speak to some deep-rooted, perhaps primitive, fear of the uncontained, and an especial fear of all that uncontained brownness; you do not need to be a psychoanalyst to see why this might be so. But there are also more straightforward explanations: many people, shuddering at memories of the gristle and gloop ladled out menacingly in their childhood, are put off stews for life. It's true: a bad stew, floury and flavourless, the meat boiled in the liquid until each chunk curls up in desiccated defence, is an emetic proposition. And perhaps it is the legacy of just such culinary abominations that makes the word 'stew' – even for me, the keenest of casserolers – seem a synonym for 'slop'. I'm never hesitant of saying there's stew for supper at home, but I've often shied away from it on the page (as the recipe titles that follow certainly indicate) in the sad knowledge that for many readers it is not always the most compelling of invitations.

But what we surely know is that it is always more rewarding to cook to comfort rather than to impress. I don't want applause when I bring food to the table, but rather silence to descend as people begin to eat. Rest assured, I don't insist on it – lively talk around a table is one of the joys of life, and one I pointedly miss at time of writing – but it speaks gratifyingly to the cook, more than words can ever say.

However comforting, though, a brown bowl of something doesn't scream showstopper. Everything has to make a statement these days all of the time (including us) and brown food most definitively doesn't do that: it gently beckons us with a whisper rather than a shout. And the truth is, we need the calm that it bestows. The vibrant, the splendid, the sprightly and bright: all these have a place at the table, but not at the cost of cosier, quieter pleasures. And while I hold by my view that a conker-shiny, wine-dark stew is a beautiful sight, I gladly concede that so much of my favourite food is not picture-book pretty: fat-pearled black pudding; chopped liver, in all its visceral mauve-grey glory; slow-cooked peas, their hyper-green perkiness braised to a sweet-tasting, khaki drabness; beautiful red chicory roasted in the oven until a wilted and scorched dried-blood maroon; the Italian way of cooking greens to an olive-oil-soused pond mulch. As my notebook reminds me, and in capital letters what's more: COLOUR FADES AS FLAVOUR DEEPENS; a metaphor for much of life, I suggest.

I once described a very beige chicken fricassée as having a face only a mother could love. To me, all the recipes that follow are beautiful in their brownness, and on them I rest my case.

BURNT ONION AND AUBERGINE DIP

This recipe nestled impatiently in my subconscious for quite some time before a bout of insomnia allowed it to percolate properly, and although I very much wish sleeping were one of my gifts, I am very happy with this brown bowl of silky savouriness. I class it as a dip, but in truth it is as much a spread or a sauce. I first made it, though, to go alongside the very much brighter Beetroot and Chickpea Dip and Coriander and Ginger Salsa (both on p.199), to dip my usual blue corn tortilla chips into over drinks before dinner, and haven't been able to stop making it. True, anyone in the habit of changing nappies regularly might not find it the most appetising of sights, but I love its manila-tinted, speckled brownness. Besides, one taste of it – full of rich, deep smokiness – and even those not immediately attracted come back for more.

Should you have leftovers – and I make enough to ensure I do – you can turn it into a pasta sauce, add it to soups or stews to thicken and add flavour, and were you to want to make, say, a vegan mushroom risotto, you can stir this in at the *mantecatura* stage, when all the stock has been absorbed, in place of butter or cheese. Or eat it, simply, on toast.

Just to give you a pointer, to make it into a pasta sauce for 200g of linguine (or pasta of your choice), mix 5 tablespoons of the dip, thinned with some pasta-cooking liquid, add salt and chilli flakes to taste (and a squeeze of lemon juice if you feel it needs brightening up), toss through the drained pasta in the saucepan it was cooked in and add chopped parsley or whatever herbs you want.

If you don't have a baking tray large enough for all the aubergines and onions and need to use two, then be prepared for the cooking time to be longer, and swap the trays around in the oven after about 40 minutes.

And if at all possible, I recommend using 3 aubergines as stipulated below, rather than say 2 that come to the same total weight. Obviously, if that choice isn't open to you, it does work with 2, but you will need to cut them into long quarters.

MAKES 600ml

6 x 15ml tablespoons (90ml) olive oil

3 onions (approx. 500g)

3 medium aubergines (approx. 250g
  each)

1 bulb of garlic

2 teaspoons sea salt flakes (or
  1 teaspoon fine sea salt)

1½ teaspoons dried mint

2 x 15ml tablespoons lemon juice

2 x 15ml tablespoons (approx. 25g)
  tahini

1 teaspoon ground cumin

1 teaspoon sweet smoked paprika

6 x 15ml tablespoons (90ml) extra-
  virgin olive oil

For make-ahead, store and/or freeze notes, see p.333

1. Heat the oven to 220°C/200°C Fan, and get out a large baking
tray (not a tin with high sides, or the aubergine and onion will
braise rather than roast); I use one of 42 x 33cm, measuring from
the outside of each shallow lip. Pour in the 90ml of olive oil.

2. Quarter the onions, remove the skins, then cut each quarter in
half lengthways, leaving (if you can) the onion attached still at root
end, and arrange on your baking tray.

3. Halve the aubergines lengthways, then with a sharp knife, cut
diagonal slashes into the fleshy sides in a cross-hatched pattern,
and add these, flesh side down, to the baking tray with the onions.
Schmoosh everything about, really smearing the fleshy side of the
aubergines with the oil, and making sure the onions are covered.
Then turn the aubergines cut side up.

4. Lop the top off the bulb of garlic so that the cloves are just
peeking through, and wrap in foil, making a tightly sealed but
baggy parcel. Add this to your baking tray if there's room, otherwise just pop it into the oven as it is, at the same time as putting in
the onions and aubergines. Depending on the fierceness of your
oven and the materials of your baking tray (the darker it is, the
faster everything will brown), the onions and aubergines will take
around an hour to cook to scorched softness. Check on them at
about 40 minutes and throw in 90ml of water (I use an American
⅓ cup measure for ease), and turn the onions where needed.

5. As soon as the baking tray has gone into the oven, spoon the sea
salt and dried mint into a cup, add the lemon juice, stir to mix, and
leave while the onions and aubergines are cooking.

6. When the onions are soft and browned and burnt at the edges,
the aubergines darkened and floppy-fleshed, remove from the oven
and let stand for 5–10 minutes, just to let them cool down a little

before handling. Get the garlic out, unwrap it, and allow it to cool a little too.

7. Transfer the onions, scraping every bit off the bottom of the tin, to a bowl that you can use with a stick blender. When you can touch the aubergines comfortably, use a spoon and your hands to get the flesh out of the charred skins, though you won't be able to separate it all, nor do you need to. Bits of charred tender skin will add to the taste. When you've got as much of the flesh out as you can comfortably manage, you can squeeze the skins in your hands over the bowl to get out the last bits of pulp. Add a tablespoonful of the burnt-onion-and-aubergine juices from the tray to your bowl. If the tray is dry by now, add a little water from the kettle to sluice it out. Once the aubergines are in the bowl, squeeze the caramelised garlic out of its papery skin on top on them. Don't burn your hands, but do try and get out every last bit you can.

8. Before you blitz everything together, add the waiting minty, salty lemon juice, tahini, ground cumin, sweet smoked paprika and the extra-virgin olive oil, and blend until smooth and silky.

9. Taste for seasoning – it may need more smoked paprika – then decant into a bowl, and dip tortilla chips into it, spread it on toast, or eat it however you like.

SOUPY RICE WITH CELERIAC AND CHESTNUTS

Although the focus of this chapter is brown food, I feel it can generously spare some space for the beige, too. But it's not so much the colour of this recipe that needs defending – although it most certainly has an appearance that does not endear itself to our image-obsessed age – but rather its modest demands on the eater. You will not get blown away by this. It won't be the most electrifying thing you have ever eaten. This is not to disparage it: it is a favourite in my home. If I felt it weren't worthy of your time or your table, I wouldn't include it. There is just something quiet and lovely about it that seems to still the air around you as you eat.

I think of this rather as an autumnal or wintry version of *risi e bisi*, Venice's celebration of spring in the form of a pea risotto that is just this side of a soup. It has a certain elegant calm about it. Its flavour is not muted exactly – the sweet grassiness of the celeriac, the fragrant woodsiness of thyme, the richness of Marsala and the warmth of garlic all make their presence lightly felt – but it has a gentleness that feels so very unmodern and so very precious.

If you wish to use mushroom stock (either from a cube or made by soaking dried porcini) you certainly can, and if using porcini, fry them, once soaked, along with the leek. This would also make it vegetarian. While simply ditching the cheese and using oil in place of butter – on top of the switch of stocks – would make it vegan, you will need to provide more oomph; I suggest a couple of teaspoons of miso or 2–3 tablespoons of the Burnt Onion and Aubergine Dip that precedes this recipe. Or roast a whole bulb of garlic as per the directions in the dip recipe and squeeze into the soup at the end.

SERVES 4

300g celeriac

1 leek (150g trimmed weight – approx. 250g if you're buying it untrimmed)

A large bunch of flat-leaf parsley

A bundle of fresh thyme

2 fat cloves of garlic

3 x 15ml tablespoons extra-virgin olive oil

50g butter

½ teaspoon ground mace

225g Arborio rice

4 x 15ml tablespoons (60ml) Marsala

1.5 litres chicken stock

100g cooked and peeled chestnuts (I buy these in vacuum-sealed packets)

2 x 15ml tablespoons (approx. 15g) freshly grated Pecorino Romano or Parmesan, plus more to serve

For make-ahead, store and/or freeze notes, see p.333

1. Peel the celeriac and cut into 1–2cm cubes. Wash the leek to remove any mud, if needed. Halve the leek lengthways then finely slice it. Roughly chop enough parsley to give you 3 tablespoonsful, strip and measure out 1 teaspoon of thyme leaves, and peel the garlic cloves in readiness.

2. Get out a heavy-based pan that comes with a lid – I use one of 22cm diameter – and to it add 1 tablespoon of the oil and 25g of the butter. Warm over medium heat and, when the butter's melted, add the sliced leek and cook, stirring, for 3–5 minutes, until it loses its brightness and starts to show the first signs of softening.

3. Add the 3 tablespoons of chopped parsley and the teaspoon of thyme leaves, then mince or grate in the garlic. Take the pan off the heat for this if it helps.

4. Add the remaining butter to the pan, stir everything together, then, when the butter's melted, tip in the cubes of celeriac and cook, stirring regularly, for 8–10 minutes or until you can feel that the celeriac cubes are beginning to soften and fuzz a bit around the edges.

5. Stir in the ground mace, pour in the remaining 2 tablespoons of oil, and give another good stir, turning the heat up as you do so.

6. Add the rice, stirring until it is well coated, and pour in the Marsala, letting it bubble up and reduce a little, before adding the stock.

7. Finally add the chestnuts, breaking them up a bit with your hands as you drop them in.

8. Bring to the boil, then put on the lid, turn the heat down, and cook at a jaunty simmer for 15 minutes, giving it a stir halfway through to make sure it's not sticking to the bottom of the pan.

After 15 minutes the rice should be cooked and the celeriac soft, but if not, give it another 5 minutes. At this stage it will still be quite liquid.

9. Take off the heat and leave to stand for 10 minutes with the lid off. It will become thicker but still be comfortingly soupy. While it's standing, chop some more parsley to give you about 6 tablespoons' worth. When the soup has had its 10 minutes, stir in the just-chopped parsley and 2 tablespoons of grated Pecorino Romano or Parmesan, and taste to see if you want more.

10. As you serve, sprinkle with some thyme leaves and maybe a sprig or two and put the cheese on the table for people to grate over as they eat.

SHORT RIB STEW FOR TWO

This is the meatiest of stews: the rich short ribs, with their deep beefy flavour and luscious marbling, are headily intense; and although I mush up shallots, chilli, ginger and spices to create a paste to flavour and thicken the gravy, no vegetables are added in the pot alongside.

Not only are short ribs a favourite of mine, they lend themselves perfectly to a small-scale stew. Normally, I'd worry about not making enough for people to have a second (or third) helping, but even I find one plenty. And I like the idea of a stew for two. Of course, it's possible to make any of the stews in the book and simply bag them up into smaller portions and freeze them, but this recipe makes a virtue out of the fact that short ribs, when cooked for large numbers of people, can get a bit unwieldy. And I happily make this recipe just for me, saving the second rib to be eaten another time, either in identical fashion to the first, or shredded in its rich gravy (with some water and a splosh of red vermouth added) to make a divine and succulent sauce for pappardelle. Indeed, if you wanted, you could easily make this recipe for two into a rich meat sauce for four.

Ideally, you need a small casserole for this, and I use one of 18cm diameter. Should you not have one that small, be prepared to add quite a bit more water, and bubble it away – with the meat removed – to let the juices reduce and thicken just before serving.

When you get the short ribs, do ask for them both to be cut from the meatier side, and to be of equal sizes, and specify the length rather than the weight. Obviously, if you're using a larger casserole than I do, you could get them longer, but you certainly don't need to.

I like polenta with this, and although you should check the instructions on the packet you have, I make mine here with 200g of fine polenta and 1 litre of water, adding seasoning, a little Parmesan and a big lump of butter at the end. If using instant polenta replace the water with stock, adding lots of butter and grated Parmesan before serving. But the Root Vegetable Mash on p.206 (you could make a half quantity) is also wonderful with this.

I should warn you before you go any further that you need to cook this stew at least a day ahead (and up to 3 days). And when you reheat it, I suggest you roast some red chicory to go with it for and at the same time; its silky bitterness is just right with the rich stew. Just quarter a couple of heads of red chicory lengthways and put in a small baking tray or dish. Pour over 3 tablespoons of dry white vermouth (or half freshly squeezed orange juice, half water), 1–2 tablespoons of olive oil and a sprinkling of sea salt flakes.

A LOVING DEFENCE OF BROWN FOOD

SERVES 2

2 meaty short ribs (approx. 12cm
  long)

125g banana shallots

25g fresh ginger

1 red chilli

4 fat cloves of garlic

15g stalks from a small bunch of
  coriander

Seeds from 3 cardamom pods

¾ teaspoon ground turmeric

¾ teaspoon ground cinnamon

15g beef dripping or
  1 x 15ml tablespoon oil

2 x 15ml tablespoons tomato purée

300ml hot water from a just-boiled
  kettle, plus more as needed

1 teaspoon sea salt flakes (or
  ½ teaspoon fine sea salt)

1 teaspoon maple syrup (optional)

For make-ahead, store and/or freeze notes, see p.333

SHORT RIB STEW
FOR TWO

1. Take the short ribs out of the fridge, and let them get to room temperature. Once they've reached it, heat the oven to 150°C/130°C Fan. Tear off a piece of baking parchment just a little bigger than the diameter of your casserole (I use one that's 18cm in diameter), and set aside for now.

2. Peel the shallots, and quarter them, and peel then slice the ginger into fat coins, putting both into a bowl you can use with a stick blender.

3. Deseed the chilli and bruise the garlic with the flat side of a heavy knife to help remove the skins, then add the peeled cloves and deseeded chilli to the bowl, too, along with the coriander stalks, cardamom seeds, turmeric and cinnamon.

4. Use a stick blender to turn everything into a paste. Be patient: at first you'll think it's never going to happen, but after a while, everything will turn obligingly into a vibrantly coloured mush.

5. Melt the dripping or heat the oil in your little casserole on the hob. Add the paste and fry for about 5 minutes over medium-low heat, stirring most, if not quite all, of the time. As it cooks, the paste will seem to condense and tighten; it will also lose its cheery brightness.

6. Stir in the tomato purée, and cook for another minute. Then add the water and salt, stirring well, to combine.

7. Add the ribs to the pot, bone side up, and press down so that the liquid only just covers them; it doesn't matter if the bones them-selves peek out. If you need a little more water for this, then add it. And if you're using a much bigger casserole, you might need quite a bit extra water. Bring to a bubble, then get your piece of parch-ment and scrunch it up, then open it up again, and place on top of

the stew, tucking the edges in and up around the inside of the pan. This is your cartouche; it will help prevent the scant liquid from evaporating. Place the lid on the casserole and transfer to the oven. Cook for 3 hours, by which time the meat should be meltingly tender.

8. Once out of the oven, remove both the lid and cartouche – a thing of beauty, like an ancient map on an unfurled papyrus scroll, as you can see from the photograph on p.92) – and, when it's not too piping hot, have a taste. Only you will know if you want to add the maple syrup: sometimes the pungency of the rich juices seems to need it for balance; ingredients always vary, and you need to respond to them accordingly.

9. Leave to cool, then refrigerate, with the lid on. About 2½–3 hours before you want to eat, take the casserole out of the fridge, and remove the firm, thick orange fat.

10. Once the fridge chill is well and truly off it, heat the oven to 200°C/180°C Fan. Add water so that the meat is just covered, though don't worry if the bones themselves aren't completely submerged. Tear off a sheet of baking parchment to make a new cartouche and place over the ribs, tucking it in well, then put on the lid, and cook for 45 minutes, or until piping hot.

11. Remove the short ribs from the casserole – don't worry if the meat comes away from the bone: it just makes it all even easier to eat – and put the pan of juices on the hob to bubble away for a minute or two to reduce and thicken. Obviously if you've had to use a big pan and have added a lot of water, you'll have to bubble it away for considerably longer to get a thick sauce-like gravy.

12. Sit the short ribs on your polenta or mash and pour the sauce over. If you want a sprinkle of something on top, consider some finely chopped chives, although it certainly might make sense to go for the coriander left from the stalks you used in the paste, but taste first before you decide.

MARROWBONE MINCE

This is a favourite in my household, and there is much jubilation when I announce that I'm making it. It is not, so resolutely not, for fatphobes but, for those who like the feel of the divinely mucilaginous melted marrow coating their lips stickily as they eat, it is a rich and rare treat.

While you are, of course, entirely free to eat it as you would a meat sauce, over pasta, I don't advise it. Our house rules dictate that it is eaten either on toast or with dumplings. While I often make this big batch and freeze it in individual portions to be eaten on toast whenever needed, mince with dumplings is the cosiest of Sunday night suppers. And to make the dumplings, mix together 150g of plain flour, 2 teaspoons of baking powder, ½ teaspoon of fine sea salt and lots of freshly ground pepper. Add 75g of grated beef suet. It really makes an extraordinary difference using proper suet, and since you need to go to the butcher's for the marrowbone, you might as well get some while you're there. The butcher should grate it for you, although it is very easy – and curiously pleasurable – to do it yourself, using a processor. Mix to a dough with cold water – you'll need anything from 3 to 6 tablespoons – and roll into 8 balls (or 12 smaller balls) using floured hands. Cook on top of the mince for the last 30 minutes. The dumplings swell puffily as they cook so you will need to use a bigger pan – the one I've used here is a shallow casserole, 30cm in diameter.

For the mince, cooking the onions for so long at the beginning makes all the difference, so please be patient. I quite often cook the onions the day before. And incidentally, slow-cooking onions to avoid what I should in fact be doing is one of my favourite displacement activities. You will never regret having a supply of soft, sweet, soused onions. Even just on toast they are magnificent. Here, they are transformational.

While this recipe is unapologetically a celebration of saturated fat, if you are making the suet dumplings I will grudgingly understand if you wanted to give the marrowbone a miss. However, if making the mince to go on toast, don't even think about it. Speaking of which, the fact that the picture of this on p.111 looks uncannily like a map of the UK in mince-on-toast form, is entirely unintentional. Of course, I cannot account for the deep and mysterious workings of the unconscious.

SERVES 4–6

500g onions

45g beef dripping or 3 x 15ml
  tablespoons oil of your choice

250g carrots

4 fat cloves of garlic

1 stick of celery

1 teaspoon dried thyme

Approx. 400g marrowbone, cut in half
  lengthways like canoes

500g minced beef

200g minced pork

100ml red vermouth (or red wine)

1 x 400g tin of chopped tomatoes

1 x 15ml tablespoon tomato purée

250ml beef stock

2 teaspoons Worcestershire sauce
  (gluten-free if necessary)

2 fresh bay leaves

1½ teaspoons sea salt flakes (or
  ¾ teaspoon fine sea salt)

A good grinding of pepper

For make-ahead, store and/or freeze notes, see p.333

1. Peel and chop the onions. Melt the dripping or warm the oil in a large heavy-based casserole (I use one of 24cm diameter or a 30cm one if I'm making dumplings, in which case you might need a bit more fat for the pan) and add the onions. Stir well and cook over medium heat for 10 minutes, stirring frequently, then turn down to low and cook for a further 30–40 minutes, stirring and pressing on them every now and again, until they are soft, golden and jammy.

2. While the onions are cooking, peel the carrots and chop into 1cm dice, peel the garlic and finely slice the celery.

3. Heat the oven to 170°C/150°C Fan.

4. Once the onions have had their full cooking time, sprinkle over the dried thyme and mince or grate in the garlic, giving a good stir. Turn the heat up to medium, add the prepared celery and carrots and cook, stirring, for another 5 minutes. Tip this vegetable mixture into a bowl, scraping out every last bit from the pan.

5. Using a spoon – and a robust one at that – dig out the marrow from the bones into the casserole, then put the casserole back on the heat, over a lowish flame, and help the marrow melt by giving it the odd stir. When it's almost completely melted – some bits will blobbily resist – turn the heat up, and when the fat is hot, crumble in the minced beef and pork, stirring well to turn it in the marrowfat. Once it's largely lost its raw look, add back the sweet-soused onion mixture, again scraping to get every last bit out of your bowl.

6. Pour in the red vermouth (or wine), the tinned tomatoes, the tomato purée and the beef stock. Add the Worcestershire sauce, bay leaves and salt and give a good grinding of pepper, and then stir well before dropping in the scraped-out marrowbones.

7. Clamp on the lid and cook in the oven for 2 hours. If you're going for the dumplings – see recipe intro for directions – add them on top of the mince after 1 ½ hours (removing the bones first), and put the lid back on and cook for a further 30 minutes. Some people like to give a bit of time with the lid off to crisp up the dumplings – I don't. If eating with dumplings, serve immediately as they will lose all their inexplicable lightness on standing.

BEEF CHEEKS WITH PORT AND CHESTNUTS

This a deeply flavoured and elegantly cosy stew, perfect for when the nights are drawing in. It warms body and soul, and lifts the spirits; eating it feels like you're instantly sitting in front of a crackling log fire. Show me a stew that isn't comforting, but this one has something undeniably festive about it, too. It's like wearing party shoes you can actually walk in.

The chances are you will have to get the beef cheeks from a butcher's, and so you might as well get them to cut the meat up into chunks for you at the same time. After long, slow cooking beef cheeks become lusciously tender, but they certainly don't start off that way: if you're cutting them yourself, proceed with care. And if you can't get beef cheeks, use shin.

I often make a horseradish sauce to eat with this, and if you want to do likewise, just stir together 3 tablespoons (packed) of finely grated fresh horseradish, 3 tablespoons (45ml) of double cream, 4 tablespoons (60ml) of full-fat Greek yogurt (or replace the cream and yogurt with 100ml of crème fraîche or sour cream) and add a drop of vinegar and salt to taste. You can do this in advance, but just before serving add – if you so wish – a tablespoon or so of finely chopped chives. However, if you're thinking of eating the beef cheeks with baked potatoes, then I'd boost the quantities of sauce.

Jacket potatoes are certainly an easy accompaniment, and always a good one, but I have to say my absolute favourite partner for this is the Celeriac and Anchovy Gratin on p.23. And if that's the plan, you don't need the horseradish sauce. Either option is gratifying, but which I choose depends on how much time I have at my disposal.

While this is enough for four people, there are not likely to be left-overs, but I'm happy to cook this when there are three or even two of us. In which case, should you have leftovers, I can excitedly tell you to slightly shred the meat in its sauce and reheat gently on the hob, adding a little more water as needed, and maybe a small splosh of the port you used to cook it, and turn it into a pasta sauce. If you've only got a teeny bit left, do bump it up with some cream.

Warning: this needs to be made at least a day (and up to 3 days) before you plan to eat it.

SERVES 3–4

1kg beef cheeks

500g leeks (trimmed weight –
approx. 750g if you're buying them
untrimmed)

2 fat cloves of garlic

2 carrots (approx. 200g)

1 large or 2 small sticks of celery

A small bunch of flat-leaf parsley
(approx. 20g)

45g beef dripping or 3 x 15ml
tablespoons oil of your choice

1 orange

1 teaspoon fennel seeds

A very generous grating of nutmeg

200ml ruby port

350ml beef stock

2 teaspoons Worcestershire sauce
(gluten-free if necessary)

1 teaspoon sea salt flakes (or
½ teaspoon fine sea salt)

A good grinding of pepper

150g cooked and peeled chestnuts
(I buy these in vacuum-sealed
packets)

For make-ahead, store and/or freeze notes, see p.333

1. Heat the oven to 150°C/130°C Fan. Tear off a generous piece
of baking parchment a bit bigger than the diameter of your
casserole (I use a heavy-based one of 24cm diameter) and set aside
for now.

2. Cut the beef cheeks into large chunks, about 6cm; if the cheeks
are still covered in membrane, carefully cut it away and peel it
off first. Wash the leeks to remove any mud, as needed. If your
leeks are chunky, cut them in half lengthways, and then into
2½cm slices; if they are relatively slender, just slice them. Peel
the garlic cloves.

3. Peel the carrots, cut into chunks, drop into the bowl of the
processor, and add the peeled garlic. Tear the celery into smaller pieces and add, too, along with the parsley (leaves and tender
stalks), and blitz until very finely chopped. Or just chop everything
finely by hand.

4. Melt 30g of beef dripping or warm 2 tablespoons of oil in your
casserole and, in two batches, brown the meat over medium-high
heat, then remove to a bowl.

5. Add the remaining 15g of dripping (or tablespoon of oil) to the
pan, turn the heat down to medium-low, then add the carrot mixture and cook, stirring, for 3–4 minutes.

6. Finely grate the orange zest into the pan, and stir in the fennel
seeds and grate in the nutmeg – which smell heavenly as they hit
the heat – then add the leeks. Turn up the heat to medium and
cook, stirring frequently, for about 5 minutes, by which time the
leeks will have wilted a bit.

7. Return the meat to the pan, scraping in any juices that have collected in the bowl, and stir well so that everything is mixed together.

8. Pour in the port and let it bubble up before adding the beef stock, Worcestershire sauce and salt, and grind pepper generously into the stew. Add the chestnuts, stir well and, when bubbling, squish the meat down in the pan with your spoon or spatula so that it is just submerged in the liquid. Scrunch up your piece of baking parchment, unscrunch it and press it down on top of the stew, tucking the edges in and up around the inside of the pan, then put on the lid and cook in the oven for 3 hours, by which time the meat will be gorgeously tender. Remove lid and parchment and let cool before refrigerating for up to 3 days. Though you certainly should taste for seasoning before letting it cool too much.

9. To reheat, take the stew out of the fridge, remove any of the now solidified fat on the top if you wish, and let come to room temperature.

10. If the meat isn't just covered by its jellified stock, add a little water so that it is. Tear off a sheet of baking parchment to make a fresh cartouche and replace the lid and, if serving with the Celeriac and Anchovy Gratin, put in a 190°C/170°C Fan oven for 50 minutes to 1 hour, making sure the gratin is on the shelf above the casserole. If you want to bake potatoes in the oven at the same time – although you'll need to give them a head start – you can reheat at 200°C/180°C Fan for 40–50 minutes. Make sure the stew is piping hot before you serve it.

OXTAIL BOURGUIGNON

I don't need much of an excuse to make an oxtail stew. I love its rich fattiness, its sweet viscosity: words that alarm the lean team, but bring joy to the brown-food brigade.

I'm not sure how Burgundians feel about this tinkering with their most revered classic, but I must tell you that I feel very good about it indeed. And so, I hope, will you when you eat it.

Peeling a pile of pearl onions would be a daunting prospect, but happily the universe provides, in the form of packets of frozen peeled ones (of French provenance) which I found at the supermarket, and now always keep in my freezer. If you can't find them, add another onion at the beginning.

The first time I cooked this was for a low-carber, and so I made a cauliflower mash to go with it, an emphatically cheesy cauliflower mash, I should say, and although it is an unexpected accompaniment, it is a compelling one, and I commend it to you. To make this, you will probably need 2 cauliflowers, or about 1.5kg total weight, and once you've halved them and removed the core, you can either finely slice the florets so that they crumble into little pieces, or blitz them in the processor. Melt 75g of butter in a wide pan (I use one of 26cm diameter), add the cauliflower confetti and stir it into the butter along with 1 teaspoon of ground mace and 1 teaspoon of sea salt flakes (or ½ teaspoon of fine sea salt). Cook over medium heat, stirring regularly, for 5 minutes then cover – or just about cover: it will bob up a bit – with boiling water from the kettle, drop in a couple of fresh bay leaves, and bring to the boil. Clamp on a tightly fitting lid, and leave to cook until very tender. This will probably take around 20 minutes, though check at 10, and give it a good stir at the same time. Once it's very soft, you shouldn't have much liquid left in the pan, but if you do, tip it out into a bowl or jug for now, and discard the bay leaves. With a stick blender, blitz the buttery cauliflower until smooth, adding any reserved liquid as needed, then stir in 75g of grated Emmental or Gruyère and blitz again. Give a good grinding of pepper, and taste to check for seasoning and to see if you want any more butter or cheese.

I put a bowl of the Savoy Cabbage with Turmeric (see p.192) on the table alongside too. Its spicy bite works so well with the richness of the stew and mash.

There may not be much left over if you're making this for four, but I gladly make it for two, freeze one portion and eat the remainder – the sweet meat shredded into the rich sauce – reheated on the hob with some extra water and some orzo (and sometimes frozen peas as well) cooked in it, to be eaten comfortingly from a bowl, with a spoon.

I know, of course I know, that caraway has no place in proper boeuf bourguignon (and the same goes for the other spices I add), but just before making it, I'd eaten some caraway-studded black bread (for which there's a simple recipe on p.305), and knew instantly I wanted its deep aniseed sweetness in this stew; I have never wanted to make it any differently since. Sometimes I have to, though, as my children don't have the same enthusiasm for its liquorice intensity. If you, or those you're cooking for, feel equally antagonistic to aniseed, simply leave it out.

This is another stew that needs to be made at least a day (though you can leave it for up to 3 days in the fridge) before you plan to eat it.

OXTAIL
BOURGUIGNON

SERVES 4

1.75kg oxtail

1 large onion (approx. 200g)

1 stick of celery

3 fat cloves of garlic

1 x 15ml tablespoon fresh thyme leaves (or 1 teaspoon dried thyme)

250g field/flat or portobello mushrooms

200g baby chestnut or button mushrooms

250g pancetta or 225g lardons

1 x 15ml tablespoon olive oil

1 teaspoon caraway seeds (optional)

35g plain flour

½ teaspoon ready-ground black pepper

1 teaspoon ground cumin

1 teaspoon ground coriander

30g beef dripping or 2 x 15ml tablespoons olive oil

500ml full-bodied red wine (though, as the name of the stew suggests, it should properly be a Burgundy)

500ml beef stock

250g peeled pearl onions (I use frozen; if you can't find them, add another onion at the beginning)

3 fresh bay leaves

For make-ahead, store and/or freeze notes, see p.333

1. Take the oxtail out of the fridge to get to room temperature. Heat the oven to 150°C/130°C Fan. Tear off a large piece of baking parchment slightly bigger than the diameter of the casserole you're using – I use one of 26cm diameter – and put to one side for now.

2. Peel and chop the onion, and finely slice the celery. Peel the garlic cloves, and strip the leaves from the stalks of thyme. Chop the dark-gilled field or portobello mushrooms into 3–4cm chunks.

3. Cut the rind off the pancetta, put it with the tablespoon of olive oil into your casserole and leave over lowish heat to render the fat, while you chop the rest of the pancetta into strips approx. 1½ x 2½cm. If you're using lardons, you will naturally dispense with this step.

4. Add the pancetta cubes (you can leave the rind in the pan) and cook for about 8 minutes, stirring frequently, by which time they will have rendered quite a bit of fat, and be bronzed and crisp.

5. Remove the pancetta – discarding the rind or, if you have any sense, eating it yourself – to a bowl big enough to take the onion and mushrooms later, too. Cook the chopped onion in the warm bacony fat, on low, for 10 minutes, keeping an eye on it, and stirring every now and again to make sure it isn't burning. Mince or grate in the garlic cloves and stir in the sliced celery, thyme and – if using – caraway, and cook for a bare minute.

6. Add the chunked field mushrooms to the pan and stir well for a minute or so, then add the whole baby chestnut or button mushrooms and cook altogether, stirring regularly for 4–5 minutes. Remove to the bowl with the pancetta, and take the pan off the heat for a moment.

7. Get out a large shallow dish, and in it mix the flour, pepper, cumin and coriander, then dredge the oxtail pieces in the spiced flour on all sides.

8. Melt half the beef dripping or heat half the olive oil in the pan, and over medium-high heat sear half the oxtail pieces, transferring them, once browned, to the bowl, too. Do the same with the remaining fat and oxtail.

9. Add whatever flour is left behind in the dredging dish to the pan, and gradually stir in the red wine, followed by the beef stock. Stir well, and whisk to get rid of any floury lumps, and let it bubble a little before adding back the oxtail. Then add your frozen pearl onions if using (no need to thaw), then the remaining contents of the onion and mushroom bowl, using a bendy spatula to scrape out every last drop of flavoursome juices. Drop in the bay leaves, and press everything down into the liquid as best you can.

10. Let the pot come to a bubble, make a cartouche by scrunching up your piece of baking parchment, then unscrunch it and place it on top of the stew, tucking the edges in and up around the inside of the pan. Then clamp on the lid, and transfer to the oven to cook for 3½ hours.

11. Remove from the oven, take off the lid and parchment, press down – with a spatula or large spoon – to keep the meat and

vegetables submerged, then leave to cool, before putting into the fridge, covered, for at least a day and up to 3 days. If you want, you can remove the layer of solidified fat when it's cold, but for me the fat is the point of oxtail.

12. On the day you want to eat this, take the stew out of the fridge in good time to reach room temperature. Heat the oven to 180°C/160°C Fan. Make a fresh cartouche, and cook, lid on, for about 1¼ hours, by which time it should be piping hot. While this is enough, I like to give it another hour turned down to 140°C/120°C Fan and it won't come to any harm if it stays there for considerably longer. Should you wish to reheat in a hotter oven to accommodate other dishes you might want alongside, simply reduce the time the oxtail has in the oven. Make sure it's piping hot before serving.

BLACK PUDDING MEATBALLS

I'm not sure that these beauties, bobbing about in their cheerfully red tomato sauce, count as brown food exactly, but I decided they belonged here since they are probably going to be fully appreciated only by true brown-food lovers. Even unapologetic meat eaters can be disgusted by the dark mysteries of blood. And while it's not entirely rational, our emotional responses so rarely are. Besides, I make no attempt now to convince anyone about these: I love them too much to waste making them for people who fail to appreciate them, no matter how brave they feel for trying.

And cooking is by no means always altruistic. The quantities below make for a big old batch of black pudding meatballs, simply because they are one of my absolute favourite things to eat, an instant sparker of joy; I honestly feel so much better about life knowing there's always a container or three of them in the freezer. I thrill at their deep gloriousness every time I eat them.

It's up to you what you eat them with but I must tell you that the Brown Butter Colcannon (p.209) is sensational with them. But if I'm eating alone, I like them best with good bread and butter.

Broadly speaking, black pudding comes in either a nubbly, crumbly texture or a smooth, moussy texture. I tend to favour the latter for these, but use either happily.

SERVES 4–6 (or 1 person 4–6 times)

FOR THE TOMATO SAUCE

400ml cold water

2 onions (approx. 300g)

45g beef dripping or 3 x 15ml
  tablespoons olive oil

2 fat cloves of garlic

3 x 15ml tablespoons finely chopped
  flat-leaf parsley

1 teaspoon dried thyme

2 x 400g tins of chopped tomatoes

1 x 15ml tablespoon tomato purée

2 teaspoons Worcestershire sauce
  (gluten-free if necessary)

2 teaspoons sea salt flakes (or
  1 teaspoon fine sea salt)

FOR THE MEATBALLS

500g minced beef (not low fat)

250g black pudding (gluten-free if
  necessary)

2 fat cloves of garlic

3 x 15ml tablespoons finely chopped
  parsley, plus more to serve

2 x 15ml tablespoons finely chopped
  chives, plus more to serve

1 teaspoon dried thyme

2 teaspoons sea salt flakes (or
  1 teaspoon fine sea salt)

A very good grinding of pepper

¼ teaspoon dried chilli flakes

2 x 15ml tablespoons porridge oats
  (not jumbo, gluten-free if necessary)

2 large eggs, at room temperature

BLACK PUDDING
MEATBALLS

For make-ahead, store and/or freeze notes, see p.333

1. Take the minced beef and black pudding out of the fridge so they lose their chill while you get on with the sauce. Pour 400ml of cold water into a measuring jug and put it by the stove in readiness.

2. To make the sauce, peel and roughly chop the onions. Melt your dripping or warm the oil in a large heavy-based casserole – I use one of 26cm diameter – then add the onion and cook over medium heat, stirring every now and then, for about 15 minutes, or until beginning to soften and get golden in parts. If you want to do this for longer on low heat, do, after you've given them a 5-minute start on medium.

3. While the onions are cooking, peel the garlic and finely chop 3 tablespoons' worth of parsley. When the onions are ready, stir in the dried thyme and chopped parsley, and mince or grate in the garlic. Add the tomatoes, swilling out the empty tins with the water in your jug before pouring it into the pan.

4. Stir in the tomato purée, Worcestershire sauce and salt and then turn up the heat to bring to the boil. Once boiling, turn down the heat a little and leave to simmer for 10 minutes.

5. Meanwhile, make the meatballs. Loosen the mince with your fingers as you drop it into a large bowl. Add the black pudding, crumbling it in by hand as well.

6. Peel the garlic cloves, and mince or grate them into the bowl. Now finely chop another 3 tablespoons worth of parsley and 2 tablespoons of chives and transfer both to the bowl.

A LOVING DEFENCE OF BROWN FOOD

7. Add the dried thyme, salt, pepper and chilli flakes. Then sprinkle over the oats and crack in the eggs. Mix this all together with your hands, making sure it's evenly incorporated.

8. Get out a large baking sheet or a very large chopping board. Then tear off walnut-sized lumps of the mixture and roll them between your palms to make meatballs, placing them on the baking sheet or board as you go. You should end up making about 40.

9. Drop the meatballs into the sauce in concentric circles, easing them in gently. Try to get the meatballs covered by the sauce and then bring to a bubble. At which point, clamp on the lid, turn the heat down a bit, and let it simmer robustly for 15 minutes.

10. Take off the lid and give the pan a very gentle stir, then leave without a lid for another 15 minutes, simmering a little less robustly now, by which time the meatballs should be cooked through, and the sauce divinely intense.

11. Check the sauce for seasoning, then leave off the heat for 5–10 minutes. While you wait, chop some chives (and parsley if wished) to sprinkle over. Ladle into bowls and eat joyfully with bread and butter or a buttery bowl of colcannon.

RHUBARB

For much of the world, the coming of rhubarb heralds the arrival of spring; for those of us in England, it appears brightly in the bleak midwinter, absurdly, improbably pink, the colour of hope, filled with all the light that is missing from our skies. My heart lifts every time it comes into season towards the end of December. How could it not? Yorkshire forced rhubarb, which is started off outside, but then transplanted inside, cultivated in the dark and harvested by candlelight, is one of our greatest culinary treasures: hot pink from the cold earth, its stalks are more tender, their texture more delicate, and the taste purer and more vibrant than the hefty red rhubarb that comes later, out in the open, and which, as the year moves on, and the stalks grow thicker and greener, all too often cooks to a fibrous khaki mush.

That's the rhubarb I remember from school, and you'd think it would have put me off for life. But as soon as I discovered, in my twenties I think, proper pink Yorkshire forced rhubarb, I became a woman obsessed. Over the years I have made, and written recipes for: a rhubarb upside-down cake (the cake itself more of a giant buttery scone); a rhubarb steamed pudding going by the name of Pig's Bum; rhubarb crumble (of course); baked rhubarb custard (the primrose rippled with pink); rhubarb fool; rhubarb ice cream; rhubarb meringue pie; rhubarb, Muscat and mascarpone trifle; rhubarb and Muscat jelly; rhubarb brown sauce (a rescue operation for a chutney that went too far); rhubarb cornmeal cake; rhubarb crumble kuchen; rhubarb grunt; rhubarb schnapps; rhubarb tart; rhubarb muffins; rhubarb vanilla mincemeat (the sort destined for mince pies rather than a curious Yorkshire take on spag bol); and various rhubarb compotes.

And I think it is the simple compote that showcases the earliest, pinkest rhubarb best. If a rhubarb crumble is the second thing I make to celebrate the arrival of those slender Schiaparelli stems in my kitchen each year, a compote is always the first. I call it a compote, as that is what it turns itself into once cooked, but really I mean roast rhubarb. For if you want rhubarb to keep its shape, its colour, its intense, rampaging tartness, never do more than chop it, toss it in sugar, cover it with foil and cook it in the oven. Do not be alarmed at the amount of sugar you need to add: rhubarb loves sugar as meat loves salt. So, for 800g of rhubarb, by which I mean its trimmed weight (even if you still have to top and tail) or two supermarket packets, you'll need 200g of caster sugar. Chop the rhubarb into about 5cm lengths (or half that size if the rhubarb is chunky rather than slender), put it into a roasting tin or dish in which it can, ideally, sit in one layer, add the sugar and gently but thoroughly mix together so that the sugar is evenly dispersed. Once you've got your rhubarb back in its single layer, flat in the tin, cover with foil, making sure the edges are sealed tightly and roast in a 200°C/180°C Fan oven for 30–40 minutes, until the rhubarb is just tender, but still very much holding its shape.

Remove from the oven and leave the rhubarb in its tin for 20 minutes, before gently transferring to a dish with a slotted spatula. As it stands, the rhubarb gets pinker and pinker, until it seems to glow. There is a great trick played by it: it looks so pertly pretty, so positively candied, like Brighton rock in fruit form, or something Barbie might cook in her Malibu Dream House, and yet it isn't sweet. Or, rather, the syrup doesn't overwhelm its fierce tang, but rather sets its fragrant sherbettiness into stark relief.

Most of the time, I let the rhubarb sing its sharp song without adding other notes, but I don't deny it pairs well with other flavours. So, when you're roasting it, feel free to add some pared orange zest, very finely sliced or chipped fresh ginger, a couple of fresh bay leaves, or 2 star anise. While vanilla, with its rich sweet perfume, is of course a glorious match for tart rhubarb, I prefer not to add it – unless in the form of vanilla sugar with its gentle, blossomy kiss – to the fruit (and yes, I do know that botanically speaking it is a vegetable) when making a simple compote, but to deploy it alongside, most pleasura-bly in the form of custard (see p.141). But I also love roast rhubarb with the cardamom-and-vanilla-infused Marzipan Loaf Cake on p.70, both when it's freshly cut, and when it's toasted in the oven after a few days. And, indeed, you could bake some rhubarb in the cake; you need just 175g or so of slim, tender stems cut into 1cm slices. What I do is take out half the cake batter once it's mixed, and fold into it half the sliced rhubarb. Scrape into the prepared loaf tin and bake for 10 minutes, and then fold the rest of the rhubarb into the rest of the batter, scrape into the tin, too, and bake for a further 40 minutes or until cooked.

If you're eating the compote with yogurt (and full-fat Greek yogurt would be my choice) for one of the sprightliest of breakfasts, try it with some thyme leaves or a small amount of fresh mint, cut into fine strips, sprinkled over.

But a plain, pink rhubarb compote, glossy with lucent syrup, is, if you want to go beyond custard, a ravishing treat alongside the cheesecake on p.251, the Rice Pudding Cake on p.238 and spooned on to crêpes while they're still warm. First dollop a little mascarpone or crème fraîche (spiked, if you felt like it, with a drop of rum or Frangelico) on to half of the pancake before you then – using a slotted spoon – top with some rhubarb and fold the other side of the crêpe over, place on a plate, and carry on with the rest of the pile. Drizzle over a little of the syrup, though it may be wise to reduce it so that it's thicker first (see instructions on p.142) and scatter over some chopped toasted hazelnuts. Crêpes are easy enough to make: melt 2 tablespoons (30g) of butter, and set aside while you whisk together 150g of plain flour with an egg and 325ml of milk until completely smooth, then stir in the melted butter; smear a crêpe pan or other shallow frying pan (of 20cm or 21cm diameter) with a little butter, put it on the hob to melt, then wipe it off and add 4 tablespoons (I use an American ¼ cup measure for this so I can add the batter for each pancake in one go) of pancake batter to the hot pan. Swirl it in your hand so that the batter coats the bottom of the pan thinly, cook it for about 1 minute before flipping it – as dramatically or cautiously as you wish – and cooking for about 30 seconds on the other side. Continue until you've finished your batter, which should give you 6 crêpes in all. But I wouldn't set the kitchen police on you for using shop-bought.

Pavlovas are best topped with tart fruit, and a rhubarb pavlova is in particular a joyous creation. You can use the recipe for the base from the blood-orange-and-passionfruit one on p.243 or, if you want one of more generous proportions (which would be right were you to want to use the entirety of the compote for it), follow the guidelines for the petite version but use 4 egg whites, 250g of caster sugar, 2 teaspoons of cornflour, 1 teaspoon of white wine vinegar, and add ½ teaspoon of vanilla extract along with the vinegar and cornflour, and, once the oven temperature is turned down, cook for 1 hour. Just before you serve the pav, add ½ teaspoon of vanilla paste (or extract) to 250ml of double cream and whip until airy and thick. Remove the rhubarb from its liquid with a slotted spoon, letting the juice drip back into the dish as you go, and add half to the whipped vanilla cream, folding it in gently with a spatula. Sit the pavlova base on a plate or stand, with the underside now facing up, pile what is really rhubarb fool over it, and top with the remaining rhubarb, making sure again to strain as much liquid off it as possible. I wouldn't be against adding a drop – but just a drop, mind – of rose-water on to the rhubarb here, either. And, although I'm sure you'd do this anyway, I should say that I use any overcooked or fraying lengths of rhubarb for folding into the cream, leaving the prettiest pieces for the top.

You can also make a wonderful, and very easy, rhubarb tart. For this, you need not pastry, but 250g of ginger nuts and 75g of soft unsalted butter. Blitz the biscuits in the processor until reduced to rubble (or bash in any other way you like), then add the butter and blitz again until the mixture begins to clump together, resembling damp sand. Tip this into a 23cm loose-bottomed flan tin, and patiently press onto the base and up the sides of the tin. You can use the back of a dessertspoon for this, but I find it easier to use my fingertips. Put the tin into the fridge to set the base for 1–2 hours (depending on how cold and full your fridge is) or up to 2 days.

Before you add the rhubarb, make a cream for it to sit on. Stir together 175g of room-temperature cream cheese or mascarpone with 200ml of double cream, add 1½ teaspoons of Bird's custard powder or cornflour, 1 teaspoon of vanilla paste (or extract), 3 tablespoons (40g) of caster sugar and, if you have some, an eggy splash or two of advocaat. Then, either by hand or with an electric whisk, softly whip until smooth and aerated. Taste to see if you want more sugar, vanilla or advocaat; you may even want to add a squeeze of lemon juice. And if it gets too thick, just gently stir in a little milk. You can make a rather more luxe and moussy version by whisking the sugar with an egg yolk (reserving the white for a mo) before adding, combining and whipping the other ingredients as before. And when you've done that, whisk the egg white just firm – but still frothy rather than dry – then fold it into your cream mixture. (Since you have the egg, you don't need the advocaat.) Carefully line the gingernut base with it, and then top with rhubarb, carefully draining as much liquid as possible from it first. And it looks exquisite with a few chopped pistachios sprinkled on top.

To remove the rhubarb tart from its case, sit it on a vase or something tall that has a flat top with a smaller diameter than the flan tin, and let the ring fall away, before transferring your beautiful creation very tenderly to a large flat plate, being careful not to touch the fragile edges; I use a large cake-lifter, which is a bit like a flat, round pizza shovel of 25cm diameter. I'm rarely confident of lifting the tart from the base of its tin, though often foolhardy enough to try, and sometimes succeed. I think it's safer to leave it be.

I must apprise you of the welcome fact that whenever you roast this forced pink rhubarb you will get a gorgeous amount of sharp-sweet, intensely flavoured syrup (more, for some reason, than if you were roasting later, outdoor rhubarb). You can boil this until reduced by half (obviously timings will vary depending on how much liquid and what size pan you're using, though see the Rhubarb and Custard Trifle recipe on p.142 for more details) and use it to pour over yogurt, pavlova or tart as you eat; it's also excellent with the No-Churn Cheesecake Ice Cream on p.235, as well as with any good shop-bought vanilla or pistachio ice cream. And it would be gorgeous dribbled over some baked custard. But not so fast. If you leave the syrup as it is, it is a glorious addition to cocktail hour. Yes, you can certainly add around 100ml – but go slowly and taste – to a bottle of Prosecco for a pink, perfumed rhubarb fizz, or add to vodka in equal parts and shake together over ice to make a Rhubartini, but I love this best with Campari. A Campari soda is my favoured *aperitivo*, and when I have this light syrup about, I add a splash to the Campari in my glass, and add a handful of ice, before topping with soda. It also goes into my Rhubarbicano, a take on that other great delight of mine, the Americano (a Negroni without the gin, give or take, and much the better for it in my book). In this case, you need 1 part rhubarb syrup, 1 part sweet red vermouth and 2 parts Campari in a glass with a lot of ice, top with a spritz of soda, and add an orange slice. But there is a new development in my life, and it is the Shaken Campari or Campari Shakerato. This is no more than Campari and a lot of ice, shaken for quite a bit, and then strained into an iced glass. It needs to be drunk almost immediately, as it loses its seemingly ice-emulsified consistency very fast. You can also turn it into a Campari Slush, by mixing with ice, not in a shaker, but in a bullet blender. Both are even better with the addition of rhubarb syrup. So, for 60ml of Campari, add a tablespoon of rhubarb syrup; you may prefer 2 tablespoons. There are plenty of other drinking opportunities here, alcoholic and non-alcoholic. Frankly, it's smile-inducing enough simply added to some fizzy water. Occasionally, I want to make a generous batch of the syrup from scratch and, unsurprisingly, this is easy to do: chop 300g of rhubarb up small, put it into a saucepan with 500ml of cold water and 100g of caster sugar, stir and bring to the boil, then turn down the heat to low and let simmer for 30 minutes. Turn the heat off and leave the pan to stand for 15 minutes, then strain through a non-metal fine-mesh sieve, pushing down on the now pulpy rhubarb, into a jug. I reckon on getting 400ml of rosy syrup out of this, but it's best to give this about 8 minutes bubbling on the hob to reduce it to 300ml. What's left behind in the sieve is a not terribly attractive mush, but it's still wonderful eaten with some Greek yogurt for breakfast, or with custard at any time.

The most recent addition to my rhubarb repertoire, however, comes in flapjack form. I was cooking my supplies down at the beginning of the lockdown and, faced with a packet of oats and a jar of crystallised ginger well past their recommended use-by dates, along with the limp remnants of a box of rhubarb, I couldn't start melting the butter, sugar and golden syrup fast enough. The nuggets of hot ginger and sudden bursts of rhubarb-sharpness are sublime counterparts to the deeply sweet, buttery bars. Now, there are some who like their flapjacks relatively thin and crisp, and those that like them dense and chewy. I belong most definitely in the latter camp; if you are among the former, I'd advise you to bake your Rhubarb and Ginger Flapjacks in a 23cm square tin rather than the 20cm one I use. Although having said that, the sherbetty dampness of the rhubarb means that these flapjacks will never be very crisp.

You need first to heat the oven to 190°C/170°C Fan and line a 20cm square tin with baking parchment and stand something heavy on it – a bag of sugar, for example – to keep it in place.

You need 150–175g (trimmed weight) of rhubarb, which is probably about 3 sticks of slender forced rhubarb, cut into thin slices; I aim for ½cm, but am happy so long as I don't go bigger than 1cm. If you're using outdoor summer rhubarb (which would be fine here, although I wouldn't recommend it for any of the other recipes I've already mooted) it might be better to chop rather than slice it. Either way, roughly chop, if you have it, 50g of crystallised ginger. Then, in a large heavy-based saucepan of 22cm diameter, melt 125g of golden syrup, 200g of butter (I use unsalted and add a pinch of salt, but you can use whatever's easier) and 50g of demerara sugar. Once you have a smooth, golden pool, turn off the heat and, with a silicon spatula, stir in 300g of porridge oats (gluten-free if necessary). Just use regular, unfancy oats: I sternly advise against jumbo or steel-cut oats; they make excellent porridge but terrible flapjacks. Stir the sliced rhubarb and chopped crystallised ginger into the sticky oat mixture and tip and scrape into the prepared tin. Use the spatula you stirred it all with to press the mixture into the tin in an even layer, tamping down as you level it. Sprinkle a teaspoon of demerara sugar over the top before baking in the hot oven for 35–40 minutes, or until golden brown on top (though it will feel soft) and a darker brown at the edges. Immediately, cut into the still sizzling mixture, to give yourself 9 flapjacks, or 12 smaller ones, and leave in the tin to cool. It's tempting to eat them still warm, and I nearly always do, but I need to tell you that they will not hold their shape firmly enough to be eaten by hand until they're cold. However, I'm more than happy to hold my other hand underneath to catch any falling clumps as I eat. And they make for an excellent emergency sundae, broken up over ice cream.

Indeed, I am now thinking that one could do a very good rhubarb flapjack crumble, just by preparing the fruit as if you were making a crumble, then topping with the flapjack mixture. Still, I don't know. There is something so purely perfect about a rhubarb crumble that it would be hard to cast it aside. And yes, I have given recipes before, but since there is a crumble recipe on p.235, I feel it is only right to suggest that you could use it too with some Yorkshire forced rhubarb. So, for the topping amount in the Cherry and Almond Crumble recipe, you need 800g (trimmed weight) of rhubarb, cut into 2–4cm pieces (depending on how thick it is). Put into a pan with 1 tablespoon (15g) of unsalted butter, 2 teaspoons of vanilla extract, 3 tablespoons (40g) of caster sugar and 1 tablespoon (12g) of cornflour, and cook over medium heat for about 5 minutes, stirring regularly, until the rhubarb is just beginning to soften on the outside, reducing a tiny bit in the process, and is covered with sugary, buttery, now pink-tinted, gloss. Turn into a 23cm pie dish, using a bendy spatula to get every last bit of scant sticky syrup out of the pan. You can

either use the topping from the Cherry and Almond Crumble as it is or, more traditionally, forget about the ground (and flaked) almonds, upping the amount of flour to 200g to make up the weight. All other instructions remain as for the crumble on p.235.

Before I leave the sweet world of rhubarbary for now, I must suggest an alternative topping to create a rhubarb version of Eve's Pudding, which is cooked traditionally, as the name might indicate, with apples. I'm not sure anyone cooks it much anymore, though many of my vintage might remember it from school, where it was made in vast trays, the slightly gloopy apple covered with bumpy sponge. I remember it with particular clarity as – until I was stripped of my stripes for abusing my position – I held the high office of Custard Monitor, and so spent many a lunchtime stationed by it and its sister offerings; dry chocolate sponge with mauve-pink custard haunts me to this day. Still, I have plenty of time for Eve's Pudding, especially if served with proper rather than school custard, and even more time for the rhubarb variant which, according to the invaluable *Cook's Companion*, by the great Stephanie Alexander, is known in Australia as Blushing Betty. This is not quite her recipe, but I gladly purloin her title.

You need the same amount of rhubarb as you do for the crumble, but this time cut it into 1½cm slices, and put it into a saucepan, along with 1 tablespoon (15g) of unsalted butter, 2 teaspoons of vanilla extract, and 3 tablespoons (45g) of sugar. Cook over medium heat for about 3 minutes, until the juices just start to run, stirring most of the time, then cover with a lid, turn down to low, and give it a further 2 minutes. Take off the lid and cook for another 2 minutes, until just holding its shape, before adding 2 tablespoons (25g) of cornflour. Stir this in for 30 seconds or so, before tipping the tender tart rhubarb – scraping out every bit of dense pink sauce covering it – into a buttered 23cm round pie dish that is around 5cm deep, and heating the oven to 180°C/160°C Fan, popping in a baking sheet at the same time. The easiest way to make the sponge topping is by putting 75g each of butter and caster sugar, 2 large eggs, 150g of plain flour, 2 teaspoons of baking powder and 2 teaspoons of vanilla extract into a food processor and blitzing to mix. Give a good scrape down, and then blitz again as you add 4 tablespoons of full-fat milk down the funnel with the motor running. And eggs, butter and milk should all be at room temperature. Dollop this gently over the rhubarb and, with a small offset spatula for ease (though the back of a spoon would do) and patiently smooth the yellow batter over the pink rhubarb so that it's completely covered. Bake in the oven for about 30 minutes, until the top is golden and risen, firm to the touch in the centre and beginning to come away from the sides, the rhubarb soft underneath it, and let stand for 5–10 minutes before eating it. With both crumble and Blushing Betty, custard is mandatory. Fortunately, there is a recipe on p.141. Follow the method for this, but since you're after a pouring custard, rather than a set one, use 4 egg yolks, 1 tablespoon (12g) of caster sugar, 1 tablespoon (12g) of cornflour, 150ml of full-fat milk and 250ml of double cream. One last note about Blushing Betty: like all sponges, she can't be made in advance (though the fruit part can be); however, leftovers can be perked up impressively in a microwave.

While you will find the savoury world of rhubarb amply explored in restaurants, it's rare now to come across rhubarb in anything other than sweet confections in homes. My maternal grandmother would often make a rhubarb sauce to accompany grilled mackerel (as she did also with gooseberries) and I rather think that must have been my earliest introduction to its particular, pronounced tartness; I savour it still. It's wonderful with pork, too, as an alternative to the more traditional apple sauce. I make it simply by chopping rhubarb into short lengths (you need about 175g, trimmed weight, to make a sauce to go with pork chops for two or three of you eating) and putting them into a saucepan with 2 tablespoons of sweet red vermouth and 2 tablespoons of water, ½ teaspoon of finely grated or minced ginger, 1 star anise and 2 tablespoons (30g) of sugar. Bring it to bubbling, let it bubble for a couple of minutes with a lid on, and then uncover, and cook until the rhubarb has collapsed and you have an elegantly muted, soft pink mush. Keep an eye on it: it won't take long. Depending on the age of the rhubarb, you might need to add more water (or sugar); conversely, if the sauce you have is too liquid, remove the rhubarb to a bowl, and boil the juices down a little. If you want to make more, just increase quantities of all but the star anise. One star anise will be enough to lend its deep, almost liquorice-like scent easily to three times this amount of rhubarb. If I'm making this to go with the Norwegian Pork Ribs on p.265, I'd go for four or even five times this amount and then I'd add 2 star anise. Orange juice would be a fine alternative to the vermouth in the sauce, though blood orange juice would be even better, in which case add a little more sugar.

I happily eat this sauce hot or cold: it's hard to say which I prefer, although when I say hot, I don't mean piping hot, and by cold, I most certainly don't mean it should have even a whisper of fridge-chill about it. Either way, it's perfect with any oily fish or fatty meat – lamb ribs or shoulder, duck, goose and grilled or fried black pudding in particular – and it offsets perfectly the moussy sweetness of calves' liver. And please consider it, too, in lieu of chutney with some good Cheddar or other cheese of your choice.

I am always ready to dunk a tortilla chip into a dip, and this is where my Roast Rhubarb Salsa comes in. As the name suggests, this is made in the oven, so get out a large baking sheet (you can't use an oven tin with deep sides or everything will braise rather than roast) and on it, arrange 2 large red onions, of about 200g each, peeled and cut into long eighths, 3–4 red peppers (total weight 450–500g) cut into strips following the lines of the ribs, 250g rhubarb (and it doesn't matter here if it's the greener summer rhubarb) cut into about 5cm logs, 3 red chillies, just as they are, and 2 fat cloves of garlic, peeled. Pour over 3 tablespoons of olive oil, and sprinkle with 2 teaspoons of sea salt flakes, 2 teaspoons of ground cumin and ½ teaspoon of ground allspice. Give a good mix with your hands so that everything is well coated, then spread the ingredients out as much as possible in one layer, and roast in a 220°C/200°C Fan oven for 40 minutes until the vegetables are soft and cooked, and scorched in parts. Let the hot pan sit out of the oven for 10 minutes, then remove the stems from the chillies, and scrape everything into a bowl and blitz with a stick blender until you have a rough, terracotta-tinted purée. Stir in 1 tablespoon of freshly squeezed orange juice (if it's blood orange season, so much the better) and coarsely grate 30g of fresh ginger onto a small plate; there is no need to peel it if the skin's tender. Get out a square of kitchen paper and, standing by the salsa, spoon the ginger into the centre, pull up the edges of the paper to make a little swag bag and, holding it over the salsa, press on it to squeeze out the heady ginger juice. Stir the salsa, and taste it to see if you need more orange or ginger juice or salt. And don't think this is just for dippage: it also doubles as a kind of sharp ketchup, to be splodged onto a plate alongside the Norwegian Pork Ribs on p.265, or wherever you feel its combination of sweetness, heat and acerbity would enliven what you eat.

Meat and rhubarb are mixed together in Claudia Roden's rhubarb *khoresh*, which I came upon in her magisterial *Book of Middle Eastern Food* decades ago, but it is only recently that I have started cooking it – or, rather, a stew inspired by it – and now I can't stop. I make it in small quantities, perfect to be divided, one half stashed in the freezer, to make another solo supper later. It needs anyway to be made in advance, but for me the process adds to the gratification later.

Khoresh is the Persian name for stew, generally one that is cooked in fairly scant amounts of water; my beef stew with rhubarb is probably a little more liquid than is authentic, but I love the strongly flavoured stewing juices too much not to be generous to myself with them. I use beef cheek, for the richness and thickness it brings to the gravy, and one of 500g does me well for two meals. If you're not a beef eater, you could also use the same weight of boneless lamb neck or shoulder.

The only difficult thing about this recipe is cutting the beef cheek, so I advise doing this first, very carefully, and leaving the meat, cut into large chunks, on the chopping board, ready to go into the stew. While traditionally this stew would be cooked on the hob, I much prefer to cook it in the oven; it's much easier to regulate the heat, and you need not tend to it anxiously. So heat the oven to 150°C/130°C Fan. Then, in a smallish heavy-based casserole with a tightly fitting lid, gently fry 2 onions, chopped fairly fine, in oil or butter for about 20 minutes, until they are beginning to turn golden; 30 minutes would be even better. Stir in ½ teaspoon each of ground turmeric, cumin, cinnamon and allspice, and ½ teaspoon, also, of dried mint. Mince or grate in 2 fat cloves of garlic, stir everything together, and then add the chunks of meat, turning them well in the spiced onion. Pour in about 500ml of water, or as much as you need more or less to cover the meat. Add 1 teaspoon of sea salt flakes (or ½ teaspoon of fine sea salt), 1 teaspoon of brown sugar and 1½ tablespoons of tomato purée. Stir well again, and let it come to the boil. When it does, tear off a piece of baking parchment, scrunch it up, unscrunch it, and press it down onto the surface of the meat, tucking the edges in and up around the inside of the pan. Clamp on the lid, and cook it in the oven for about 2½ hours, or until the once-tough meat is lusciously tender.

Remove the lid, discard the parchment, and leave the stew to cool, when you can freeze one half, and refrigerate the other. So, in a day or two, or at some future defrost date, gently reheat the single portion of stew on the hob. When hot, get out a frying pan, and melt a little butter in it. Add about 100g of rhubarb, cut into 4cm lengths, and stir for a minute or two before adding a spritz of lemon. Gently scrape the butter-slicked rhubarb into the stew, and cook for about 7 minutes, until the rhubarb is just soft. The fragrant sourness it brings is not unlike the tang of preserved lemons, and it strikes me that you could add rhubarb – though at the last minute, turned in butter first, as here – for stews which call for preserved lemons if you don't have a jar in your kitchen.

I advise eating this with rice (and I often make a mini version of the oven-baked rice on p.164 using 75g of basmati, a sprinkling of salt, a drop of oil and 150ml of water, in a small, shallow ovenproof dish), with a little freshly chopped mint or dill or, even better, a mixture of both.

While I have exercised my rhubarb enthusiasm extravagantly in these pages, I cannot quite stop here; nor would you expect me to. What follows are three more recipes that make magnificent use of early, tender, pink forced rhubarb, and one which I make with rougher red rhubarb. I have arranged these in the order the rhubarb comes into season, which means, for once, dessert comes first.

RHUBARB AND CUSTARD TRIFLE

I have published many recipes for trifle and made even more, and this is the one I return to most, even though it is the first time I have actually written it down. This simple, joyous pile-up of sponge, rhubarb, custard and cream remains my favourite, and will always remain my favourite; it's time I shared it with you.

It's true, it does involve the making of a custard, but since I have relaxed my previous no-cornflour rule, and also make it these days with double cream, rather than a mixture of cream and milk, it thickens quickly and is the least anxiety-provoking custard you could imagine. Still, if, for ease, you prefer to use ready-made custard from the chill cabinet of the supermarket, I won't stop you. It will be both runnier and sweeter than the one that you make here – and you will probably need 750ml, which is likely to be a tub and a half – and since it won't need time to set in the fridge, you can simply pour it over the fruit-sodden sponge, just before you add the softly whipped cream before serving.

This custard is really no trouble, though. If you feel at all anxious, do fill the sink with cold water, enough to come halfway up the sides of the pan you're using, ready to plunge the pan in to cool down should you feel that the custard looks in danger of splitting at any time. Whisk it assiduously while it's there, cooling in the sink, and danger should be averted. Not that I want to highlight any potential difficulties, as the short time this custard needs to cook pretty well ensures it doesn't get too hot. But as you cook it, keep taking the pan off the heat while stirring or whisking (I do both, swapping from wooden spoon to whisk) so that the heat doesn't get too intense. The only other thing I should say about the custard you see here, in its thick rich yellow layer, is that I actually used 7 yolks and 700ml of cream; I had a spare 100ml that needed to be used up, so I went for it. I added, along with the extra yolk, another teaspoon each of sugar and cornflour. Oh, and its deep colour is due to the glorious yolks of the Burford Brown eggs I use. Should you be using perfectly good standard eggs, and want to give them that Bird's brightness, then you could add a few saffron strands to the milk while you infuse it. You can freeze the leftover egg whites, bagged in pairs, in an airtight container to give you the wherewithal for three of the pavlovas on p.243. As for the vanilla, if I'm not using a vanilla pod I prefer to substitute with paste, which speckles its way through the custard, but of course regular extract will do.

Rhubarb and custard is a hallowed combination, and one I'm loath to depart from, but I don't make this once the beautiful, pink forced rhubarb is out of season, preferring to use other fruit rather than the infinitely less beguiling and more fibrous, greener summer rhubarb. I've made this in summer with strawberries, ones that might disappoint if eaten simply with cream, but whose relative firmness and sourness lend themselves perfectly to being roasted, so that they soften and become more intense in flavour. For this you will need a 1kg of strawberries: roast 850g of them, with 100g of caster sugar, ⅛ teaspoon of salt and 2 tablespoons of lemon juice, in a foil-covered dish (that will take them in a single layer), much as you do the rhubarb, but only for 20 minutes at 200°C/180°C Fan. You will get some liquid from them to add to the red vermouth to soak the sponge, but not quite enough, and it certainly won't yield any extra for a syrup to dribble on top of the cream. So, blitz the 150g of strawberries you have remaining with 2 tablespoons (25g) of caster sugar and 1 tablespoon of lemon juice (amending either, depending on the sweetness or sourness of the fruit) and keep a little of this to drizzle on top of the trifle, mixing the rest with the liquid from the roast fruit and the vermouth.

Otherwise, and in the dead of winter, frozen fruit is your best bet. I tend to go for raspberries, which bring that desirable sharpness, though mixed berries would do on that score too. So, put 800g of frozen raspberries in a saucepan, along with 3 tablespoons (40g) of caster sugar and 4 tablespoons of orange juice and give a good stir, before putting over lowish heat with the lid on for about 5 minutes. Stir again, adding 2 teaspoons of vanilla paste (or extract), then leave off the heat for 15 minutes with the lid on. They won't be completely thawed, but nearly, and will be a deep, almost divinely illuminated red. Once they've stood for a quarter of an hour, stir in the 175ml of red vermouth then pour fruit and juice over the sponge in your trifle dish; it will continue to drip down onto the sponge. To replace the rhubarb syrup for drizzling on top later, simply warm together, in a small pan, a tablespoon of seedless raspberry jam, ¼ teaspoon of lemon juice and 2 tablespoons of water, whisking to help the jam melt. Once it comes to a bubble, pour into a little jug and allow to cool completely.

I've given precise quantities for all the ingredients below, but please bear in mind these are based on the proportions of my trifle bowl, which is 20cm in diameter and 13cm deep. If you are using a wider bowl you will need to boost quantities or the layers will be too shallow.

And I think that's it. Time to dive in.

RHUBARB AND CUSTARD TRIFLE

SERVES 8–10, although I still make this if there are fewer of us; leftovers are to be relished, or generously boxed up and given to people to take home

FOR THE CUSTARD

600ml double cream

1 vanilla pod or 2½ teaspoons vanilla paste (or extract)

6 large egg yolks, at room temperature

2 x 15ml tablespoons plus 2 teaspoons caster sugar

1 x 15ml tablespoon plus 1 teaspoon cornflour

FOR THE BASE

1kg pink forced rhubarb (trimmed weight)

250g caster sugar

175ml red vermouth

12 trifle sponges

FOR THE TOPPING

300ml double cream

Approx. 3 x 15ml tablespoons (20g) chopped or nibbed pistachios

For make-ahead, store and/or freeze notes, see p.333

1. Get on with the custard first. Pour the 600ml of double cream into a heavy-based saucepan (I use one of 22cm diameter), split the vanilla pod lengthways (if using), and use a pointy coffee spoon or the tip of a knife to scrape the damp black seeds into the cream. Drop in the pod, as well. Bring to a bubble but don't let it boil, then take it off the heat straightaway and cover with a lid to let it infuse for 20 minutes. Remove the vanilla pod, run it under the water from the tap to get any cream off, then leave it to dry and use it to scent sugar. If you're not using a vanilla pod, just warm the cream and add vanilla paste or extract once your custard is made.

2. Gently whisk the egg yolks, caster sugar and cornflour in a batter jug or whatever suits you. Keep whisking while you gradually pour in the warm cream and make sure it is all smoothly amalgamated. Wash out the saucepan and dry it – just use water, you don't need soap. Pour the custard mixture from your jug into the pan (using a bendy spatula to scrape out every last eggy bit from the bottom) and cook over medium heat for a minute, stirring with a wooden spoon (preferably one with a pointy bit to help scrape up bits from the bottom), and then on low heat, still stirring mostly with a wooden spoon, but transferring to a little whisk every now and again, too, until thick enough that it coats the back of a wooden spoon and, when you run your finger through it, it doesn't run into the bare stripe. I reckon this takes about 5 minutes altogether. Mind you, I do like to live dangerously. Go more slowly

if you wish, and, at whatever speed you're going, take the pan off the heat regularly, and whisk the custard, to make sure it doesn't get too hot, especially around the edges of the base of the pan.

3. As soon as it's cooked, take it off the heat and scrape it into your batter jug (adding vanilla paste or extract if you haven't gone the vanilla pod route), then cover with a damp scrunched-up piece of baking parchment to stop it forming a skin. (Even writing 'skin' in conjunction with custard makes me feel quite ill.) Once the custard has cooled down, put it into the fridge to chill.

4. Meanwhile, get on with the rhubarb. Heat the oven to 200°C/180°C Fan. Cut the trimmed rhubarb into about 5cm lengths if the ribs are slender; if chunky, cut into about 2½cm pieces. Put into an ovenproof dish in which they can (mostly) sit in a single layer – I use a large baking tin measuring 37 x 34cm, though you could get away with one a bit smaller – and sprinkle over the 250g of caster sugar. Mix together well with your hands, leaving the rhubarb in a single layer, as much as possible, then cover the tin or dish with extra-wide foil, sealing the edges, and cook in the oven for approx. 30 minutes until the rhubarb is tender but still holding its shape.

5. Once the rhubarb is just cooked, let it stand out of the oven with the foil removed for 20 minutes. You might be disappointed with the colour the moment it comes out of the oven, by the way, but after a few minutes it will begin to glow a bright candy pink. Gently transfer with a slotted spoon or spatula (or both) to another dish for now. You should have about 300ml of liquid in the tin, although if you wait about 5 minutes, you will see more juice collecting under the rhubarb in its dish; add that to the juice in the tin.

6. Set aside 125ml of the rhubarb juices for now and measure out another 175ml of the rhubarb juice (I should say that by the end of the forced rhubarb season it seems to make less liquid; if you don't have enough, I suggest you make up the amount with orange juice), then add to it the red vermouth. Taste one teaspoon just for the joy of it, although once you do so, it will be hard not to drink the rest.

7. Now make the rhubarb syrup for the top of the trifle. Pour the re-served 125ml of rhubarb juice into a small heavy-based saucepan,

bring to the boil and bubble away to reduce to a viscous syrup. I reckon if I start off with 125ml, it takes about 4 minutes to bubble away (in a small, 14cm diameter saucepan) to 60ml. If you start off with more, still aim to reduce it by half; any further than that and it will turn to rhubarb toffee. And if that does happen, just stir in a little hot water from the kettle to get it to a thick pouring consistency.

8. Arrange your trifle sponges at the bottom of your trifle bowl, brushing off as much as you can of the sugar coating as you go. Squodge them in as you like, tearing them up as needed to fill any gaps; I tend to go for a layer about 5–6cm deep. Pour your very delicious rhubarb-vermouth liquid over, as evenly as you can, and let the dry little sponges drink it up thirstily, as any sensible person would.

9. Top the drenched sponges with the rhubarb and pour over any juices that have collected in the dish. Once the custard is properly cold, carefully scrape it into the trifle dish on top of the rhubarb, smoothing it to the sides, trying not to smear the glass. The pink of the rhubarb underneath the yellow of the custard is a sight that makes me smile; a fond reminder of the boiled rhubarb & custard sweets of my childhood. Cover the dish with food wrap and put into the fridge overnight.

10. Take the trifle out of the fridge a good 2 hours before you intend to eat it. Shortly before serving, probably just before you sit down to the meal itself, whip the double cream – I like mine quite softly whipped – and spoon gently over the set custard. Use the back of your spoon to create a few whorls and whirls. Drip as much as you want of your reduced rhubarb syrup pinkly over the top and scatter over chopped or nibbed pistachios.

TOASTED MARSHMALLOW AND RHUBARB CAKE

This is a relatively new addition to my rhubarb repertoire, but it has been heavily in rotation ever since I first made it nearly two years ago. Anyone who has a birthday when the forced pink rhubarb is in season gets it (and I do even have alternatives for those dim days when it isn't, and I'll get to them later). It is splendidly celebratory, but not dauntingly difficult. You need a bit of elbow grease and a blowtorch; I can't tell you how much I enjoy teasing out the snowy spikes of marshmallow-meringue and then scorching them. Actually, I positively exult in it: the very act of making this feels like a jubilant part of the celebration itself. And I thank cake consigliere Stella Parks, who, in the pages of her compendious *BraveTart: Iconic American Desserts*, provided the hand-holding inspiration for the marshmallow icing.

You do need to be prepared to whisk the whites until truly thick, but if you have a mixer, this does most of the work. The yolks are used to make two tender and celestially light golden sponges, and the rhubarb that goes between them provides its emphatic tang, offsetting the intense sweetness of the marshmallow icing. Out of forced-rhubarb season, I favour a mixture of raspberries and redcurrants: 300g of the former and 100g of the latter. I put them into a small saucepan with 1 tablespoon each of caster sugar, undiluted elderflower cordial and water, and warm them over low heat with a lid on for 3 minutes, or until the juices start to run, then give them 2 minutes with the lid off, before transferring them to a dish to cool. If you want to use just raspberries, straight from a punnet, uncooked, you may, and you won't need many, but you should mash some with a fork – leaving a generous handful whole – before topping the marshmallow layer that sandwiches the cake with them. When I make the original rhubarb version, I like to bring a bowl of roast rhubarb or rhubarb compote (p.127), however you like to think of it, to the table for people to spoon onto their cake plate, but I don't regard it as obligatory; when I do the raspberry version, I regard extra berries on serving as non-negotiable.

While I have made the cake in its entirety the evening before when there has been no alternative, I prefer not to. The icing certainly keeps the cake airtight, but the potential for drippage and slippage overnight is just too tense-making. I haven't had any disasters yet, but feel it's only fair to warn you that it is a risk. The cakes, on their own, if made in advance will become both too dry and too frangible.

It's not for me to tell you how to do your birthday candles, should you be making this for just such a celebration, but I favour a single black candle stuck into a plain white holder. It's hard to make birthday candles chic – and

I'm not saying they should be – but this does it; besides, there is no point interfering with the sumptuous vulgarity of the cake itself.

One last – important – comment: since you will be blowtorching this cake, it is imperative that the cake stand you put it on is heatproof.

GIVES 8–12 slices

FOR THE RHUBARB LAYER

400g pink forced rhubarb (trimmed weight)

100g caster sugar

FOR THE CAKE

6 large eggs, at room temperature

1 lemon

100ml full-fat milk, at room temperature

25g cornflour

100g plain flour

2 teaspoons baking powder

½ teaspoon bicarbonate of soda

¼ teaspoon fine sea salt

150g caster sugar

150ml vegetable oil, plus more for greasing

FOR THE ICING

6 egg whites, from eggs above

350g caster sugar

¼ teaspoon fine sea salt

½ teaspoon cream of tartar or ½ teaspoon lemon juice

2 teaspoons vanilla extract

For make-ahead, store and/or freeze notes, see p.333

For make-ahead, store and/or freeze notes, see p.333

1. Start by cooking the rhubarb. Heat the oven to 200°C/180°C Fan. Cut the trimmed rhubarb ribs into 5cm lengths if slender, 2½cm if chunky. Put into an ovenproof dish in which they will be able more or less to sit in a single layer – I use a 20 x 26cm Pyrex dish – and sprinkle over the 100g of sugar. Mix together with your hands, leaving the rhubarb in a single layer, as much as possible, then cover the dish with foil, sealing the edges well, and cook in the oven for approx. 30 minutes until the rhubarb is tender, but still holding its shape.

2. Remove the foil, and leave the dish of rhubarb out on the counter, watching it glow ever more pink as it cools. Turn the oven down to 170°C/150°C Fan. Line the bottoms of two 20cm loose-bottomed sandwich tins, and lightly grease the sides.

3. Separate the eggs, dropping the whites into a large mixing bowl or bowl of a freestanding mixer (whichever bowl you're using should be thoroughly washed and grease-free) and the yolks into another. Cover the bowl of whites with food wrap, and put to one side while you mix and bake the cake.

4. Finely grate the zest of the lemon and add to the bowl of yolks. Measure out the milk, juice the lemon and add

2 tablespoons of juice to the milk, and leave to stand for a mo. Mix together the cornflour, flour, baking powder, bicarbonate of soda and salt, and set this aside for now, too.

5. Add the 150g of sugar and the oil to the yolks and whisk on medium-high speed for 3 minutes, by which time the mixture will be rich, gleaming and billowy. Actually, it looks rather like a glorious mayonnaise.

6. Still whisking, but slightly more slowly now, gently pour and scrape in the now curdled milk and, once it's in, carry on whisking until combined; the mixture looks like custard at this stage. Finally, whisking more gently now, gradually spoon in the dry ingredients. Once in, use a spatula to scrape down the sides, and fold everything gently together, before dividing the airy mixture between the prepared tins.

7. Bake for 20–25 minutes, by which time the cakes will have risen up extravagantly, the tops a golden brown; they will feel soft and puffy to the touch, but a cake tester should come out clean. Remove to a wire rack and let the cakes cool in their tins for 15 minutes – sinking a little as they do so – before very carefully turning out. You'll need to loosen the edges with a small offset spatula first. These are tender sponges, so don't rush or be rough. Once unmoulded, gently pull back and remove the lining papers straightaway.

8. When the cakes are completely, completely cold – which will take about an hour – you can get on with the icing. But first, tear off four strips of baking parchment, scrunch them, then unscrunch them and lay them flat to make the outline of a square on top of a cake stand. (This is to stop you covering the cake stand with sticky marshmallow icing later. It may sound a faff, but I wouldn't advise you to leave out this step.) Place one of the cakes on it, top-side down, the paper strips under the edges. Also, now's the time to lift the rhubarb pieces out of their syrup in the tin and on to a plate.

9. So, to the icing: get out a tall pan that you can sit your big bowl o' whites on (without the bottom of the bowl touching the water) and heat a little water in it until just about to come to a simmer. Mix the 350g of sugar, the salt and the cream of tartar (or lemon juice) together and add to the egg whites. Then sit the mixing bowl on top of the pan, so it's gently warmed by the barely simmering water underneath and, just using a balloon whisk (thoroughly washed

and grease-free, again), keep whisking for 3 minutes, to dissolve the sugar. I couldn't say this is hard to do, but you can really feel it in your forearm. I'm always grateful when my 3-minute timer goes off.

10. Once the sugar's dissolved and you have a smooth opaque mixture that's warm to the touch, remove the bowl from the saucepan. Whisk at high speed for 5 minutes in a freestanding mixer, or for 6–7 minutes if using an electric handheld whisk, by which time the whites will be very, very thick and ludicrously voluminous. Whisk in 1 teaspoon of the vanilla extract, and when it's incorporated, whisk in the remaining teaspoon, then give a good fold by hand to make sure every bit is mixed in.

11. Dollop a generous amount of marshmallow icing on to the waiting cake, and smooth right to the edges, so that you have a layer about 1cm thick: this should use about a quarter of the icing. Cover this with the rhubarb, though leave about ½cm perimeter around the edge; I go slowly here, using a couple of dessertspoons to ferry the rhubarb to the cake. And you might want to tilt the rhubarb plate away from you slightly as you transfer the slices, to make sure you leave any pooling liquid behind.

12. Top with the second cake, right way up, and use just under half the icing left in the bowl to cover the top, going just beyond the edges. Then carefully spread the rest of the icing thickly around the sides – leaving a tiny bit in the mixing bowl – until the whole cake is completely covered. Now for the really fun part: dip your fingers in the bit of icing left in the bowl and then dab the top and sides of the cake, lightly pulling up and teasing out spikes of marshmallow icing; I feel like an '80s hairdresser doing this. Bear in mind that sometimes, as you do the sides, you will pull bits of the icing off, leaving a hole, but don't panic, just pat it back on. Gently pull out the strips of paper from beneath the cake and discard, then seal the bottom of the cake with any remaining icing should you need to. Then, slightly dampen a piece of kitchen towel with cold water, and rub off any stray bits of icing or sugar smear from the plate.

13. Take the cake somewhere you can kindle fire safely. Light a blow-torch and, holding it fairly near the cake and with not too timorous a flame, toast the top and the sides of the icing.

14. I find this cake easiest to slice if left to stand for a couple of hours before serving. And you need to slice generously, as with all layer cakes.

PICKLED RHUBARB

A simple pickle is quite one of the easiest things to make, and when the early pink rhubarb is in season, you should celebrate its shortish season with this. As with the spiced rhubarb sauce on p.135, it pairs tangily with oily fish and rich meats; it also makes a beautiful addition to a cheeseboard, in place of chutney.

You will have to sterilise a preserving jar, but it's scarcely hard work. Indeed, I consider a jar sterilised if it's come straight out of the dishwasher and not so much as a finger has touched the inside of it. Or you can just wash the jar in soapy liquid, rinse it well, and dry it in a 140°C/120°C Fan oven. Leave to cool before filling.

This pickle will last for 4 weeks in the fridge, but if you feel like planning for a longer future, then you will need to hot-process the filled jar (and you might then want to do several batches to make it worthwhile). By this, all I mean is that the filled sealed preserving jar should be immersed in a large pan of boiling water so that the jar is covered by a good 10cm of water. After the jar's had 10 minutes, carefully remove it (you will need special preserving jar sterilising tongs) and let it cool before putting it into the fridge, where it will last for a year. It makes me feel very *Little House on the Prairie*.

Pink peppercorns are softer than actual peppercorns – despite the name, pink peppercorns are dried berries in fact related to the cashew family and are only so called because of their resemblance to the pepper we grind in mills – and you can bite into them without fear of cracking a tooth. I love the pops of piquant heat as you eat, but if you don't have any pink peppercorns, replace with some ginger cut into short, fine chips rather than black or white peppercorns.

FILLS 1 x 1.5 litre jar

600g pink forced rhubarb (trimmed weight)

375ml raw, unfiltered apple cider vinegar

375ml cold water

125g caster sugar

3 fresh bay leaves

4 star anise

2 teaspoons pink peppercorns

2½ teaspoons sea salt flakes or 1¼ teaspoons fine sea salt

For make-ahead, store and/or freeze notes, see p.333

1. Sterilise a 1.5 litre jar following the instructions in the recipe introduction.

2. Cut the young, pink rhubarb into roughly 4cm lengths, and drop them into your preserving jar.

3. Pour the vinegar and cold water into a saucepan, and stir in the sugar. Add the bay leaves, star anise, pink peppercorns and salt, and bring to the boil, giving another stir to make sure all the sugar's dissolved and pour the sharp-sweet pickling liquid over the rhubarb. The pink peppercorns will rise to the surface, where they'll stay, but that's fine.

4. When you've filled the jar, seal the lid tight, leave it to cool, then stash in the fridge for 2 days before eating it, though it will last for 4 weeks.

BEETROOT, RHUBARB AND GINGER SOUP

Sharp and sweet, rhubarb and beetroot were made for one another, and this soup is a fitting celebration of their union. I had intended to make a beetroot and apple soup (hitherto a favourite) one day, only to find I had no apples, so substituted the rhubarb instead, and have never looked back. (Though if you want to make the apple variant, simply use 2 Granny Smiths in its place. Or, for a Christmassy version, use 200g of cranberries and an extra 100g of beetroot.) The rhubarb undercuts what can, for me, be the cloying candied intensity of beet. Deep in colour and sprightly in taste, this is a soup to have in a jug in the fridge for a tangy bowl of instant comfort whenever needed.

    You can eat it just as it is, or swirl over a horseradish cream made by mixing 175ml of regular dairy or oat-milk cream with a pinch of salt, 3 tablespoons of freshly grated horseradish, ¼ teaspoon of apple cider vinegar and ½ teaspoon of Dijon mustard. But I have grown to love it particularly with the Green Tahini Sauce – either the coriander version or the wild garlic one – on p.223. Or you can simply squiggle over some cream.

MAKES 1.5 litres

400g rhubarb (trimmed weight)

500g raw beetroot

1 large onion (approx. 200g)

2 x 15ml tablespoons olive oil

3 fat cloves of garlic

2 teaspoons ground cumin

1 litre cold water

2 teaspoons sea salt flakes (or
  1 teaspoon fine sea salt)

50g fresh ginger

For make-ahead, store and/or freeze notes, see p.333

1. Break or cut each rhubarb stalk into 2 or 3 pieces, just so they fit in the pan, and set aside. Wash the beetroot, remove the stalks and leaves (see p.199 for what to do with them), and trim each beetroot, cutting away the barnacly bits; there's no need to peel. Roughly chop into 2cm chunks. Peel the onion and roughly chop it.

2. Warm the oil in a decent-sized saucepan or casserole that comes with a tightly fitting lid – I use one of 24cm diameter – and cook the onion for about 10 minutes over medium-low heat, stirring frequently. It won't soften much in that time, but enough for now.

3. Peel and roughly chop the garlic, and stir it into the pan of onions. Cook for about 2 minutes, then stir in the cumin and tumble in the rhubarb and beetroot. Add the water and salt, turn the heat to high and bring to the boil. Once it's bubbling, turn the heat down, clamp

on the lid, and let it all cook at a robust simmer until the beetroot is utterly, utterly soft. This always takes more time than you'd think: I'd reckon on 1½ hours, though it easily could take longer.

4. With a stick blender (and if yours comes with a soup-blending attachment, so much the better), blitz until you have a smooth and velvety ruby soup.

5. If the skin's tough, peel the ginger with the tip of a teaspoon, then coarsely grate it onto a plate. Moving fast, get out a piece of kitchen paper and spoon half the grated ginger into the centre, then bring together the edges of the paper and twist. Holding this little swag bag over the soup, press on it to squeeze out the intense juice. Now get another square of kitchen paper, and do the same with the remaining half of grated ginger. Taste for seasoning, ladle out into waiting bowls, and drizzle over each a little horseradish cream or Green Tahini Sauce as you wish.

MUCH DEPENDS ON DINNER

It's a strange thing to begin a book in one world and finish it in another. This chapter – or the chapter it was going to be – was originally called 'How to Invite People for Supper Without Hating Them (or Yourself)'. And I am almost winded by the inappropriateness of this title now.

The gap between my finishing this book and its being published means I do not know if, by the time it comes out, inviting people over for supper will still be an empty proposition or whether our tables will be brimming with conviviality (though I suspect something nearer the former). It isn't simply the absence of guests that renders my initial – only slightly facetious – title obsolete. After all, we shall be inviting friends for supper again, even if we're not sure when that 'again' will be; we shall not be eating in isolation forever. I sense that the period of enforced unsociability can't help but change the way we'll feel for a very long time about having people over. It seems such a privilege now, the idea of being able to cook for other people, and not because we have to, but because we want to. How lucky it seems, how nourishing, to have friends in our home, eating, drinking, laughing, and talking, talking, talking.

I don't deny that even in normal times, this can be a joy. But all too often plans made in expansive hopefulness, issuing from the generous, human need to feed those we hold dear, can turn, as the date gets nearer, into a prospect we either exhaustedly regret or cook for with sullen resentment. What a waste all that sociability-through-gritted-teeth seems now.

Perhaps, over the months of the lockdown, many have learned how misjudged our attitude to cooking can be. Yes, of course, it can be drudgery and it can be draining, but it is also a way to make a substantive difference to the emotional temperature of the days. There is so much around us that we cannot control, but food gives shape to our pleasures and offers both immersion and escape. We focus on food, not just out of appetite, but because it satisfies our need, our greed, for connection. What we cook links us to those who've cooked it before, as well as to the earth, what grows from it, lives off it, and to that essential human drive – not always benign, to be sure – to transform it, and thus ourselves. Cooking is about imposing order on the natural world and ourselves. It is also an essential ritual, turning feeding to eating, mixing animal hunger and our civilised habit of assuaging it. Even done alone, it is something we share.

Cooking is not an art, it is a craft: art is demanding, it needs to last, making claims for posterity; craft expresses our need to make something beautiful and useful. I don't think a bad meal can ruin a good day, though it can make a dent in it, but I do believe a good meal can save a bad one. And because we eat daily, and more than once each day, we have so many occasions of potential pleasure to reach for. When we cook for those we live with, we accept that sometimes what we set out to achieve escapes our grasp. But when we invite others to our table, we lose sight of this, aiming for artistry, and making ourselves anxious in the process. Jane Grigson has some wonderful words on this subject in *Good Things*, which I think about often:

> Cooking something delicious is really much more satisfactory than painting pictures or throwing pots. At least for most of us. Food has the tact to disappear, leaving room and opportunity for masterpieces to come. The mistakes don't hang on the walls or stand on the shelves to reproach you for ever.

And I think that is essential to our enjoyment of it. Once you feel you are having to create something extraordinary that will live evermore in the memories of those who eat it, cooking becomes performance, complete with, all too often, crippling stage fright. And even though we might like to feel we're thinking only of our guests, the fraught and freighted desire to please can be so much more a measure of our own needs – for approval, affirmation, applause – and somewhere we know that, and that knowledge is a source of discomfort and shame. Is it any wonder, then, that inviting people for supper can be so emotionally exhausting?

So, whenever we can have friends around a table again, I think we have to build on what we've learned through lockdown: that cooking and eating are daily ways to find pleasure, and to share it, and that companionship is as much the measure of a good dinner as the food. What and how I eat matters immensely to me and I can be overwhelmed by despondency if I make something to eat for myself that disappoints. But even I feel that if, having had friends over for supper, the best thing to be said about the evening was that the food was great, I'd consider it a failure. I may not want the food to have been bad, but the mark of a good evening for me is to be able, as I sit in idle post-mortem mode with my mug of tea the next morning, to recall the room warmed by friendship, chaotic with the zigzag of conversation across the table, or at odd moments throughout the day, find myself laughing at a remembered joke. It's the sort of liveliness that calms.

The recipes in this chapter – and indeed, throughout the book – are to help usher in that sense of animated serenity, whether you have guests around the table or not. In a piece for the *New York Times*, the critic Frank Bruni wrote beautifully of the martini's near-instant ability 'to blunt the day and polish the night'. And yes, I'd concur, but I fervently believe that the evening meal has the power to do this, too.

This is not too lofty a claim for a quotidian exercise. And it does not rest on the cook's putting in long hours to produce elaborately transcendent food. The kitchen is a vital decompression chamber for me, but this is predicated on meals – whomsoever I am feeding – being manageable and the cooking itself being enjoyable. The recipes that follow are for the food that I cook for my family; the only difference when I have people over is that I rustle up a dip or three to eat over drinks before sitting down at the table, and provide pudding after. And if I don't start here with those dips, it's because the dinners we depend on most are those we look forward to daily, those one-course affairs that bring cheer, comfort and contentment: delicious deeds in a sometimes dark world.

If I start with chicken, it's because when I ask myself what I'm going to cook for dinner, it is the answer I most often come up with, and the bedrock of my cooking life. In fact, if I'm putting a reminder into my phone calendar, I only have to type the letters 'Ta' and, eager to please and boast of its impeccable memory, it will immediately fill the rest in, offering up the completed command: 'Take chicken out of fridge', no matter if what I actually intended to enter was 'Tape up parcel for post office' or 'Tax return'. The truth is, it is nearly always 'Take chicken out of fridge' that I am actually setting a time for in my calendar but, even when it isn't, I find the reminder popping up smile-inducingly soothing. So I will never be the person who dissuades you from making roast chicken for supper yet again. I will never find it boring, and take comfort from an act so often repeated I could probably do it in my sleep. It feels almost like a sacred ritual, taking said chicken out of fridge, letting it come to room temperature in a roasting tin, smearing it with butter or oil, sprinkling it exuberantly with sea salt flakes, stuffing half a lemon and a handful of herbs inside it, squeezing the other half of lemon into the tin, splashed up with a little water, before roasting it in a 220°C/200°C Fan oven for an hour or so.

'Shall I roast a chicken?' has the same emotional resonance for me as 'How about a nice cup of tea?' And the answer is always yes. I do try and make an effort not to serve the same vegetables alongside every time, although in my house it would be considered an act of egregious negligence not to bring a small casserole of my House Special Slow-Cooked Peas to the table at the same time. The recipe for these sweet, soft peas, along with other suggestions for vegetables to make a roast chicken (or whatever plain dish it is that you have on auto-repeat) feel just a little bit different, can be found on p.195. But I can dispense with the peas and just make a salad if I serve the roast chicken on a dish which I have first filled with crisps. Clearly this is a serving suggestion rather than a recipe, however you should know that the chicken in the picture opposite was cooked as for the Chicken with Garlic Cream Sauce (p.164) only instead of making the sauce, I sprinkled over some finely chopped rosemary. The crisps under the chicken pieces become gooily sticky and sodden with savoury juices; the crisps around the edge remain just as their name suggests.

CHICKEN IN A POT WITH LEMON AND ORZO

This is not exactly the same as perhaps the most precious recipe in my repertoire, My Mother's Praised Chicken, which found a home in my eighth book, *Kitchen*, but it owes a lot to it. A family favourite, it's a simple one-pot dish which brings comfort and joy, and it is my pleasure to share that with you.

It's not in the spirit of things to be utterly specific with this kind of cooking: if you're feeding small children, for example, you may not want to add the chilli flakes. Similarly, you may want to use just one lemon, rather than the two I like. Your chicken may weigh more or less: the ones I get tend to be between 1.5kg and 1.7kg. And although I have specified the casserole I always use, you obviously will use the one you have, which will make a difference to how quickly everything cooks, how much evaporation there will be, and so on.

Don't let these things trouble you unduly; this is a very forgiving dish. It doesn't rely on precision timing: the chicken, leeks and carrots are meant to be soft, and I even like it when the orzo is cooked far beyond the timing specified on the packet. It's also open to variation, owing to what's in your kitchen. You can, for example, replace the orzo with rice if you prefer, although you need to know that it will be slightly puddingy cooked this way; I don't mean this disparagingly, but to indicate the soft, swollen texture. Barley works well, too, though will need to go in sooner, or you can use ditalini or any other small pasta you want. If you prefer to use dried thyme in place of the dried tarragon, by all means do; I also like it with dried mint. I could go on, but there is no need to add complications: this is a simple recipe that brings deep contentment.

A final note: although this isn't easily scale-downable, in light of the fact that a whole chicken has the starring role, I do often make a version of it for a soothing solo supper. For this, you don't need the oven, as it's frankly easier to cook it all on the stove; you could, of course, cook the recipe proper on the hob and not in the oven, but I find there is more evaporation of the flavoursome liquid that way. Anyway, get out a small pan that comes with a tightly fitting lid, heat 1 teaspoon of olive oil, and put a large chicken thigh (bone-in and skin-on) in it, skin-side down, and let it fry for a good 10 minutes over medium heat until it's golden brown. While that's happening, peel and finely dice a smallish carrot, slice a small leek, or half a large one, and peel a fat clove of garlic. Once the chicken skin has browned, take the pan off the heat, turn the chicken thigh skin-side up and finely grate the zest of half a lemon into the pan, then mince or grate the garlic in as well, followed by ½ teaspoon of dried tarragon or thyme. Add the prepared carrot and leek, and pour 500ml of light chicken stock over, though this doesn't have to be homemade. (You don't get enough flavour from one chicken thigh cooked for a relatively short time to be able to use water alone.) Add a pinch of dried chilli flakes, and ½ teaspoon of sea salt flakes (or ¼ teaspoon of fine sea salt) unless the stock you're using is salty enough, give a bit of a stir, and put back on the heat, this time at high, and bring to the boil. Once it starts bubbling, clamp on a lid and turn the heat to low (or medium low, depending on how big the burner is) and cook at a firm simmer for about 40 minutes. Check that the chicken and cubes of carrot are cooked through; it is as essential that the carrots are soft as it is that the chicken is well cooked. Add 50g of orzo to the pan, making sure it's all submerged, replace the lid, and cook over medium heat for 10–12 minutes until soft. Leave the pan on the hob, with the lid still on but the heat off, for another 10 minutes or so, and then shred the chicken thigh with a couple of forks (the skin will be flabby, so you may want to remove it along with the bones) and decant to a large bowl, adding freshly chopped parsley, some leaves and sprigs of thyme or feathery fresh dill.

SERVES 4–6

1 chicken (approx. 1.5kg)

3 fat cloves of garlic

2 medium carrots (approx. 300g)

2 medium leeks (approx. 400g trimmed weight, or approx. 600g if you're buying them untrimmed)

1 x 15ml tablespoon olive oil

2 lemons

2 teaspoons dried tarragon (or dried thyme)

2 teaspoons sea salt flakes (or 1 teaspoon fine sea salt)

½ teaspoon dried chilli flakes

1.5 litres cold water

300g orzo pasta

6 x 15ml tablespoons finely chopped flat-leaf parsley, plus more to serve

Freshly grated Parmesan, to serve

CHICKEN IN A POT WITH LEMON AND ORZO

For make-ahead, store and/or freeze notes, see p.333

1. Untruss the chicken, if it comes trussed, and remove all the string. If time allows, let it stand out on a board for 40 minutes or so to let the chill come off it. Heat the oven to 180°C/160°C Fan.

2. Peel the garlic cloves, and peel and cut the carrots into three lengths across, and then into batons. Wash the leeks to remove any mud, if needed, and cut into approx. 2½cm rounds.

3. Heat the oil in a large heavy-based casserole with a tightly fitting lid; I use an enamelled cast-iron oval casserole 29cm long, in which the chicken fits neatly, leaving just a small space all around it to fit the vegetables later. Place the chicken in the hot oil breast-side down to colour the skin; I do this over high heat for 3–5 minutes, or until the skin is richly golden. Then turn the chicken the right way up.

4. Take the pan off the heat and, aiming for the space around the chicken, finely grate in the zest from the 2 lemons, then grate or mince

in the garlic (obviously some can end up on the chicken itself), add the dried tarragon (or thyme) and give a quick stir into the oil as best you can.

5. Scatter the vegetables around the chicken, followed by the salt and chilli flakes (if using), and squeeze in the juice from your zested lemons.

6. Pour in the cold water – covering all but the very top of the breast – and put back on high heat, then bring the pot to a boil. Once it's bubbling, clamp on the lid and carefully transfer to the oven to cook for 1¼ hours, though check to make sure the chicken is all but cooked through and the carrots soft.

7. Take the pot out of the oven, and add the orzo all around the chicken, and push it under the liquid, giving something as approximating a stir as you can manage in the restricted space. Put the lid back on, and return the casserole to the oven for another 15 minutes, by which time the orzo should be soft and swollen.

8. Let the casserole stand, uncovered, out of the oven for 15 minutes before serving. The orzo will continue to soak up the broth as it stands.

9. While you're waiting, chop the parsley. Stir in 4 tablespoons, and then sprinkle over a little more. You could shred the chicken now, but it looks so wonderful in its pot I like to bring it to the table whole.

10. Place a dish by the casserole, and then pull the chicken gently apart with a couple of forks, removing any bones and skin that come loose to the dish. (For me, these bits are a particular treat: I live for the cartilage.) I find it easiest to do this while the chicken's still in the pot but, if you prefer, you can try and remove it to a carving board; go carefully as it's likely to fall to pieces a bit as you do so. Stir the chicken and orzo again and ladle into bowls, sprinkling with parsley as you go. You may also want to offer Parmesan to grate over: I prefer it without, but there is a strong pro-Parmesan contingent in my house.

2 hrs +

CHICKEN WITH GARLIC CREAM SAUCE

There is something old-fashioned and comforting about a cream sauce. It's so rare to come across these days, and I think it's time we welcomed it back. My paternal grandmother was very keen on chicken with finely sliced button mushrooms and cream, which I remember fondly if blandly, and although you could certainly fry a panful of mushrooms in butter and add cream to it, I much prefer this funghi-free and fiercely garlicky version. While I'm always happy to have simply steamed new potatoes with it, crushing them delectably into the chickeny, garlicky, creamy sauce as I eat, there is something so particularly perfect about plain rice alongside. And, for an easy life, if you don't have a rice cooker, you can cook it in the oven on a shelf underneath the chicken (but not until the chicken is about halfway through its cooking time). Put 250g basmati rice in a shallow ovenproof dish of 23cm diameter (no deeper than 5cm). Stir in 1 of teaspoon sea-salt flakes (or ½ teaspoon of fine sea salt) and perhaps – for all that this is intended to be plain rice – the seeds from a couple of cardamom pods, add 2 teaspoons of olive oil and then pour in 500ml of hot water from a just-boiled kettle, cover tightly with foil and cook in the oven for 20–25 minutes. I more often cook the rice at 200°C/180°C Fan, when it needs the full 30 minutes, though that's with nothing else in the oven, so take a look after 25. The water should be fully absorbed when it's cooked, and the rice tender. Remove the foil and cover the dish with a clean tea towel, and leave for 10 minutes or so before fluffing the rice up with a fork; you'll find this much easier if you decant the rice into a larger bowl, though warm the bowl first.

And this recipe can very simply be turned into a supper for one. I use a small cast-iron frying pan for this, though you can use any small pan that can go both on the hob and in the oven (which should be at 200°C/180°C Fan) and in which a couple of chicken thighs can sit fairly snugly. Heat a drop or two of olive oil in the pan and when good and hot, though not smoking, put 2 bone-in, skin-on chicken thighs in the pan, skin-side down, sprinkle the fleshy side with sea salt, and cook over medium-low heat for 10 minutes, preferably with a splatter guard resting on top of the pan as there is a lot of fatty spitting, until the skin is beautifully golden and crisp. Take off the heat, turn the chicken pieces over so they are now skin-side up, and stand back a bit as you pour in 60ml each (or 4 tablespoons or a ¼ cup) of water and dry white vermouth, or replace the vermouth and water with 120ml of light chicken stock if you prefer. Let it bubble up, which it does even off the heat if you're using cast iron, then transfer to the oven and roast for 30 minutes until the chicken is completely cooked through. Do check after about 20 minutes that there is still liquid in the pan and add a little water if it looks dry. Let the chicken stand in the pan for as long as you need to make your cream sauce, which is essentially the same as the one below only I make it with 75ml of cream and 1–2 cloves of garlic depending on my mood, and the size of the cloves. Once the cream is thickened and reduced a little, transfer the chicken thighs to a warm plate and pour the garlic cream into the chicken pan so you don't waste the flavoursome juices left in it, adding parsley and chives as wished and stirring well. And you can put it back

on the heat to reduce and thicken further as needed. Just before you pour this now golden sauce (which owes its colour, in contrast to the elegant pallor of the sauce below, to the initial frying in the cast iron) over and around the chicken thighs, taste for salt. I should also tell you that it is perfectly possible to bake a single portion of rice in the oven too, providing you have a shallow ovenproof dish small enough; I use one of 18cm diameter, cooking 75g of rice in 150ml of water (and only a sprinkling of salt and a drop of oil), as above.

If you prefer, you can replace the spatchcocked chicken in the recipe that follows with 8 chicken thighs or 12 if you want to feed 6. There's more than enough sauce. And should you wish to add anchovies to this sauce, go right ahead. Just chop up as many fillets as you want, adding them to the cream along with the garlic.

SERVES 4, or 6 if you get a bigger chicken or boost with extra chicken portions

FOR THE CHICKEN

1 chicken (approx. 1.5kg) spatchcocked (or see step 1)

1 teaspoon sea salt flakes (or ½ teaspoon fine sea salt), plus more for sprinkling

2 fat cloves of garlic

2 x 15ml tablespoons (30g) soft unsalted butter

75ml dry white vermouth (or wine) combined with 75ml cold water (or use 150ml light chicken stock in place of the vermouth and water, if preferred)

FOR THE SAUCE

300ml double cream

4 fat cloves of garlic

A good grinding of pepper

Sea salt flakes to taste

3 x 15ml tablespoons finely chopped flat-leaf parsley

3 x 15ml tablespoons finely chopped chives

For make-ahead, store and/or freeze notes, see p.333

1. If you haven't got a butcher to spatchcock the chicken for you, do not worry: it's easy enough to do yourself; indeed, it's a task I take perhaps unseemly delight in. Put the chicken, breast-side down, in a large but fairly shallow roasting tin (I use one that measures 34 x 37 x 5cm) and push down on it until you hear a satisfying crunch. With some good kitchen scissors or poultry shears, cut through each side of the backbone, remove it, leaving it in the tin, then turn the chicken the other way up, and now press onto the breast to flatten it a little more.

2. Flip the chicken breast-side down again and sprinkle ½ teaspoon of sea salt flakes (or ¼ teaspoon of fine sea salt) over the inside of the chicken. Peel the 2 cloves of garlic and mince or grate over the

chicken, too, and rub lightly into the meat. Leave for 30 minutes or so to let the chicken come to room temperature.

3. Pour the cream into a small saucepan (I use one of 14cm diameter). Peel the 4 cloves of garlic, and mince or grate into the cream, add a good grinding of pepper, stir well, and bring to a boil, then turn down and let it bubble away for 3 minutes. Don't worry about the cream boiling, just don't let it boil over. Stir regularly with a silicon spatula so that you can scrape down the sides as well. Take the pan off the heat, cover with a lid or foil and let it steep while the chicken cooks.

4. Heat the oven to 220°C/200°C Fan. Turn the chicken the right way up, smear the soft butter over the skin, and sprinkle with the remaining ½ teaspoon of sea salt flakes (or ¼ teaspoon of fine sea salt.) Pour the vermouth and water (replacing both with light chicken stock if you prefer) into the tin around the chicken and transfer to the oven to cook for approx. 45 minutes, by which time the skin should be golden and crisp, and the meat completely cooked through. The juices should run clear if you use the tip of a knife to pierce where the thigh meets the body (or just waggle the thigh to see if it feels loose). Transfer the chicken to a carving board and let it rest for 10 minutes. Pour the juices from the roasting tin into your saucepan of cream, scraping up any golden sticky bits.

5. While the chicken is resting, bring the cream sauce to just under a boil, then turn the heat down and let it simmer gently for 5 minutes, keeping an eye on the pan and stirring regularly. Taste to see if you want to add salt and pour into a warmed jug. Add most of the chopped parsley and chives to the jug and stir.

6. Cut the chicken up and arrange on a warmed platter. Pour a little of the sauce over, and sprinkle with the remaining herbs. Bring the jug to the table with the chicken so that people can pour more over as they eat. It's a lot of sauce, but that's the way we like it. Should you have any left over, warm it up, add a little grated Parmesan and some more freshly chopped parsley or chives, toss with pasta or drizzle over steamed new potatoes or, frankly, anything you'd like.

ONE-PAN CHICKEN WITH APRICOT HARISSA AND SWEET POTATOES

When you're feeling jaded and lacking in brio, this is just the supper for you. It's an instant pick-me-up: ebulliently bright and deeply flavoured, and a joy to bring to the table. Should you have already made a jar of the Apricot Harissa (p.218) to keep in the fridge, which I suggest you do, for anointing and enhancing whatever takes your fancy (and see the Harissa Roast Potatoes on p.216, Harissa Roast Parsnips p.278, and Roast Cauliflower with Apricot Harissa and Spinach on p.216 for other suggestions for its use), then this is blessedly quick and simple to rustle up. But if you haven't, and my suggestion that you do comes at a bad time, then use shop-bought harissa. Do taste it before using all 4 tablespoons, as it might well be a lot fiercer than the apricot harissa here. But then, even if you've made a batch of your own apricot harissa, you should taste before you decide how much to add: you may be after raging fire, or merely flickering warmth. Besides, we all tolerate the heat of chillies differently. I don't feel this is particularly hot but it does give – when combined with the sweetness of the potatoes, peppers and leeks, offset by the lime, and enriched by the deep savouriness of the chickeny juices – an aromatic and rambunctious tang.

While you need no more with this than a crisp salad – as ever, I move towards bitter leaves territory – it does make a lot of intensely flavoured and exuberantly orange juice, so you might well want some good, sturdy bread for dunking. And should I have some of the pink sauce (aka Beetroot, Chilli and Ginger Sauce, p.225) in the fridge (and I try to, always) I most certainly bring it out to ladle on top for more tang, more heat, and an upliftingly riotous clash.

To turn this into a solo supper just divide everything by four, give or take, but use one whole pepper.

SERVES 4

900g sweet potatoes

2–3 red peppers (approx. 400g)

2 leeks (400g trimmed weight – or approx. 600g if you're buying them untrimmed)

3 x 15ml tablespoons olive oil

4 x 15ml tablespoons (60ml) Apricot Harissa (see p.218)

8 chicken thighs, skin-on and bone-in

3–4 limes

1–2 teaspoons sea salt flakes (or ½–1 teaspoon fine sea salt)

For make-ahead, store and/or freeze notes, see p.334

1. Heat the oven to 200°C/180°C Fan.

2. Wash the sweet potatoes, then cut into 4–5cm slices or chunks. Deseed the peppers and cut into 4–5cm pieces, discarding the pith, and slice the leeks into 2cm rounds, washing first to remove any mud, if needed.

3. While you need a large roasting tin for this, it's better if it's relatively shallow. I use one that's 34 x 37 x 5cm. Get out whichever tin fits the bill best, and pour in the oil, spoon in the harissa, and whisk or use a fork to mix, then add the prepared sweet potatoes, peppers and leeks and toss well together.

4. Add the chicken thighs and toss again, and really rub the chicken skin with the harissa-brightened oil, then arrange the chicken skin-side up, jostling among the vegetables. You'll have to crowd everything in a bit.

5. Juice 1 ½–2 of your limes to give you 2 tablespoons. Add this to the tin, sprinkle in the salt, then roast for 1 hour – turning the tin around halfway through if needed – by which time the chicken should be cooked through and crisp-skinned. If the skin isn't crisp enough, leave it in the oven for a bit longer.

6. I bring the tin to the table – along with a side plate of lime wedges – and serve straight from it, making sure to spoon the bright juices, like a crazy fluorescent gravy, over everyone's plate too. And should you have any of the gravy and vegetables left over, they can be made (once defatted a bit) into a glorious soup, with or without the addition of coconut milk.

LASAGNE OF LOVE

This is what I make for my children's birthday celebrations, for parties to send them off before they go away, and for the dinners to welcome them back when they come home again. And it's always made, of course, in the same dish (which I have in triplicate). But then, every family has its own much-loved recipes that absolutely have to be repeated for special occasions, year in, year out, through the ages, and this is one of ours. I love the ritual of making it: the anticipation, the preparation, the soothing repetition of the layering up, all suffuse me with celebratory cosiness; even writing about it now, I find that I have an idiotically fond smile playing about my lips.

This lasagne of ours is not limited to filial festivities: fashionable variants can come and go, but a traditional, meat-sauce-and-cheesy-béchamel lasagne is always, always popular. And although I wouldn't say the recipe were exactly faff-free, no part of it is difficult. I find it invaluable when I need to feed a lot of people – the stuff of blessed memory now – but can't be fiddling about on the night: I layer it up in advance, ready to be popped into the oven as needed; and if more than one is required, as it often is, it's easy enough, when you get into the swing of it, to fill any number of lasagne dishes.

I have referred to it as a traditional lasagne, but I am aware that an Italian might look askance at this. For one thing, I don't make my own lasagne sheets; while I have done in the past, I now routinely use dried ones out of a packet and, what's more, I don't boil them first. In order, then, to ensure they soften properly, I make a slightly more liquid meat sauce than is usual, and rather than have the béchamel on top, I finish with a layer of meat sauce. It's not quite *come si deve*, that's to say, how it should be from a proper Italian perspective, but it's our way, and it would feel wrong now for me to change it. And so, I apologise to all Italians, but more particularly for the fact that I vulgarly top that erroneous final meat layer with mozzarella. You don't have to follow suit, but I would never dare leave it out at home.

Even if you don't have eight people to feed (it would stretch to more, no doubt, but I wouldn't feel comfortable requiring it to) I really don't think it's worth going to the trouble of making lasagne on a smaller scale. It freezes well, so you could easily wrap or tub up individual portions for near-instant, enduringly blissful solo suppers at a later date. Especially useful if you have teenagers in the house.

I always just serve a green salad with this, and in particular a green salad with the shallot and chive dressing on p.197. It's a family law. But since it's not your family's law, feel free to dress your salad as you wish.

LASAGNE OF LOVE

MAKES 9–12 slices depending on how you cut it, though I wouldn't want to feed any more than 8 with this in my house

FOR THE MEAT SAUCE

2 large-ish onions (approx. 350g)

3–4 x 15ml tablespoons olive oil

125ml full-fat milk

4 x 15ml tablespoons (60ml) tomato purée

2 carrots (approx. 250g)

1 stick of celery

4 fat cloves of garlic

150g rindless pancetta (or bacon)

A small bunch of flat-leaf parsley (approx. 20g)

1 x 15ml tablespoon fresh thyme leaves (or 1 teaspoon dried thyme)

⅛ teaspoon dried chilli flakes

350g minced beef

350g minced pork

250ml red wine (good enough to drink) or red vermouth

500ml beef stock

2 x 400g tins of chopped tomatoes

2 teaspoons sea salt flakes (or 1 teaspoon fine sea salt)

3 fresh bay leaves

FOR THE BÉCHAMEL

Vegetable prep detritus from meat sauce, above

1 litre full-fat milk, plus more as needed

1 teaspoon sea salt flakes (or ½ teaspoon fine sea salt)

A good grinding of white pepper

2 fresh bay leaves

100g unsalted butter

100g plain flour

3 x 15ml tablespoons (approx. 25g) freshly grated Parmesan

FOR ASSEMBLING

18–20 dried lasagne sheets

1 ball mozzarella, not bufala

5 x 15ml tablespoons (approx. 40g) freshly grated Parmesan

For make-ahead, store and/or freeze notes, see p.334

1. Chop the onions, dropping the peeled skin into a saucepan big enough to make the béchamel shortly. I use one 22cm in diameter and 9cm deep.

2. In a large, heavy-based casserole or pan that comes with a lid – I use an enamelled cast-iron casserole of 26cm diameter, with a capacity of 5.3 litres, and wouldn't advise going any smaller – warm 3 tablespoons of the oil and, over medium-low heat, cook the onions for 5 minutes, then turn down to low and cook for a further 15 minutes, stirring every now and again until the onions are beginning to soften and colour.

3. While the onions are cooking, first stir the tomato purée into the 125ml of milk, and set aside for a mo. Peel the carrots if they need it (if they're organic, or the skin looks tender, I don't bother) and chop them each into 3 or 4 pieces, dropping them into the bowl of a food processor and the peelings and any discarded pieces into the saucepan with the onion skin. Tear the celery into pieces and add to the processor, then peel the garlic (dropping the peelings into the béchamel pan) and add the cloves to the processor. Cut the

MUCH DEPENDS ON DINNER

[173]

pancetta (or bacon) up a bit and add to the processor as well, along with the parsley (you can use all the tender stems too). Strip enough thyme leaves from the stems to give you 1 tablespoon, add this too (or use 1 teaspoon of dried thyme) and blitz until everything is finely chopped, but not mush. Obviously, you could chop everything by hand. In which case, don't drive yourself mad trying to get everything as fine as the processor version.

4. When the 15 minutes is up on the onions, heat the oven to 170°C/150°C Fan. Scrape every last bit of the bacony vegetable mixture from the processor into the pan, turn the heat up to medium-high, stir well and cook for 5 minutes, then turn the heat down again to medium-low, sprinkle in the chilli flakes, and cook for another 5 minutes.

5. At this stage, I feel I should tell you to remove all the vegetables in order to brown the meat properly, but I have taken to simply adding it on top of what's in the pan already. So, turn the heat to high, crumble in the minced beef and pork and turn well in the pan for about 5 minutes. If you need to add another tablespoon of oil, do.

6. Add the wine (or vermouth), let it bubble up, and then pour in the beef stock, the tins of chopped tomatoes, the tomato purée and milk mixture, salt and bay leaves and bring to a bubble. Taste to see if you want to add any more salt, and then clamp on a tightly fitting lid and transfer to the oven, leaving it to cook for 1 hour.

7. Straightaway, pour the litre of milk for the béchamel over the vegetable peelings, add the salt, pepper and bay leaves, and bring almost to the boil, but don't let it boil. Turn off the heat, cover with a tightly fitting lid (which will stop it from getting a skin, as well as making the flavours infuse better) and leave while the meat sauce cooks. When the meat sauce has been in the oven for 45 minutes, strain the milk into a large batter jug. If, when all the milk has dripped through, you are short of your full litre, just pour in a little more milk to top up.

8. Clean out the pan (just with water's fine, you don't need soap), dry it well and melt the butter in it, then add the flour and mix together, over medium heat, for a couple of minutes, forming your roux, and cooking it a little; you should have a dingy primrose paste that, somehow, magically, seems to come away from the pan and cleave to itself as you stir and move it about.

9. Take the pan off the heat, swap your wooden spoon for a whisk, preferably a little one that's good for removing lumps, and slowly whisk in the milk. Don't worry, by the way, that the milk (thanks to the onion skins) will have a slightly peachy tone about it. I rather like it, actually, not that it is visible in the finished sauce.

10. When all the milk is whisked in, carry on whisking until you've got a smooth cream in the pan, and then put back on the heat, lowish, and keep whisking until you have a very, very thick sauce, with all taste of flouriness banished; this will take 5–7 minutes. Off the heat, quickly whisk in the 3 tablespoons of Parmesan and then scrape every last bit back into the batter jug, tasting for seasoning as you go.

11. Take the meat sauce out of the oven, and give a gentle stir with a large ladle. Once you can taste it without burning your mouth, check for seasoning: it may well need more salt; do not be timid.

12. Now, it's just a matter of layering up. My lasagne dish measures 24 x 35 x 6cm and it's a pretty tight fit. Sit the dish on a baking tray. Line the dish with a couple of ladlefuls of the meat sauce, aiming to get more liquid than meat, and cover with a layer of lasagne sheets. I get 4 sheets in the bottom layer but find that for subsequent layers I need extra, which I snap into pieces for patching gaps. Put a couple more ladlefuls of the liquidy bit of sauce into a jug or bowl, and set aside for now.

13. Put a third of your béchamel on top of the lasagne sheets and use a spatula to help spread it a little, but don't worry about making an absolutely even, edge-to-edge covering. Top with a third of your remaining meat sauce, then cover with another layer of lasagne sheets, followed by your second third of béchamel, second third of meat sauce and third layer of lasagne sheets. Add your remaining béchamel and meat sauce in order and top with a final layer of pasta sheets and then add the set-aside liquidy meat sauce to cover, pressing down if you need to make sure the top layer of pasta is, if not submerged exactly, then lightly covered. Leave now for at least 30 minutes, but longer (up to 2 days) if needed; if you're leaving it for more than about 2 hours, you will need to refrigerate it.

14. When you are ready to bake your lasagne, heat the oven to 200°C/180°C Fan. Finely chop or shred the mozzarella and

sprinkle over the top of the unbaked lasagne, then sprinkle over the Parmesan. Cover with foil, trying not to press it down on the top of the lasagne, and bake for 40 minutes (if it's been refrigerated it'll probably need 1 hour). Remove the foil (pull off any cheese that's stuck to it and add it back to the top of the lasagne) and cook for a further 30 minutes until it's slightly scorched in parts, the cheese gooey, the pasta swollen and runkled on top, and everything piping hot all the way through.

15. Leave to stand, if you can bear it, for 20–30 minutes before diving in.

PAPPARDELLE WITH CAVOLO NERO AND 'NDUJA

This is a gorgeous, wintry, rib-sticker of a dish, just right to bolster and brighten where skies are dark and the air is chill. If you haven't come across 'nduja before (pronounced en-doo-ya, with the 'en' mumbled, and the stress on the 'doo'), I can best describe it as being like a fabulously fiery salami pâté, or a chorizo-ish spread (I can only imagine that 'nduja is a Calabrian rendition of the French andouille), and once you start cooking with it, you won't be able to stop. I always use the 'nduja that you buy cut into soft slabs, but it works just as well with the 'nduja paste that comes in a jar; it has perhaps a slightly more bitter edge, but you hardly notice that given its intense heat. Add it to anything – a bowl of chickpeas, a pan of mussels, a chicken stew – when you want to bring smokiness and heat; or, just eat it as it is, spread on toast. Here, it binds with the potato to make a fuzzy, buttery sauce to coat the thick pasta and minerally greens, and although two large pans are involved, very little work is required of you.

If you can't find 'nduja, or are vegetarian, then do use harissa in its stead, though you probably won't need more than a tablespoon or two, and I'd add a generous handful of halved cherry tomatoes, frying them in the butter until they give up some of their gloop; should you be vegan, use 60ml of olive oil in place of the butter.

If it's a solo supper you're after, I suggest you generously divide everything by 5, give or take; use a tablespoon of butter and a larger potato, by all means. And you don't have to use pappardelle: I recently made this with fusilloni – comically giant fusilli – and the sturdy spiral shapes were a perfect foil for the full-bodied 'nduja sauce.

SERVES 6

1 large floury potato, such as Rooster (approx. 300g)

500g cavolo nero or other kale or dark leafy greens

500g pappardelle (preferably not egg pappardelle)

60g unsalted butter

150g 'nduja (see recipe intro)

3 x 15ml tablespoons extra-virgin olive oil, plus more to serve

For make-ahead, store and/or freeze notes, see p.334

1. Fill a large pan with cold water, and add salt with abandon.

2. Peel the potato (as you want to help it break down a little as it cooks with the pasta) and cut it into 1cm cubes, then add these to the pan of salted water and bring to a boil.

3. Meanwhile, pull the leaves off the stalks of the cavolo nero, tear them into smaller pieces, and leave in a colander for now.

4. Once the water in the pan has come to a boil, cook the potato cubes for 10 minutes, and then add the pappardelle; I don't use egg pappardelle, but the sturdier durum wheat kind, which take around 7 minutes to cook; if you have only the finer egg pappardelle, which take about half the time, add the cavolo nero to the water first. Give the pappardelle a good stir, and once the water has reached boiling point again, add the cavolo nero.

5. Set your timer for just under the recommended cooking time on your packet of pasta, though start checking before that, and get on with the sauce. I use something called a stir-fry pan for this, which looks like a large wok, really. You need a pan that's big enough to take all the ingredients later, and with room to toss the pasta comfortably. Melt the butter gently in your pan of choice, and then, over low to medium heat, add the soft, squidgy, spicy 'nduja and stir it into the butter to make a sauce.

6. When the pasta's nearly ready, scoop out a cupful of pasta-cooking water, and then add about 3–4 tablespoons to the buttery 'nduja, and stir it in.

7. Then, once the pasta is done and the cavolo nero soft, drain both and tip into the 'nduja pan. It doesn't matter if the pappardelle and greens are wet; you will just have to add less water later.

8. Turn everything together carefully, as your pan will be very full indeed, and add more of the pasta-cooking water as needed to help emulsify the sauce.

9. Pour over the extra-virgin olive oil, and toss again, adding more if wished, and serve immediately. Bring the bottle to the table, to pour, greenly and greedily, over your pasta as you eat.

SPICED BULGUR WHEAT
WITH ROAST VEGETABLES

This is one of my most repeated suppers, particularly when I have vegetarian or vegan friends over, but not only then; even meat-eaters do not need to eat meat every day. And while it's certainly enough for four, I don't decrease quantities for two; this is most definitely something you want in a tub in the fridge to eat later in the week, whether reheated or as a salad. But it also serves as a glowingly beautiful and glamorously practical side dish – starch and vegetables in one – alongside a roast chicken or slow-cooked lamb, say. And I especially like it, too, with some quickly cooked (and tonally congruent) red mullet fillets. Heat a little olive oil in a pan, fry the fillets skin-side down for 2 minutes, sprinkle some sea salt flakes on the fleshy side as it faces you, then turn them over and give them another minute. Check they're all but cooked – they'll continue cooking as they stand – then transfer to a warmed plate, their beautiful pink skin uppermost. Put the pan back on the heat, pour in extra-virgin olive oil, mince or grate in garlic and stir it in the oil before adding a juicy spritz of lemon, though you could squeeze in a little orange juice as well, or replace both with a slug of rosé (which is the wine I'd want to drink alongside) or dry white vermouth. Let it bubble up quickly and pour it over the fish, then sprinkle with sea salt flakes and some chopped chives or a few sprigs of thyme, and you're done.

Do, please, bear this recipe in mind without the roast vegetables, too: when you're searching for a starchy side dish, a bowl of bulgur wheat is the effortless answer to your prayers. Use the recipe that follows as a blueprint. You can use lemon instead of orange, replace the coriander with parsley, add a little fresh mint, use different seeds, replace the lentils with a drained tin of chickpeas, or leave them out entirely, stir in toasted flaked almonds at the end, or some cooked and drained short lengths of green beans: in other words, this is a basic formula that can be both repeated and varied.

But back to the recipe in its full glory. If it makes your life easier, you can prepare the vegetables and sit them in their tin ready for you a good couple of hours in advance. I don't cover them, but you could if you don't want the scent of raw leeks to pervade the air. I find it very much more relaxing to give the bulgur wheat its 15 minutes of cooking time quite a bit in advance because it will stand happily for up to 2 hours; it doesn't need to be piping hot.

I feel a particular wistful fondness for this dish as it was what I cooked the last time I had friends for supper in the Old Life, just before lockdown. I served the roast butternut and the pink sauce (p.225) alongside; the Blood Orange and Passionfruit Pavlova (p.243) after. It was a beautiful evening.

SERVES 3–4 as a main course (more when a side dish, obviously)

FOR THE BULGUR WHEAT

A small bunch of coriander (approx. 25g)

2 fat cloves of garlic

1 teaspoon fennel seeds

1 teaspoon cumin seeds

1 teaspoon coriander seeds

⅛ teaspoon dried chilli flakes

375ml cold water

1 x 15ml tablespoon olive oil

1 orange

200g bulgur wheat

50g red lentils

1½ teaspoons sea salt flakes (or ¾ teaspoon fine sea salt)

FOR THE ROAST VEGETABLES

400g leeks (trimmed weight – or approx. 600g if you're buying them untrimmed)

400g (2–3) red peppers

200g cherry tomatoes

1 teaspoon cumin seeds

1 teaspoon fennel seeds

1 teaspoon sea salt flakes (or ½ teaspoon fine sea salt)

3 x 15ml tablespoons olive oil

150g radishes

For make-ahead, store and/or freeze notes, see p.334

1. You don't have to start on the bulgur wheat straightaway, but as it stands so comfortably once cooked, I tend to do it this way round. Finely chop some of the tender stalks of coriander, just enough to give you about a tablespoon; peel the garlic; measure out the seeds and chilli flakes; and have water in a jug by the hob in readiness. If you are in a hurry to eat you could get on with preparing the vegetables now too.

2. Get out a not-too-large heavy-based casserole or pan that comes with a tightly fitting lid – I use an enamelled cast-iron one of 20cm diameter – and very gently warm the oil over low heat. Finely grate in the zest of the orange, and stir it into the oil. Mince or grate in the garlic, add your spoonful of finely chopped coriander stalks and stir these into the now golden oil for about 30 seconds. Turn the heat up a little, just to medium-low, and add the fennel, cumin and coriander seeds, followed by the chilli flakes, and give everything a good stir.

3. Turn the heat to high, and quickly add the bulgur wheat and lentils, and stir again, and well, to make sure everything is mixed together. Now add the water and salt and bring to the boil.

4. Once it's started bubbling, clamp on the lid and turn the heat back down to low, then leave to cook gently for 15 minutes – you can start chopping your vegetables – by which time all the water should be absorbed.

5. Heat the oven to 220°C/200°C Fan. Wash the leeks to remove any mud if needed, and cut them into approx. 3cm logs, and drop into a sturdy and fairly shallow roasting tin in which, ideally, all the vegetables will sit snugly; I use one that's 29 x 25 x 5cm. Cut the red peppers (deseeding, and discarding any pith in the process) into large bite-sized pieces and add them to the roasting tin along with the whole cherry tomatoes.

6. When time's up on the bulgur wheat, turn off the heat, cover the pan with a clean tea towel, clamp the lid back on and leave for 40 minutes, though it will stand happily for a lot longer than this. I routinely leave this for 2 hours.

7. Sprinkle the seeds and salt over the waiting vegetables, then add the oil and schmoosh to mix. Pour 2 tablespoons of cold water and 2 tablespoons of juice from your zested orange into the tin and roast in the hot oven for 30 minutes, by which time the vegetables should be cooked and soft, and the leeks beginning to scorch in parts. While the vegetables are in the oven, halve the radishes from top to bottom.

8. When the leeks, peppers and tomatoes have had their 30 minutes, take the tin out of the oven, add the radishes, and mix. Because the vegetables – ideally – fit so snugly in their tin, they make a wonderful strongly flavoured juice as they cook. However, if you've had to use a bigger tin, you may find that they're going a little dry, and might be sticking to the tin in places; if so add another tablespoon each of orange juice and water or more as needed. Put back in the oven to roast for another 10 minutes. Take the tin out of the oven and let stand while you put the finishing touches on the bulgur wheat.

9. Chop the coriander leaves. Remove the lid and tea towel from the bulgur wheat and use a couple of forks to mix everything together in the pan and, importantly, to separate and fluff up the grains.

10. Tip into a serving bowl or dish, add most of your chopped coriander and fork it in. Add a third of the roasted vegetables and mix in well but lightly with your two forks. Taste for seasoning – I often want to add more salt at this stage. Top with the remaining roasted vegetables, and sprinkle with the rest of the coriander.

FEAR-FREE FISH STEW

I know a lot of people are hesitant about cooking fish, and I do understand why, but this, my friends, is the recipe to allay your anxieties and free you from fear. Your fissues will be a thing of the past.

It's also very useful when you have to get dinner on the table fast, for although the sauce takes around an hour to cook (and for a good half of this time you can be lying languorously on a sofa, should your life allow for such luxuries), you can make it quite a bit in advance, actually; indeed, I think it is better for having time to steep and mellow. Then, when you're ready to eat, you just heat the sauce, adding 60ml of water, chop up your fish chunkily, drop it all into the simmering pan, and supper's pretty much on the table.

Furthermore, you should regard the sauce as a welcoming base, ready to accommodate a good variety of fish. I've specified firm white fish to give you leeway, depending on what's available, but there is no reason why you couldn't use salmon either. And I have made this, too, with a couple of packets of raw prawns from the freezer. Nor is there anything to say this couldn't be turned into a vegetable stew. In which case, increase the sweet potato, cutting any extra you add into bite-sized pieces rather than small dice (I still like to have some cut finely as below, since it helps give body to the sauce), along with parsnips, an aubergine and some courgettes, if they're in season; the courgettes should be added towards the end of the cooking time; feel free to add a can of drained chickpeas along with them. And you can stir in 250g or more of young spinach leaves once everything's cooked, letting them wilt in the heat of the pan for a couple of minutes.

Serve spectacularly with plain black Venus rice if you can get it. Or make up the bulgur wheat following the preceding recipe, ignoring the roast vegetable part, and boosting the quantities to 300g of bulgur wheat and 575ml of water.

SERVES 4

¼ teaspoon ground mace

½ teaspoon ground ginger

½ teaspoon ground turmeric

½ teaspoon hot smoked paprika

½ teaspoon ground cumin

¼ teaspoon ground cinnamon

1 large sweet potato (approx. 250g)

A small bunch of coriander (approx. 25g)

Approx. 20g fresh ginger

2 fat cloves of garlic

1 onion (approx. 175g)

400ml cold water

2 x 15ml tablespoons olive oil

1 orange

2 x 400g tins of chopped tomatoes

1 x 15ml tablespoon tomato purée

1 teaspoon sea salt flakes (or ½ teaspoon fine sea salt)

1 teaspoon runny honey or maple syrup

750g skinless firm white fish, in 1 thick piece or thick-cut fillets

For make-ahead, store and/or freeze notes, see p.334

1. Measure all the spices into a little bowl, and then peel the sweet potato and cut into 1cm dice, and leave to one side. Finely chop the tender stalks from the bunch of coriander, to give yourself 3 tablespoonsful. Peel and finely grate the ginger, to give you 1 teaspoonful, and peel the garlic. Peel and roughly chop the onion. Fill a measuring jug with 400ml cold water.

2. Warm the oil in a heavy-based pan or casserole that comes with a lid (I use one of 22cm diameter). Add the onion, and cook it gently for about 20 minutes until it's beginning to soften and colour.

3. Finely grate in the orange zest, mince or grate in the garlic, add the chopped coriander stalks and the grated ginger, and stir everything over gentle heat, then add the spices.

4. Tip in the diced sweet potato, and stir into the spiced onion over medium heat for a minute or so. Add the tinned tomatoes, and half fill the empty cans with your water and swill out into the pan.

5. Spoon in the tomato purée, and add the salt and honey or maple syrup. Halve your zested orange and squeeze out enough juice to give you a tablespoon and add that too, giving everything a good stir.

6. Turn up the heat to bring to the boil, then clamp on the lid, turn the heat right down, and leave to simmer for 40–45 minutes until the sweet potato is completely soft and the sauce has thickened slightly. You can do all of this in advance, heating up when you are ready to cook the fish, or move straight on to the fish now.

7. Cut your fish into large bite-sized pieces and add to the simmering sauce. Turn the heat down and put the lid on. Depending on how chunky or how cold the fish is, it'll need 3–5 minutes to cook in this gentle heat. Remove the pan from the heat, take off the lid and let it stand for a further 2 minutes.

8. Chop the leaves you have left from the stalkless coriander, and sprinkle over the stew on serving.

Even if you're the most carnivorous of meat-eaters, it remains unequivocally the truth that the best way of feeling as if you're not always eating the same thing is to vary the vegetables. I don't mean that you have to try and find ever more recherché roots and tubers, or that salads must be made with only lesser-known leaves, although novelty can certainly revitalise when you feel in a rut, but rather that you could think of cooking the vegetables you do like a bit differently now and again. I'd need a whole book to accommodate my enthusiasms with sufficient expansiveness, but – with the proviso that you check the index for mentions of and suggestions for any specimens staring up at you reproachfully from the vegetable drawer – allow me to take a running jump at the side dishes I repeat to zhuzh up the evening meal from one long day to the next.

Since no laborious preparation is needed for green beans, I rely on them particularly when I want to make life easy for myself. There's nothing wrong with them plain (and by plain, I do of course mean with butter, lots, or extra-virgin olive oil, ditto), but they do just feel like more of a treat if, while they're cooking, you toast some flaked almonds in a dry pan, and then once the beans are cooked, drained, returned to the pan they cooked in and doused in butter, toss some of the toasted almonds with the beans, then turn out into a warmed bowl, taste for seasoning and scatter with the rest of the flaked almonds (which could equally well be replaced with chopped toasted hazelnuts).

I have in recent years become ever keener to cook with wild garlic, which used to be the province of foragers and country-dwellers, but now these pungent leaves can be found at the greengrocer or supermarket, if you're lucky. Of course, if you don't pick your own, you will be looked down on by those eager to tell you about their gorgeously scented ambling walks, where they can gather more than they need for free – much as the aristocracy sneered at those of less illustrious lineage who, as the old phrase had it, 'had to buy their own furniture' – but I refuse to be cowed by that. If you can find any of these beautiful leaves, which look rather like the foliage of lily of the valley (though don't confuse them, as the latter are poisonous) during their season – from March to June – use them with abandon. I may have gone a bit overboard with wild garlic suggestions in this chapter, but I've been able to get hold of them at the shops only in the past three years, so my excitement is still young.

You can simply wilt the leaves in butter, and toss them through some boiled or steamed green beans, but I advise turning them into pesto, and using a couple of spoonfuls – the quantities below will give you 150ml – diluted with the teeniest bit of water, as a rich green sauce to toss the green beans in. I make my wild garlic pesto by blitzing, with a stick blender, 50g of wild garlic, tender stems included, 4 tablespoons (30g) of freshly grated Parmesan, and 100ml of extra-virgin olive oil. You can add 2 tablespoons of pine nuts, but I prefer to leave them out, toasting them separately to scatter over the pesto-slicked beans. This leads me to the wild garlic variant of an old favourite of mine, the Ligurian classic of pasta cooked with potato and green beans (similar to the way the pappardelle are cooked on p.177) and tossed in pesto. Cook 250g each of potato and linguine following the method for the pappardelle on pp.177–178 and when they have about 5 minutes to go, throw in about 100g of green beans, cut into shortish lengths. Reserve a mugful of the pasta-cooking water before draining, and then turn the potatoey pasta and beans in the wild garlic pesto, diluted with as much pasta-cooking water as you need to help create a thick, felty sauce. If you feel you want crunch, add toasted pine nuts at will.

Before I go back to my beans, I need to tell you that this wild garlic pesto is wonderful stirred into a bowl of soft-cooked chickpeas (as a vegetable dish as they are, or as a main course with ditalini or other sturdy small pasta) or cannellini beans. Even a small amount spooned into soups on serving can breathe instant life into them. I'm not the greatest fan of cooked carrots (although do see p.13) but I can eat a crazy amount if they're cut into chunky batons, boiled with a lot of salt and a squeeze of lemon juice, then tumbled into a pool of melted butter and a dollop of this pesto. And it makes a great dressing (whisk a teaspoon or so into a couple of tablespoons of extra-virgin olive oil, adding lemon juice to taste) for tomatoes. Actually, for pretty much anything you like: the other day, I scraped a smidgeon out of the bottom of the jar of wild garlic pesto in my fridge, mixed it with probably two or three times its volume of extra-virgin olive oil, and let it drip, shiny as flecked green glass, over the white flesh of a sea bass I'd roasted for 10 minutes in a blisteringly hot oven and then rather badly filleted.

While you can fill an ice-cube tray with a batch or two of this pesto for using throughout the year, I have come to realise that I use it more exuberantly because I know I have to snatch the opportunities while they're there. Still, it doesn't do any harm to keep some in frozen reserve.

Obviously, you can turn the wild garlic pesto back into proper pesto, as it were, by replacing the wild garlic leaves with basil, and adding a clove of garlic, and your green beans will thank you. But I think I'd still leave the pine nuts out of the sauce, and sprinkle them over the beans instead.

I'm rather afraid this is all amounting to a mountain (rather than the much disparaged hill) of beans, but I have two words to say to you: warm salad. Those of my generation will remember those *salades tièdes* of yesteryear, most memorable of which was the then ubiquitous frisée tossed with searingly hot lardons and toasted walnuts straight from the oven, the dressing made by whisking red wine vinegar and a little Dijon mustard into the hissing bacon fat in the pan.

Certainly take that route with some cooked and drained beans (and you can cook them in advance, so long as you dunk them straight from the colander into some icy water and drain them again, only to have them warmed slightly later by the bacon, walnuts and hot dressing), but I have a couple of other plans in this regard. Both, again, rest on a panful of cooked and drained beans; let us say, 350g of them. For the first, gently drop 2 or 3 (depending on their size) ripe tomatoes into a bowl and pour over boiling water from a kettle to cover, and let them stand for 10 or so minutes, and then plunge the tomatoes into a bowl of iced water; this is just to make them easy to peel. As you take them out of the bowl of cold water, nick a bit of the skin near where the stalk would have been, and peel them. Cut them in half, remove the core and discard the seeds, then chop the flesh finely – you can either leave them as visible small cubes, or carry on chopping until you have a pinky-red fuzz. Pour a generous amount of extra-virgin olive oil into the dried-out pan the beans cooked in, mince or grate in a couple of fat cloves of garlic, and stir over gentle heat for a minute, then scrape in the chopped tomato pulp and 1 tablespoonful of capers, then return the drained beans to the pan and toss in the warm dressing. Taste for seasoning and to see if you want to add any lemon juice (or a little juice from the caper jar), then turn out into a dish, and leave for 10 minutes or so before serving; longer wouldn't matter. You can, as well, add some good pitted and halved black olives along with the capers, or some anchovy fillets when you're frying the garlic, pressing down on them so they melt into the pan. Finally, I suggest this, an old favourite, and much repeated over the last thirty years. Make a strong mustard dressing by whisking 2 teaspoons of Dijon or wholegrain mustard, ¼ teaspoon of sea salt flakes (or a pinch of fine sea salt), the finely grated zest of 1 lemon, 2 minced or grated fat cloves of garlic and 1 tablespoon of cold water into 3 tablespoons of extra-virgin olive oil. Finally – and trust me here – whisk in a drop of almond extract (the sort you'd normally expect to use in baking) and toss your cooked and drained beans in this. Decant into a shallow bowl and, to take us almost back to the bean-beginning, leave until you're about to serve, at which point, toss some toasted flaked almonds through the beans, and scatter some over.

There are many vegetables which can be plainly cooked, and then brightened up at the end with a quick scattering of herbs, but we could be here forever if I enumerated every possible permutation, much as I would very much like to. I shall be brief, then, as I nudge towards one, far from obvious, example. It was in Yotam Ottolenghi and Ramael Scully's *Nopi* that I learned you could roast a celeriac whole, and I've been doing it ever since. It's hard to be precise about timings, as weights can vary immensely, but I'm basing this on a celeriac of about 600g, which is not very large, but were it to weigh 700g it shouldn't need much longer. Wash the celeriac thoroughly and pat it dry with kitchen paper (or a clean tea towel) then pour about 1 teaspoon of olive oil into a cupped hand and rub this all over the celeriac, using your non-oily hand to ferry the celeriac to a parchment-lined baking sheet. Sprinkle ½ teaspoon of sea salt flakes (or ¼ teaspoon of fine sea salt) over it and roast in a 190°C/170°C Fan oven for 2 hours, by which time the celeriac will have darkened a little, caramelising slightly at the bottom where it has sat on the sheet, and it should feel soft when pierced with the tip of a sharp knife, or even a cake tester.

Shortly before the celeriac has had its time in the oven, deseed a red chilli, then chop it finely and scrape it into a small bowl. Finely chop 50g of pitted black olives (preferably the slightly squished, soft ones labelled 'dry' and often sold in packets, rather than the bouncy briny ones in a jar) and add these to the chilli confetti in the bowl. Finely grate in the zest of a lemon and squeeze in 1 tablespoon of juice, then stir in 4 tablespoons (60ml) of extra-virgin olive oil and 5 of freshly chopped flat-leaf parsley. You shouldn't need to add salt to this, but taste to see.

Put the cooked celeriac on a board, and cut into it like a cake; you should be able to get 12 slices out of it. Arrange these on a platter. Give the chilli mixture another stir and spoon it over the warm slices of celeriac and serve immediately. It really could hardly be simpler, and yet it feels like a special treat.

I have written before about my way of cooking cabbage, which is, in fact, my mother's. Her method, more precisely, was to warm quite a lot of butter in a large pan, and when melted, she'd throw in some caraway seeds, followed by shredded white cabbage, which she tossed in the spiced butter before adding a cupful of chicken stock, then clamping on a lid, letting the cabbage steam in the buttery, caraway-flecked stock until nearly cooked, but still very crunchy. She then removed the lid, turned the heat to high to let most of the stock bubble away, then added a final dollop of butter and a great deal of freshly ground white pepper. And this, more or less, is the way I always cook cabbage. That's to say, I never boil it. I vary the fats I use and the seeds – cumin is very much to be borne in mind – and more often use a Savoy rather than a white cabbage, but it is my essential cruciferous and brassica blueprint.

There are days when I chop up some bacon and fry that first, removing the bacon bits, and cooking the shredded cabbage in the bacon fat (I use my wok-like, lidded stir-fry pan, which is both light and capacious) and a little water before stirring the bacon back in at the end, but I most often stick to seeds. If I'm not using caraway or cumin, I go – ever increasingly – for fennel

seeds, and the brief recipe I'm about to explain is simply a development of that. You need a smallish Savoy cabbage, which you core, then slice thinly so you have a pile of long shreds. In a large stir-fry pan that has a lid, heat 2 tablespoons of olive oil (or, depending on what you're eating with this, coconut oil) and toss in a teaspoon or so of fennel seeds and, if you want (though I don't always bother) a minced or grated clove of garlic. Cook for a scant minute then turn the heat up, add the shredded cabbage and toss, toss, toss and toss again (I use a couple of spatulas for this) then sprinkle with 1 teaspoon of sea salt flakes (or ½ teaspoon of fine sea salt), ½ teaspoon of ground turmeric and ½ teaspoon of ready-ground black pepper and toss, toss, toss and toss again. Chuck in 250ml of hot water from a just-boiled kettle, clamp on the lid, turn the heat down a little, letting the cabbage part-braise, part-steam for about 5 minutes. Check to see if it's cooked; it may need a couple more minutes. Add more salt if needed, then transfer to a warm bowl. This has most definitely got a bit of a hit to it, but for all that is expansively versatile. It's unfair, perhaps, to highlight any one pairing but I've never served my Oxtail Bourguignon (p.116) without making a bowl of Savoy Cabbage with Turmeric to go alongside.

I also rely on this semi-stir-fry, semi-steam method for my Cavolo Nero with Chilli and Garlic. Strip the leaves from 750g cavolo nero (or curly kale), and tear them roughly. Warm a couple of tablespoons of olive oil in a stir-fry pan that comes with a lid, fry 2 cloves of minced or grated garlic, the finely grated zest of a lemon and a fat pinch of dried chilli flakes (anchovies are obviously also a contender here) for a minute, then add the cavolo nero or curly kale leaves. Toss well in the hot pan for 2 minutes. Add a spritz of lemon juice, a sprinkling of salt and enough water to create steam; in my pan that's 250ml. Clamp on the lid, turn down the heat, and cook until tender – this should take around 5–8 minutes, depending on the toughness of the leaves – removing the lid to toss everything once or twice, and adding more water if the pan looks like it's getting too dry.

Either you're someone who likes to get as much as possible done ahead of time, or you get energised by madly snapping into action at the last minute. In nearly everything but cooking (and it's a big but) I am in the latter category. When it comes to the kitchen, though, I prefer a slow build-up. Chard lends itself particularly well to being cooked in advance, or rather partly in advance. I cook the stems ahead of time, heating them up as dinner approaches, and giving the leaves a quick wilt last minute. You can cook the chard as for the pasta on p.18 (increasing the quantities) or there's this, my Sweet and Sour Rainbow Chard – though any chard will do. You need a couple of bunches (which should give you 900g). But first steep 50g of golden sultanas in 3 tablespoons of blood orange juice (or 2 tablespoons of regular orange juice and 1 tablespoon of lemon juice) and 3 tablespoons of cold water. The longer these have the better. Strip the leaves from the stems, and set them aside, then slice the stems into 2cm slices. Warm 2 tablespoons of olive oil in a large pan, mince or grate in a fat clove of garlic, and add ¼ teaspoon of Aleppo pepper or a pinch of dried chilli flakes. Stir the chard stems in the oil, turn the heat to high and stir-fry for a couple of minutes. Add the sultanas and all their liquid along with 1 teaspoon of sea salt flakes (or ½ teaspoon of fine sea salt), stir again, clamp on the lid, and turn the heat down, leaving the stems to simmer until tender, which should take 10–15 minutes. At this point, you can simply take the pan off the heat, removing the lid so everything cools down faster (unless you are making this only an hour or so ahead of time). When you're ready to eat, roll the leaves up and shred them. Put the pan back on the heat, and when the stems are warm, add the shredded leaves, turning them in the pan until they are beginning to show a bit of willing on the wilting front, then throw in 125ml of water (I use an American ½ cup measure for ease), and clamp the lid back on. Depending on how tough the leaves are, these will take anything from 5 to 10 minutes to cook. You don't want them fashionably al dente, you want them properly soft and stewed. If there is a lot of liquid in the pan by the time they're cooked, just remove the lid, turn up the heat and reduce it, until all that's left is a scant syrupy sauce. Season to taste, and pour over a little more extra-virgin olive oil – as wished – on serving.

Given that spinach takes hardly any time to cook, it might seem ludicrous to suggest you cook it in advance, too, but I am a keen proponent of the practice. The thing is, you need several sackloads to fill a teacup, and I really don't want to be stuffing bags and bags of spinach into a large pan, waiting for one load to wilt before adding the next, spilling most out all over the hob, just as I'm gearing myself to get everything else onto the table. You can wilt the spinach, bunch by bunch, or bag by bag, in a pan on the hob and leave them in a colander suspended over a large mixing bowl to drain, but I stab each bag frenziedly with a fork (which I very much enjoy), giving each a few minutes' blast in the microwave, one by one, and trying not to burn myself as I rip the bags open to tip the wilted leaves into the waiting colander. What's more, since raw spinach doesn't last very well, I often cook the spinach like this as soon as I get it into the house, then tub it up and leave it in the fridge to be reheated when needed.

You can keep this plain, simply warming some olive oil or butter in a large pan, tossing the wilted spinach in it, adding no more than sea salt flakes and a good grating of nutmeg. But it's not very much harder to add the finely grated zest of a lemon to the oil, and a spritz of lemon juice to the leaves when they hit the pan (in which case, I'd forgo the nutmeg). When hot, stir in some Aleppo pepper and toasted pine nuts, then turn into a serving bowl, and sprinkle the top with a little more of each; and you can use dried chilli flakes (though

with a light hand) or paprika (smoked sweet paprika is particularly good here) in place of the Aleppo pepper. I sometimes add a clove or two of garlic to the oil, along with the lemon zest, and often – as discussed on p.13 – stir anchovy fillets in too, pressing on them in the oil until they all but dissolve, though if I am in the mood to add double cream – which I often am – I leave out the lemon juice.

But the undisputed stars of the make-ahead vegetable show are my House Special Slow-Cooked Peas. I have mentioned these in previous books, in one guise or another, but they bear repetition. Warm a couple of tablespoons of butter or olive oil in a heavy-based casserole that comes with a tightly fitting lid. Add a finely chopped banana shallot or 50g of frozen chopped shallots and cook, stirring, over medium heat for 3–5 minutes. Add ½ teaspoon each of dried mint, dried tarragon and dried thyme. Then empty a 750g bag of frozen petits pois into the pan. Turn the heat up to medium-high, stirring as best you can (though if the peas all come out in one block, don't worry about it) for about 5 minutes, before sprinkling over 1 teaspoon of sea salt flakes (or ½ teaspoon of fine sea salt) and pouring in 125ml of dry white vermouth (and you can use wine or stock if you prefer) then clamping on the lid, giving them another 5 or so minutes on the hob before ferrying the pan to either a 170°C/150°C Fan oven, and leaving it there to cook for 2 hours or – my pref- erence – a 150°C/130°C Fan oven for 4 hours. What's more, I am perfectly happy to give them another 2 hours at 150°C/130°C Fan when I reheat them but, frankly, if I've got the oven on for something else at a higher temperature, I put them in underneath and reduce the time. I think it's pretty hard to go wrong with these peas. Although I must caution you to check on them at least once when they're cooking, and when they're being reheated, to make sure the pan isn't dry. Just slosh in a bit more vermouth (or wine, water or stock) if you think more liquid is needed. If you prefer to reheat on the hob, of course you can, but then you have to be a little more watchful, checking the liquid level, and stirring the peas regularly. However you reheat them, you'll probably find you need to salt well before serving. And any leftovers can be tubbed up for another time, and parked in either the fridge or the freezer. But if you have only a small amount left over, not even enough for a proper portion, then you have a fine pasta sauce in the making. Just warm up with some double cream (and some chopped ham if you want), stirring in grated Parmesan at the end.

The only time I ever cook peas other than by this method is for a quick last-minute affair, when I turn them in butter with radishes. And very beautiful they are too, glazed pink and green in their dish. You need to start off with the peas thawed, though you can speed this up by putting 300g of frozen petits pois in a colander in the sink and then pouring just-boiled water from the kettle over them. You don't need them to be completely thawed, but this will do the job well enough. (You can, of course, use fresh peas when in season, in which case you will need 900g of peas in the pod, to give you enough once podded.) Once they've lost their frozen look, and have drained into the sink, halve 200g of radishes from top to bottom and have them on standby. Melt 50g butter in a wide shallow pan – I use one of 26cm diameter – that comes with a lid, and once it's melted mince or grate in a fat clove of garlic, then stir it over low heat for a minute or two. Turn the heat up to medium and add the thawed (or fresh) peas and the halved radishes, turning them well in the garlic-infused butter. Pour in 4 tablespoons (60ml) of dry white vermouth (or wine) and bring to a bubble, sprinkling over ¾ teaspoon of sea salt flakes (or just over ¼ teaspoon of fine sea salt) before clamping on the lid, and leaving the peas and radishes to cook for 5 minutes. Then remove the lid, stir in a couple of tablespoons of finely chopped herbs – if I have them, I use a mixture of tarragon, chives and mint, but if all I've got is parsley, then I use just that – and serve, either in the pan you've cooked them in or turned out into a dish, with a final scattering of herbs. And should you wish to, you can cook a handful (around 125g) of mangetouts in boiling salted water for 1 minute, then drain them and stir into the peas and radishes just as soon as they're cooked but before you sprinkle over the herbs.

You might think I have gone completely mad when I suggest a salad you can make ahead, and I concede that most are not only best made at the last minute, but demand to be. However, when it comes to a cherry tomato salad, the taste immeasurably improves if you halve them, season them and sprinkle them with dried herbs at least 1 hour ahead of time, and easily up to 3 or 4 hours. And the one I make the most is a zippy little number with mint and capers. Cut 500g of cherry tomatoes across the equator and tumble them into a wide, shallow bowl. Sprinkle over ½ teaspoon of dried mint, 2 tablespoons of capers, and a good grinding of pepper. Cover the bowl tightly with food wrap, and give it a bit of a shimmy, then leave it to stand out of the fridge. Perhaps I should note here that I caution against refrigerating tomatoes at all times; I might feel differently if I lived in a hotter country where the tomatoes were better. Leave these in the bowl for as long as you need – within reason: I wouldn't leave them for longer than half a day – and once they're stashed in the corner of the kitchen somewhere, cut half a small red onion into fine half-moons, drop these into a jar (or a bowl) and cover them with red wine vinegar. Push any stragglers down to make sure they're all immersed, and then put the lid on the jar (or cover the bowl) and leave, too. In fact, these can stand for longer than the tomatoes; even a couple of days would be fine, so you could do this well ahead. You do have an alternative, though, which is to use a small banana shallot, and chop it finely or cut into fine half-moons, and stir these into the tomatoes along with the capers. Either way, all is done until, at the last minute, you uncover the tomatoes, pour over a couple of tablespoons of extra-virgin olive oil and toss gently, then add a tablespoon or two of freshly chopped mint, and salt to taste, then toss again, and tip onto a large plate (or leave in their shallow bowl, if you're happy with it). Remove the pink-pickled onions from the vinegar, squeezing them as you go, and scatter over the tomatoes, then sprinkle over another tablespoon or so of freshly chopped mint. I also make this a lot with tarragon – both dried and fresh – in place of the mint.

Generally, when I make a salad, I don't make a proper dressing. I simply put the leaves in a large mixing bowl, squeeze over a little lemon juice or dot with a cautiously small amount of vinegar, then sprinkle with sea salt, and toss well, before pouring a little extra-virgin olive oil directly over, and tossing slowly and thoroughly again. First, it is important that you add the lemon juice or vinegar before the oil (if the oil goes on first it can wilt the leaves a bit too much) and second, it is crucial that you initially use much less of everything (apart from the leaves) than you think you need. The key to not overdressing a salad is using a scant amount of dressing, and then tossing it for a long time, patiently. If, after you've done this, you feel it needs more oil, vinegar or lemon juice, add a few drops more, and toss slowly and methodically again.

I make an exception for the green salad that ritually accompanies the lasagne on p.171. For 2 romaine hearts and 1 iceberg lettuce (or 4 romaine hearts if you prefer, or indeed any lettuce you want), you will need, well in advance, to peel a banana shallot of 40–50g and slice into fine half-moons. Put these in a jar or a bowl, and pour over 3 tablespoons of red wine vinegar. Push the curls of shallot down with a teaspoon so that they're submerged, and replace the lid on the jar, or cover the bowl with food wrap, and leave to steep for at least 6 hours.

When you're ready to go on the night itself, tear the lettuces into bite-sized pieces and drop them into the largest mixing bowl in the house. Stir 3 tablespoons of finely chopped chives into the vinegar-steeping shallots, followed by 6 tablespoons (90ml) of extra-virgin olive oil, ½ teaspoon of Dijon mustard and an amber drop of honey or maple syrup. Put the lid back on the jar and shake to mix, or whisk if the dressing's in a bowl, and add salt to taste. Pour half of it over the leaves and toss gently but thoroughly for twice as long as you think it needs, then add as much of the rest as required, going slowly all the time. Turn into a very large salad bowl, or divide between two bowls, and sprinkle a couple more tablespoons of finely chopped chives over the top.

I make the shallot and chive dressing for a special treat at home, chiefly, of course, to please my children, whose eager appetite for raw onions is rampagingly greater than their poor old ma's. This combination of steeped shallots and a punchy scattering of chives is one of those rare examples of a compromise all parties are equally happy with.

More frequent house specials are either one of the following two salads. The first comprises red chicory, the tightly furled heads broken into long spears, with radishes. You can cut the radishes into halves or quarters, but I love them best sliced translucently thin with a mandolin. Dress with a scant amount of red wine vinegar, more generous amounts of sea salt flakes and extra-virgin olive oil. Add a few thyme leaves, and, once mixed and on a platter or in a shallow bowl, strew fine sprigs of thyme over.

I'm not sure there's been a day in the past few months when I haven't eaten either the red chicory salad, or its sister salad, one with fennel and radishes. The fact that chicory, fennel and radishes all last for ages in the fridge is perhaps part of the reason, but certainly not the main one. Cut the fennel and radishes in the thinnest slices you can manage safely; I put on my *Game of Thrones* glove and set to with a mandolin. Mix the thinly sliced fennel and radishes together, finely grate over some lemon zest, squeeze over a little lemon juice, sprinkle with sea salt and toss gently but well before arranging on a large plate or shallow bowl. Pour a little extra-virgin olive oil over the top, and scatter over some of the fennel fronds from the bulb or a little dill. Either salad can be sprinkled with pomegranate seeds when festivities demand, and both bring such beauty to the table, which lifts the spirits and adds poetry to the prose of everyday life.

BEETROOT AND CHICKPEA DIP

While I don't go in for starters, even when I have friends over for supper, I am – as I mention often – a dips-with-drinks devotee. This is a new addition to my stable of regulars: the beetroot not only turns the chickpeas a quite ridiculously uplifting pink, but helps you create a soft, slightly fluid texture (though it will thicken on standing), all the better for sticking a tortilla chip or a baby carrot into.

Alongside, I like to bring out a bowl of the green salsa I've been making in one variation or other for years. Most recently, it's acquired a gingery zing, and to make it, all you need to do is take a stick blender to a large bunch (approx. 100g) of coriander, trimmed stems included, 100g of green chillies (though you can halve that if you want less heat), 3 peeled fat cloves of garlic, 50g of peeled and sliced ginger, the juice of 2 limes, 250ml of light olive (or vegetable) oil, and salt to taste. On Twitter, a couple of winters ago, someone called Tom Ellis told me that he had very successfully substituted Seville oranges for the limes and now, when they arrive in January, I do too. You could always use the juice of ¼ regular orange and 1½ limes during the long months they're not around. And when wild garlic is in season, you can replace the 100g of coriander with 75g of wild garlic and 25g of flat-leaf parsley (including tender stalks), but in which case, leave out the cloves of garlic. On special occasions, this duo becomes a trio with the addition of the Burnt Onion and Aubergine Dip (p.96): the pink, green and muted ochre like tonally tinkered-with traffic lights on the table.

I admit that I call this dip Beetroot Hummus at home, although perhaps it is too mutant a version to be worthy of the name. Still, I eat it just as I would a traditional hummus; I love it spread thickly on the No-Knead Black Bread (p.305), toasted or not, topped with slim wedges of avocado, spritzed with lime and sprinkled with sea salt and those fairy fronds of dill. And it makes a fabulous light supper (or lunch) too, splodged vibrantly on a plate of dry-fried halloumi slices lying on a tangle of rocket leaves dotted with capers, with fresh mint scattered over the lot.

I use a large jar of Spanish chickpeas to make this; indeed, I always use these rather than tinned chickpeas which tend to be pebbly. The jars are quite a lot more expensive than the tins, so you can easily and affordably ape their soft and creamy texture by soaking and cooking 300g of dried chickpeas. Do keep some of their cooking liquid to add while blending.

It's not hard to roast the beetroot yourself, though it certainly adds time. I don't, I'm afraid, recommend using ready-cooked beetroot. And don't throw away the trimmed beet stalks and leaves: the offcuts from a 500g bunch

of beetroot can be cooked rather like the chard on p.18, though I leave out the anchovies, and toss them through 100g of spaghetti for a solo supper.

Finally, I advise you to seek out the more fluid and less claggy tahini from a Middle Eastern store (or online) if you can.

For make-ahead, store and/or freeze notes, see p.334

BEETROOT AND CHICKPEA DIP

MAKES approx. 900ml

225–250g raw beetroot

1 x 700g jar of chickpeas (or 300g dried chickpeas, soaked, cooked and cooled)

2–3 fat cloves of garlic

2 teaspoons sea salt flakes (or 1 teaspoon fine sea salt)

2 x 15ml tablespoons (approx. 25g) tahini

2–3 lemons

A few ice cubes, for blending

1. Heat the oven to 220°C/200°C Fan. Cut the stems and tails off the beetroot, and wrap each beetroot loosely in foil, seal the parcels tightly, and roast for about 2 hours, though be prepared to go up to 3. Open up and pierce each beetroot with a normal eating knife to make sure it's tender. When you're satisfied your beetroot is cooked, unwrap the parcels and leave to cool.

2. Peel and break apart the beetroot, and drop the pieces into the bowl of a food processor. Tip the chickpeas out of the jar, helping them loose with a bendy spatula or spoon, making sure you get all the gloop, too; it's this that will help make it all so gorgeously creamy. If using chickpeas you've cooked yourself, add a couple of tablespoons of the liquid they cooked in, or more as needed.

3. Press on 2 of the garlic cloves with the flat of a knife to bruise them and release the skin. Peel it away and add the cloves to the processor. Add the salt, tahini and 4 x 15ml tablespoons (60ml) of lemon juice. Process patiently – it will take a while to combine – and once it's well mixed, scrape down the bowl, add a couple of ice cubes, and blitz again until gorgeously smooth and radiantly, improbably pink. You can add another ice cube or two and go on for longer if you feel it needs it, until you have a light, super-smooth texture.

4. Taste to see if you would like any more lemon juice, garlic or salt, adding as necessary and blitzing again, then scrape into a serving bowl.

ROAST RED PEPPERS WITH POMEGRANATE MOLASSES AND DUKKAH

It was Sabrina Ghayour who introduced me to the idea of pomegranate molasses with peppers, though I make my dressing rather differently. And the combination is sublime: the peppers soft and sweet; the pomegranate molasses rich, fragrant and sharp. And we have Claudia Roden to thank for dukkah (as we do for so many good things), although, again, my version differs from her introductory original. And while dukkah is most often eaten sprinkled over bread first dipped in oil, it makes a perfect nubbly, nutty, spicy topping for so many salads and vegetables. Both dressing and dukkah are just as wonderful on beetroot: prepare and roast a 500g bunch, following the instructions for the Beetroot and Chickpea Dip on p.199, and when cold, break up roughly with your hands.

It's really up to you whether to peel the roasted peppers or not: it is quite finicky work, but you do end up with such tender, soft strips; you will, however, lose quite a bit of volume, so if it's bulk you're after, leave them unpeeled.

As for the pomegranate molasses, think of it as a perfumed, treacly vinegar: it can be used, sparingly, to add deep, fruity sourness to stews and soups or whenever you need the rich astringency of tamarind, or the tempered sweetness of balsamic; the Italians sprinkle the latter over strawberries to make the berries sing, and you can macerate them with pomegranate molasses likewise. You won't need much: for about 300g ripe strawberries, halved or quartered, I drizzle over 2 teaspoons each of caster sugar and pomegranate molasses, then cover the dish they're in, give it a good shake, and leave the strawberries out on the kitchen counter for 30 minutes, or up to 2 hours, after which time they will be an almost-illuminated, headily scented glossy garnet. And you can use them to make a very un-Etonian Eton Mess: gently fold your steeped strawberries into 250ml of double cream softly whipped with 50g of mascarpone. I just use a little hand whisk for this. Break up 2 small shop-bought meringues, then fold them in gently too. Spoon into 4 small martini glasses, swirl the scant but intense dark syrup on top, and add a few pomegranate seeds and mint.

But it is in marinades that I use this molasses most often in my kitchen. Mix together 2 tablespoons each of olive oil, pomegranate molasses, maple syrup, soy sauce, and 1 teaspoon hot smoked paprika, then pour over 8 meaty chicken wings. Marinate these overnight in the fridge, or for 2 hours at room temperature and then tip out wings and marinade into a small lined oven tray, give everything a good schmoosh, leaving the wings turned the right way up, and cook in a 180°C/160°C Fan oven for an hour, or a little over (basting them

after 30 minutes) by which time they will be miraculously tender and a deep burnished brown and, if not exactly crisp-skinned, then gloriously sticky. And this marinade would do equally well with chicken thighs, spare ribs, or − better still − lamb ribs, though the lamb ribs should be cooked at 150°C/130°C Fan for nearer 2 hours. Or just anoint a shoulder or neck of lamb with this heavenly marinade, then roast it at 170°C/150°C Fan, covered, for 3 hours, then uncovered for a further 30 minutes.

SERVES 4–6

FOR THE DRESSING

3 x 15ml tablespoons extra-virgin
  olive oil

2 teaspoons pomegranate molasses

½ teaspoon sea salt flakes (or
  ¼ teaspoon fine sea salt)

1 fat clove of garlic

FOR THE PEPPERS

6 large or 9 small red peppers
  (approx. 1.25kg)

2 x 15ml tablespoons olive oil

60ml hot water from a just-boiled
  kettle, plus more as needed

FOR THE DUKKAH

65g shelled pistachios

2 x 15ml tablespoons sesame seeds

2 teaspoons coriander seeds

2 teaspoons cumin seeds

½ teaspoon fennel seeds

½ teaspoon pink peppercorns

1 teaspoon sea salt flakes (or
  ½ teaspoon fine sea salt)

TO SERVE (OPTIONAL)

2–3 x 15ml tablespoons pomegranate
  seeds

For make-ahead, store and/or freeze notes, see p.334

1. I start off with the dressing (often making it in advance to give the garlic longer to infuse). Pour the extra-virgin olive oil into a small jar – an old mustard jar, for example – and add the pomegranate molasses and salt. Press on the garlic with the flat side of a knife to bruise it, then remove the skin. Add the bruised garlic to the jar (if it's broken up, don't worry) and give it a very good shake.

2. Heat the oven to 220°C/200°C Fan. Cut the peppers in half and take out the stalk, seeds and white pith.

3. Put the red peppers cut-side down into a large lipped baking sheet – I use one that is 41 x 33cm. Add the 2 tablespoons of olive oil, and schmoosh to mix, leaving the peppers cut side down again. Aiming for an unpeppered corner, pour 60ml of hot water into the tin, using a ¼ cup measure or, indeed, an espresso cup for ease. Place immediately in the oven, and roast for about 40 minutes, by which time they should be very tender and scorched in places. Do check after 30 minutes, though, and if you think they are burning onto the baking sheet, add some more water; it will be so hot at this stage, you can use cold water.

4. Get on with the dukkah once the peppers have gone into the oven. Toast the pistachios in a dry pan (big enough to accommodate them in one layer) over medium heat, giving the pan a shake and a stir regularly, for about 3 minutes. Tip the nuts into a shallow dish to cool.

5. Toast the sesame seeds for 2 minutes, again giving the pan a shake and stir frequently, and tip these into a second dish or a saucer to cool. The sesame seeds are added whole to this dukkah, which is why you can't toast them with the other seeds. Speaking of which, now toast the coriander, cumin and fennel seeds, along with the pink peppercorns, which again will take only a couple of aromatic minutes, but you'll need to shake and stir pretty much constantly. Tip these into a third dish to cool.

6. With the sesame seeds set to one side, add the salt to the mixed seeds and peppercorns and grind coarsely; if you don't have a spice or coffee grinder, and can't face a pestle and mortar, a bullet blender (should you have one) will do, but blitz very briefly: this shouldn't be a powder or a paste, but fine, spicy rubble. Transfer this to a jar or bowl.

7. Remove 1 tablespoon of pistachios and chop them roughly with a knife or mezzaluna and add to the sesame seeds. Grind the remaining pistachios with whatever method you chose for the spices. The pistachios are soft, so although you should aim for small pieces, you will inevitably get some powder, too, and that's fine.

8. Add the ground pistachios, hand-chopped pistachios and toasted sesame seeds to the jar or bowl of spicy rubble. Mix or shake well. You won't need all of the dukkah for the salad, but it lasts for ages, and you will find yourself sprinkling it over vegetables, avocado toast, salads and, of course, bread dipped in olive oil.

9. When the peppers are ready, if you want to peel them, put them straight from the oven into a bowl, cover with food wrap or a plate and leave to cool; this will help the skin lift more easily. Carefully lift off the skin with your fingers and arrange the soft peeled peppers on a platter. If you're not peeling them, you can transfer them from the oven tray to the platter and serve warm or leave to cool.

10. When you're ready to eat, stand the jar of dressing in a bowl of warm water for 10 minutes, then shake well and pour over the peppers. Scatter over the pomegranate seeds if using. Sprinkle with dukkah and serve with pride.

ROOT VEGETABLE MASH

Both uplifting and comforting, this is a regular at my table from autumn onwards. There's pretty well nothing it doesn't enhance, from stews and roasts to the plainest piece of grilled fish or meat. It is also to be borne in mind with the Norwegian Pork Ribs (p.265). And unlike proper mash, you can make it ahead and reheat it easily. Just warm a little milk in a heavy-based pan, add the gloriously orange mash, and stir regularly until piping hot.

Should you have any left over, you could also add vegetable or chicken stock for a near-instant soup.

SERVES 4–6

600g parsnips	75g unsalted butter
600g swede	A good grinding of nutmeg
300g carrots	A good grinding of pepper
2 fat cloves of garlic	1–2 teaspoons sea salt flakes (or
2 teaspoons fine sea salt	½–1 teaspoon fine sea salt)

For make-ahead, store and/or freeze notes, see p.334

1. Peel the parsnips, and cut the fat ends into thick slices or chunks – this might involve no more than cutting them into two or three – and halve the spindly tails, or leave them as they are if very small. Peel the swede, and aim to cut it into chunks that match the pieces of parsnip (obviously, you won't have any spindly pieces). Peel the carrots and as they take much longer than either swede or parsnips to cook, cut them into pieces about half the size of the others.

2. Put all your prepared vegetables in a pan; I use one of 24cm diameter. Peel the garlic and throw the cloves in whole, and cover generously with cold water. Add the salt, partially cover the pan, and bring to a boil.

3. Once the water's boiling, turn the heat down a little and, still with the lid on top of the pan at a rakish angle, let the vegetables cook at a robust simmer for about 30 minutes or until all of them are soft enough to be mashed easily. Really make sure that the carrots are very tender or your mash will be grainy.

4. Dip a cup into the pan to get a little of the cooking water, in case you need it later (or better still keep all of the liquid for making soup), then drain the vegetables and, with a stick blender (using the soup attachment, if yours has such a thing), mash them in the

hot pan with the butter, nutmeg, pepper and 1 teaspoon of sea salt flakes (or ½ teaspoon of fine sea salt). Obviously you can mash them by hand if you want.

5. Add a tablespoon of the cooking water, and continue to mash until you have as smooth a purée as possible. Add more liquid if you like a softer consistency, or indeed more butter if you feel the need, and check for seasoning, adding more salt, nutmeg and pepper as wished.

BROWN BUTTER COLCANNON

I have a particular passion for this recipe. Mash in any form has a special place in my heart, but this is simply sublime. I go dreamy-eyed every time I eat it, which is often. If you haven't come across brown butter before, then you have profound pleasure in store. It is very straightforward to make: quite simply, you heat butter until it is brown. What happens as you heat it is that the water evaporates, and the milk proteins caramelise: the result is sweet, nutty and intense. In France, it's known as *beurre noisette*: the colour is indeed hazelnut brown; and it hints at the flavour you get from it too.

Fish with brown butter and capers was a regular on the table when I was a child, and my maternal grandmother used to do the same with brains. Brown butter may be a simple sauce, but it has rich potential. Just know this: wherever you might add butter you could consider using brown butter instead.

But before I give my suggestions for what to do with it, let me give some helpful starters for making it in the first place. You need to use a light-coloured pan so that you can see what colour the butter is at all stages: I use a stainless-steel one, a rather small straight-sided frying pan of 18cm diameter when I just need a small amount; if I'm after a more serious supply, I go for a heavy-based saucepan, which helps keep the heat even. It's not essential that your butter is soft before you start, though I prefer it to be, but it must be unsalted. Keep the heat low until it's melted, giving it the odd nudge with a spatula or what have you, and then turn the heat to medium and keep stirring regularly as it bubbles away, to stop the bits that are browning first from sticking too much to the base of the pan. And I warn you, it will splatter a lot.

It's impossible to say just how long it will take until it's properly brown, as it will depend on the dimensions and materials of your pan and how much butter you're using. It does get very foamy, so spoon the foam to one side to see what's happening underneath. As soon as it's smelling nutty and is the colour of a hazelnut, pour it into a jug or bowl, and scrape in every last bit of brown speckle from the pan. If you leave it in the pan it will carry on cooking and burn. Some people strain their brown butter, but those little flecks have a wonderful caramel flavour, and it would be just criminal to waste that. (Although I am ashamed to note that in the brown-butter buttercream recipe I gave in my second book, *How to be a Domestic Goddess*, I did instruct to strain off the 'sediment'. It was a long time ago; we live and learn.) And you don't have to brown your butter as and when you need it: it will keep in the fridge for two weeks; just reheat as much as you want when you want. Not that you necessarily need to reheat it to enjoy it: take the amount you want out of the fridge and let it come to room temperature (it'll take longer to do so than regular butter) and spread it over toast or crumpets and be grateful to live in a world where such delight is possible. This fudgy-coloured butter – it gets paler as it cools – is both a flavour bomb (as overused as the term might be) and a secret ingredient ready to enhance your eating, cooking and baking pleasure.

I feel so excitedly full of suggestions that I hardly know how to marshal this undisciplined barrage of ideas. It seems right, though, for me to begin soberly with my mother's Sole with Brown Butter and Capers: dredge a couple of lemon sole fillets in seasoned flour and cook them (skin-side down first) for about 2 minutes a side (depending on their size) in a tablespoon of butter, then transfer them to a warmed plate. Get a tablespoon of capers out of a jar in readiness. Wipe the pan with some kitchen paper, and add 2 more tablespoons of butter and heat until it deepens in colour; this small amount will take a couple of minutes, if that. Once the butter is hazelnut brown underneath the foam, turn off the heat, throw in the capers, swirl the pan and pour over the waiting fillets. I like some feathery fronds of dill on this, but you may prefer chives or parsley. If you forgo the capers, you have made *sole meunière*. In either case, serve with lemon to squeeze over.

This sauce is just as wonderful poured over pork chops, though you could add some scissor-shredded sage in place of the capers, or as well as, letting the sage strips get crisp in the butter first. And gnocchi with brown butter and sage is a divine feast, though you could use pasta; ravioli would be my first choice, but there's not a pasta it wouldn't be delicious with. And I often use finely chopped rosemary in place of the more traditional sage.

If you've made a tomato sauce that tastes just a little too astringent, a spoonful or two of brown butter will counter that with toasty depth. But just alone, brown butter is gorgeous over steamed vegetables, tossed through popcorn, or added to soups. It provides emollient oomph wherever you need it.

Consider browning 125g of butter (to replace the 100g) for the Anchovy Butter Sauce on p.15: its sweet nuttiness is a perfect partner for the fiercely salty anchovies, and excellent, too, for dipping asparagus or sprouting broccoli in. You can also use it in baking. But remember, when you make brown butter, as I've said, the water evaporates, so while you can use it to exquisite effect, you do need to take this into account. Generally speaking, this means that you need to add 25% extra butter before you brown it to get the same weight of butter a recipe calls for. Keep that in mind, and then play as you will, turning brownies into caramelly brown-butter brownies, making brown-butter cookies and adapting any other recipes with brown butter potential.

As with all cooking, your palate and the contents of your fridge and cupboard will lead you to your own experiments and discoveries. Enjoy the journey. But maybe start it with this colcannon, here. We are a volubly talkative family, but when we're around the table eating this, we fall into a stunned, blissful silence, if only for a minute or two.

If the idea of using 150g of butter to make this appals you, then by all means reduce the amount – though not by too much. This is a recipe that exults in butter, not apologises for it.

While the quantities below yield enough colcannon to feed four to six, I just halve them even if I'm making it only for me, although I tend to stagger it over two nights. On the first evening, I have one of my favourite solo suppers, which is just this, in a large bowl, by itself. And for its next outing, I turn what's left over into patties. To make two of these, add 3 tablespoons of grated Parmesan, about 20g of grated Red Leicester (however geographically incorrect this might be) or other cheese that melts well, and 1 egg yolk (freeze the white to save up for a pavlova) to 1 cup (about 200g) of cooled leftover colcannon. Form into two fat patties, and put them in the fridge to firm up for at least 20 minutes. Dredge or dust the patties in flour (gluten-free if necessary) and fry fairly gently in butter or oil for about 3 minutes a side until hot all the way through with a golden crust. Eat with a fried or poached egg and I always add a splodge of the Fermented Hot Sauce on p.300.

As for what to eat the colcannon with and when, I'm finding it hard to think of any occasion it would be out of place. Perhaps in high summer it might strike the wrong note but, actually, in a British summer, there are still plenty of opportunities for it. Ham is the first accompaniment that comes to mind or, rather, boiled bacon as it's known in Ireland, where colcannon emanates, and where I first memorably ate it over 30 years ago. But on many evenings, I'm very happy to put all the cooking effort into the colcannon, and simply fry up some streaky bacon to go with it. As a family supper, it's hard to beat, but the Black Pudding Meatballs (p.122) might just be my favourite accompaniment.

The potatoes are key here. In Ireland, Kerr's Pink would be the first choice, or Golden Wonder, neither of which I can get near me in London, but I use Roosters, and suggest you do too. I'm afraid I'm also going to ask you to try and find potatoes of more or less equal size, as they need to be cooked whole. I'm not expecting you to be able to get your hands on a kilo's worth of Roosters of exactly the same size every time you make this, but it would be lovely if you could. I leave the skins on the potatoes: since you're adding kale and spring onions, you're not aiming for a smooth mash anyway.

Finally, I must tell you that I recently made the brown butter colcannon with wild garlic in place of the kale, and I look forward to doing the same next year, when it's the season.

SERVES 4–6

1–1.25kg Kerr's Pink, Golden Wonder or Rooster potatoes, preferably of a uniform size

200g kale (weight once stripped from stems – approx. 300–400g if you're buying it on stems)

250ml full-fat milk

4 spring onions

150g unsalted butter

For make-ahead, store and/or freeze notes, see p.334

1. Scrub any mud off the potatoes and put them whole into a large pan – I use one of 26cm diameter – of salted cold water and bring to the boil.

2. Without knowing what size potatoes you're using, it's hard to be precise about how long they'll take to cook: smaller potatoes will take around 40 minutes; larger ones will take around 1 hour. At any rate, cook, at a robust simmer (checking that the pan isn't boiling dry, or that the water isn't bubbling so fiercely the potatoes break into pieces) with the lid partially on, until the potatoes feel good and tender when you pierce them gently with a fork.

3. While the potatoes are cooking, strip the kale from the stems, and then tear into small pieces; even if you buy kale that's ready-chopped, you'll still need to go through it to remove any tough bits of stem.

4. Cook the kale in a small amount of salted boiling water until it's soft – this should take around 5 minutes – and then drain. When you can handle it without burning yourself, squeeze out the excess water and put the kale back in the hot pan, cover the pan to keep it warm, and leave to one side for now. Finely slice the spring onions – I like to use most of the green part as well as the white – and leave to one side for now, too.

5. Once your potatoes are tender, take them out of the pan gently (draining them in a colander may make them disintegrate, and get waterlogged) and place on a large board. Empty out the pan and, remembering it's still hot, carefully give it a quick wipe with kitchen paper. Put it back on the still-warm, turned-off hob and return the potatoes to the pan to dry out for a couple of minutes.

6. Mash the potatoes by whichever method you prefer. I like the texture from the skins, so I wouldn't use a potato ricer. I mash straight in the pan, so I warm the milk in a jug in the microwave,

pour it into the potatoes, and set to with a masher. (Whatever you do, don't use a stick blender or you'll turn them to glue.) When you've finished mashing them, fold in the cooked kale, and taste for seasoning. Put the lid on so that it all stays hot while you make the brown butter and warm a serving dish.

7. Put a small heatproof jug by the hob. Cut the butter into slabs, the better for melting, and duly melt it in a heavy-based saucepan – I use one 18cm in diameter and 8cm deep – over gentle heat. Once the butter's melted, turn the heat to medium, and carry on cooking, swirling the pan regularly, until the butter starts to turn a deep golden brown, with dark speckles at the bottom of the pan. Once it's toasty and hazelnutty, at around 7 minutes, remove the pan from the heat, and add the sliced spring onions, which will make the brown butter sizzle furiously.

8. Pour two-thirds of this into the potato pan and the rest into your little jug. Beat the brown butter into the colcannon and scrape into your warmed bowl, making swirls in the top of the colcannon with your spatula or spoon. Pour the remaining brown butter and spring onions on top and take to the table, in blissful anticipation.

FENNEL GRATIN

This creamy gratin is a special treat for fennelphiles. The nuttiness of the Gruyère partners beautifully with that gentle aniseed flavour. Frankly, I could lap up the fennel-vermouth-and-cheese-deepened cream with a spoon. And often do. While it's rich and deep in flavour, it is fairly fluid; if you want it to be thicker, make the gratin up ahead of time, since it thickens as it stands.

I often halve this for two, baking it in a shallow round ovenproof dish 23cm in diameter and 5cm deep.

SERVES 4

1kg fennel (it's best to have 2 large
   bulbs rather than several smaller
   ones)

250ml dry white vermouth

75g Gruyère

2 fat cloves of garlic

250ml double cream

2 teaspoons sea salt flakes (or
   1 teaspoon fine sea salt)

A good grinding of pepper

1 x 15ml tablespoon Dijon mustard

For make-ahead, store and/or freeze notes, see p.334

1. Heat the oven to 200°C/180°C Fan.

2. Cut off the chimney-like stems from the fennel, then halve
the bulbs, cut away most of the core and cut each half into
3 or 4 wedges. Keep the offcuts for stock and the fronds for salads.

3. Put these wedges into a heavy-based pan that comes with a
tightly fitting lid – I use one of 22cm diameter – and pour over the
vermouth, then bring to the boil over high-ish heat with the lid on,
so listen out for the bubbling. I know there's not a lot of liquid in the
pan, but so long as the lid fits tightly, it shouldn't evaporate, and
the fennel, as it softens, will give off liquid of its own. Once it
comes to the boil, turn the heat down and let it simmer robustly for
15 minutes or until the fennel wedges feel soft when you prod them
with a fork. Lift up the lid and check after 10 minutes. Remove
the pan from the heat and, with tongs or a couple of forks, transfer
the now bedraggled fennel to a round, shallow dish of about 25cm
diameter or a 2 litre gratin dish. Reserve the cooking liquid.

4. Meanwhile, finely grate the cheese and peel the garlic. Measure
the double cream into a jug, then mince or grate in the garlic,
add the sea salt flakes, grind over the pepper, and stir in the grated
cheese and the Dijon mustard followed by the vermouthy-fennel
juices from the pan.

5. Whisk to mix before pouring over the softened fennel in its dish.
Use a spoon and fork to turn the fennel in the cream, so that it's well
coated, leaving it in a single layer. You may need to press down a
bit on the fennel to make sure it's submerged, though don't worry if
some of it is poking up.

6. Bake in the oven for 1 hour, until the gratin is bubbling, its top
bronzed in places. Let the dish sit for about 10 minutes out of the
oven before serving.

ROAST CAULIFLOWER
WITH APRICOT HARISSA AND SPINACH

I know I've introduced the Apricot Harissa earlier in this chapter, but it was for this recipe that I first made it, and so here, I feel, it belongs. Not that I want to yoke it too firmly to any particular dish. Yes, it is glorious with the chicken on p.168, just as it is with the roast parsnips on p.278, but there are so many possibilities for this tangy, spicy paste. Tempting though it is to run through all of them, sadly space does not permit, but I must just urge you to make a pile of fiery roast potatoes. It's simple enough. Cut a kilo of them into cubes of 3–4cm, and toss in a bowl in which you've first mixed a tablespoonful of this harissa with 3 tablespoons of olive oil, turn these flagrantly orange beauties into a large lipped baking sheet, splash it up with about 100ml of hot water from a just-boiled kettle and roast them in a 200°C/180°C Fan oven for about 1 hour (turning them around after 45 minutes) until they're crisp, and scorched to deep crunchiness in parts.

Although the cauliflower's roasted here, it has the spicy softness I associate with a long braise. The spinach, wilted in the heat of the pan at the end, seems to bring the dish together. It tastes comfortingly familiar, and yet not quite the same as anything else.

I know that harissa doesn't traditionally contain apricots but I was talking to a friend on the phone who had bought a jar of apricot harissa and I was immediately inspired by the sound of it. And you can, of course, use shop-bought harissa here, but there is something gently rewarding about toasting your spices and making your own.

While the roast cauliflower leftovers can be heated up easily as they are, I also – perhaps strangely – like to mash some up and make a toasted sandwich with it. You'll have some Apricot Harissa left over. It will last for 2 weeks in the fridge in a jar – pour more oil over the surface to cover it before putting the lid on. Otherwise I freeze tablespoonfuls of it in ice cube trays; it will last up to 6 months.

Just knowing I have a supply of it in the fridge or freezer, ready to give a lick of its orange flame to anything I feel needs the benefit of its aromatic toastiness, makes me happy.

SERVES 4–6

FOR THE APRICOT HARISSA

20g large dried chillies (I use
  Kashmiri chillies)

1 teaspoon caraway seeds

1 teaspoon coriander seeds

1 teaspoon cumin seeds

Seeds from 4 cardamom pods

45g (approx. 6) soft dried apricots

15g fresh turmeric (or 1 teaspoon
  ground turmeric)

4 fat cloves of garlic

25g fresh ginger

2 teaspoons sea salt flakes (or
  1 teaspoon fine sea salt)

1 teaspoon sweet smoked paprika

4 x 15ml tablespoons (60ml) olive oil

1 teaspoon apple cider vinegar

**FOR THE CAULIFLOWER AND
SPINACH**

1 very large or 2 medium cauliflowers
  (approx. 1.5kg)

2 x 15ml tablespoons Apricot Harissa

4 x 15ml tablespoons (60ml) olive oil,
  plus more as needed

1 x 15ml tablespoon tomato purée

2 x 15ml tablespoons orange juice

45g (approx. 6) soft dried apricots

350g spinach

For make-ahead, store and/or freeze notes, see p.334

1. To make the harissa, put the dried chillies in a heatproof bowl
or measuring jug, and pour over about 500ml water from a just-
boiled kettle. With a spoon, press the chillies down under the water
– though they can't help bobbing up – then cover the bowl or jug
with a plate, and leave the chillies to steep and soften while you
toast your spices.

2. Put the caraway, coriander and cumin seeds into a frying pan.
Add the seeds from the cardamom pods, and then toast them all –
that's to say, dry-fry them – over medium heat for a few minutes,
giving the pan a shake and a shimmy regularly, to make sure the
spices don't burn. When you are hit by their aroma wafting up
from the pan, they should be toasted enough. Tip the seeds out
into a shallow dish.

3. Get out a second bowl that will comfortably take all the harissa
ingredients, and that you can use with a stick blender. Halve the
apricots and drop them in. Add the turmeric, sliced into about 3
(or the dried turmeric if using) and peel the garlic, add it to the
bowl, then peel the ginger with the tip of a teaspoon, cut it into a
few small pieces and add these to the bowl, along with the salt
and paprika.

4. When the chillies have had their 15 minutes of soaking time,
lift them, one by one, out of the water, give them a bit of a waggle
over the water, and pull off the stalks, letting the soaked chillies and
their seeds drop into the bowl. Tip in the cooled spices, pour in the

oil and vinegar, and blitz with a stick blender until you have a thick paste. You can use this straightaway to anoint the cauliflower.

5. Spoon 2 tablespoons of the harissa into a very large mixing bowl, add the 4 tablespoons of olive oil, 1 tablespoon of tomato purée and 2 tablespoons of orange juice and whisk to mix.

6. Get rid of any tired or discoloured outer leaves from the cauliflower, then tear off the remaining leaves and reserve them. Cut or break the cauliflower into florets, discarding the core, then add to the mixing bowl and toss so that the florets are well coated, their elegant matt pallor now slicked a glossy dayglo orange. Add the more robust leaves (holding back the tightly curled, tender inner leaves for now) and toss again. Leave to steep for 20 minutes, but they'll be fine for a few hours. If you're cooking straightaway, you should heat the oven to 220°C/200°C Fan now.

7. Tip the coated cauliflower leaves and florets into a large but fairly shallow roasting tin (I use one measuring 34 x 37 x 5cm) and spread them out evenly, and roast in the oven for 30 minutes.

8. Immediately the cauliflower is in the oven, add the reserved tender leaves to the bowl with its oily orange residue and press the leaves into this, adding a little more oil to help the paste coat them, if needed. When the cauliflower has had its 30 minutes in the oven, add these leaves to the tin, turning any florets over, should you feel it's necessary. Roast for a further 10 minutes, or until the florets are soft throughout and scorched in places.

9. While you're waiting for the florets to cook, chop up the soft dried apricots or – as I do – snip them with scissors. Once the cauliflower's ready, remove the tin from the oven, add the snipped apricots and the spinach, and gently mix together. Put the tin back in the oven, though switch it off, and let the spinach wilt into the harissa-spiced cauliflower for 5–10 minutes in the residual heat (and pop in a heatproof serving dish at the same time). It won't matter if you leave the tin in for longer; this is at its best warm rather than piping hot.

CRISP AND CREAMY ARTICHOKE HEARTS

This recipe is really a hymn of praise to the freezer. Or perhaps it owes more to my gratitude to the increasing availability of ingredients that used to require an expedition to procure. In fairness, it is a mixture of both. Until recently, I'd have to go to a Middle Eastern shop (admittedly, a pleasure in itself) to get frozen artichoke hearts, but now I find them at the supermarket, and my deep freeze has a packet of them in it at all times. I suggest yours does from now on, too. The oven banishes any hint of soddenness, turning them nutty and crisp: a simple way of transforming a packet of frozen vegetables into a feast.

You can serve this hot, straight from the oven, or let it cool to room temperature, in which case I suggest you shave some Pecorino Romano over. And if you can't get oyster mushrooms, just leave them out; other mushrooms will give off too much moisture.

It's hard to explain the particular taste of artichokes, but to me they evoke asparagus and butter, along with the boskiness of mushrooms – which is why I thought of adding them to the dish in the first place.

But if you want – and this is a favourite in my house – you can turn this into the artichoke version of chips to pick at over a drink. Dispense with the mushrooms, roast 500g of the frozen artichoke hearts for the full 45 minutes, adding the garlic and 2 tablespoons of olive oil after 30, then blot them on some kitchen paper, put in a dish and sprinkle with sea salt flakes.

SERVES 4–6

750g frozen artichoke hearts

3 x 15ml tablespoons olive oil, plus
  2 tablespoons more

1 lemon

1 teaspoon sea salt flakes (or
  ½ teaspoon fine sea salt)

½ teaspoon Aleppo pepper (or use
  ¼ teaspoon dried chilli flakes plus
  ¼ teaspoon paprika)

3 fat cloves of garlic

175g oyster mushrooms

2 x 15ml tablespoons extra-virgin
  olive oil, plus more as needed

75g rocket

3 x 15ml tablespoons chopped flat-
  leaf parsley

½ teaspoon fresh thyme leaves, plus
  a few sprigs

For make-ahead, store and/or freeze notes, see p.334

1. Defrost the artichoke hearts; you can speed up the process (and this applies to any frozen food you want to thaw) by sitting them on an aluminium tray. When they're almost completely defrosted, heat the oven to 220°C/200°C Fan.

2. Slice each heart into 3, then arrange on a lipped baking sheet in a single layer, and pour over 3 tablespoons of the olive oil. Finely grate the zest of the lemon over the artichokes. Sprinkle over the salt and the Aleppo pepper (or chilli flakes and paprika) then gently schmoosh around to mix. Put in the oven to roast for 30 minutes.

3. Peel the garlic and tear the oyster mushrooms roughly in half, so you have soft grey velvet rags. Once the artichokes have had their 30 minutes, mince or grate the garlic into the tin, add the remaining 2 tablespoons of olive oil and quickly mix together. Drop the mushroom pieces on top and put back in the oven for a further 15 minutes, by which time the mushrooms will have dried in the heat (which tastes very much better than it sounds) and the artichokes will be crisp and bronzed on the outside and creamy within.

4. Take out of the oven, and immediately squeeze over the juice from half the zested lemon, pour over the 2 tablespoons of extra-virgin olive oil and toss gently to mix. Taste to see if you need any more lemon juice, salt or extra-virgin olive oil. You can serve these straightaway, or leave on the tray until they're room temperature, or perhaps a whisper above.

5. Line a large plate with rocket. Top with the artichoke hearts and mushrooms, then sprinkle over the parsley and thyme, both leaves and delicate sprigs. Squeeze some lemon and drizzle a little extra-virgin olive oil over the rocket if you feel it needs it.

BUTTERNUT WITH BEETROOT, CHILLI AND GINGER SAUCE

It's as if I've been programmed: the minute I know people are coming for supper, I start cutting up a butternut squash. It's a rare day in my kitchen that I don't have one to hand; they keep for ages, and so it makes sense to be prepared. Butternut is easy to cook, and there are many ways its sweet orange flesh can be further enhanced to create side dishes that taste wonderful and look beautiful.

I shall be uncharacteristically restrained, confining myself to bringing to your attention just three of those ways. All of them rest on the same preparation for the butternut itself. It's only after it's been roasted that I play around.

First off, on serving, pour a thick Green Tahini Sauce over the roasted butternut, leaving the rest in a jug or bowl for people to ladle more over as they eat. I've touched on a version of this before, but the sauce I generally make now – and you'll get a cupful (250ml) from these amounts – requires you simply to take a stick blender to 75g of tahini, 75ml of cold water, 2 tablespoons of lemon juice, 1 teaspoon of sea salt flakes (or ½ teaspoon of fine sea salt), 75g of coriander, 20g of flat-leaf parsley (you can use the tender stalks as well as the leaves of both) and 2 peeled fat cloves of garlic. Blitz until you have a smooth green-flecked sauce, taste to see if you want to add any more salt or lemon juice, then leave to mellow and thicken while you cook the butternut. That's it. Except to say that when wild garlic is in season, you can use it in place of the coriander, leaving out the cloves of garlic. Both iterations give me equal joy, and can be dolloped on much else besides.

Secondly, leave the butternut to stand out of the oven once it's cooked, so that it's just warm, and turn it into a salad with radicchio, pink-pickled onions and pomegranate seeds. Instructions for the onions are on pp.61–2, and it's best if you get these steeping the night before, but if that's impossible, just leave them in the vinegar for as long as you can. To make the dressing, whisk together (or shake in an old mustard jar) 3 tablespoons of extra-virgin olive oil, 1 teaspoon of red wine vinegar, ½ teaspoon of maple syrup and ½ teaspoon of sea salt flakes (or ¼ teaspoon of fine sea salt). Once amalgamated, taste to see if you want more salt. Tear a large head of radicchio into fairly big but still manageably bite-sized pieces and, in a large mixing bowl, toss them in enough of the dressing to coat them lightly. Use them to line a large platter or shallow bowl and top with the roasted but no longer piping hot butternut; if it's at room temperature you can drizzle over a little of the dressing if you have any left. Then simply strew with pink-pickled onions, pomegranate seeds and freshly chopped coriander.

And finally there is the pink sauce, which I've called upon frequently in these pages – a sauce infused with the sweetness of beetroot, warm with ginger and hot with chilli, balanced by the tangy coolness of the yogurt. It's a show stealer of a sauce whenever it appears, but it is for draping over the orange-fleshed butternut that I first, clashingly, created it, and with which I most often serve it.

If you can, roast the beetroot ahead of time, so that you don't start worrying about whether it'll be cold, as it must be, before you want to blitz it into a sauce. I often do this a day or two before. What you can't do, under any circumstances, is use shop-bought ready-cooked beetroot instead.

But I'm always happier if I can get things done in advance, and this goes for the butternut, too. You can chop it up, toss it in the spices and oil, and let it sit in a tin for a couple of hours before you cook it. Or you can roast it ahead of time, and reheat it in a 200°C/180°C Fan oven for 20 or so minutes when you want to eat it. Though if you have the oven on at a different temperature for anything else you're cooking on the night, you can reheat at a lower temperature for longer, or at a higher temperature for slightly less time.

BUTTERNUT WITH BEETROOT, CHILLI AND GINGER SAUCE

SERVES 4–6 (makes 250–275ml)

FOR THE SAUCE

150–175g raw beetroot

200g full-fat Greek yogurt (or oat-milk crème fraîche if you need it to be vegan)

2 fat cloves of garlic

20g fresh ginger

1 red chilli

1 teaspoon sea salt flakes (or ½ teaspoon fine sea salt)

FOR THE BUTTERNUT

1 butternut

1 teaspoon ground mace

1 teaspoon ground ginger

4 x 15ml tablespoons (60ml) cold-pressed rapeseed oil or olive oil

1½ teaspoons sea salt flakes (or ¾ teaspoon fine sea salt)

For make-ahead, store and/or freeze notes, see p.335

1. Heat the oven to 220°C/200°C Fan, cut the tail and stem off the beetroot, and wrap loosely with foil, sealing the edges tightly, and roast in the oven for about 2 hours, or until it feels properly tender when pierced with the tip of a normal eating knife. Unwrap the parcel, and leave to cool.

2. Once the beetroot's cold, you can make the sauce. Put the yogurt in a bowl that you can use a stick blender with. Peel and halve the garlic cloves and drop them in. Then peel the ginger with the tip of a teaspoon, and either chop it roughly or cut it into 3 or 4 pieces, and add these to the bowl. Deseed the chilli and tear it into 2 or 3 pieces and add them to the bowl, too, followed by the salt.

3. Peel the beetroot, though unless you want more than a touch of the Lady Macbeths, it might be wise to wear gloves as you do so (I use disposable ones, and wash and reuse them). Break the beetroot up a bit over the bowl and drop the pieces in, too. Then blitz to a smooth, shocking-pink cream with a stick blender. You can also do all of this with a bullet blender. Set this amazingly vivid fluid sauce to one side for now.

4. To roast the butternut heat the oven to 200°C/180°C Fan. However, were you making this to go with the roast vegetables and bulgur wheat (p.181), for which you need the oven to be at 220°C/200°C Fan, you can roast the butternut at this higher temperature, but put it in the oven on a shelf below the tin of leeks and peppers.

5. Do not peel the butternut, just halve it, remove the seeds, and then cut into large chunks. Tumble these into a large but fairly shallow roasting tin (I use one measuring 34 x 37 x 5cm), sprinkle over the spices as evenly as possible, pour over the oil and then, with a couple of spatulas – or just use your hands – turn the butternut chunks well in the oil and spices until lightly coated. Sprinkle with the salt, and roast in the oven for about 45 minutes, or until tender; squashes vary enormously and, until you cut up and cook one, you never quite know whether its flesh will be smooth and dense, or slightly grainy and watery. Let us hope for the former. But even a disappointing butternut can be salvaged successfully in any one of the three ways mooted in the recipe intro.

6. You can keep the butternut warm in the turned-off oven if that suits you, and then, when you're ready to serve, arrange on a platter or in a large shallow bowl, spoon some of the beetroot sauce pinkly over its orange flesh, and pour the rest into a little jug for people to add more if they want – and they will – as they eat.

SPICE-STUDDED RICE WITH CRISPY SHALLOTS, GARLIC AND CASHEW NUTS

This rice makes any meal feel like the most extravagant of banquets. Indeed, it forms an essential part of one of my favourite vegan feasts, alongside the Roast Butternut with Radicchio, Pink-Pickled Onions and Pomegranate Seeds (p.223), the Roast Cauliflower with Apricot Harissa and Spinach (p.216), the Roast Red Peppers with Pomegranate Molasses and Dukkah (p.202) and the Crisp and Creamy Artichoke Hearts (p.220). The feast itself kicks off with the Burnt Onion and Aubergine Dip (p.96), the Beetroot and Chickpea Dip (p.199) and Green Tahini Sauce (p.223) with tortilla chips and crudités to dunk into them all, and ends with either the lemon polenta cake (p.257) or the gingerbread (p.312), according to the weather.

There is great jubilation in the house when I cook this, as I – never knowingly undercatered – inevitably make too much, and so my children can count on being able to find tubs of it in the fridge when they come home, a microwaveable midnight feast waiting for them.

SERVES 4–6

FOR THE RICE

2 onions (250–300g)

2 fat cloves of garlic

1 teaspoon cumin seeds

1 teaspoon coriander seeds

1 teaspoon nigella seeds

1 teaspoon fennel seeds

½ teaspoon ground mace

½ teaspoon ground turmeric

¼ teaspoon ground cinnamon

3 cardamom pods

2 x 15ml tablespoons coconut oil or vegetable oil, plus 2 teaspoons more

250g basmati rice

500ml vegetable stock

FOR THE CRISPY BITS

3 fat cloves of garlic

50g banana shallots

4 x 15ml tablespoons (60ml) vegetable oil

75g unsalted cashew nuts

For make-ahead, store and/or freeze notes, see p.335

1. Peel and chop the onions, and peel the cloves of garlic. Measure out the many spices into a little bowl.

2. Heat the 2 tablespoons of coconut or vegetable oil in a large heavy-based pan that comes with a tightly fitting lid; I use one of 24cm diameter. Add the onions, stir well, and then cook for 10–15 minutes over medium heat (turning it down if they begin to catch too quickly) until they're beginning to soften.

3. Rinse the rice in a sieve under the cold tap until the water runs clear. Set the sieve over a bowl, and bring it near to the hob.

4. Take the onions off the heat, and mince or grate the garlic into the pan, then stir in the spices. Put the pan back on the hob, turn the heat up to medium or medium-high, and stir in the 2 teaspoons of coconut or vegetable oil, followed by the rice, turning it in the pan so that it's well coated with the spiced oil. Before you add the stock, taste it to see how salty it is. If it's not very salty, add salt, then pour in the stock, turn the heat to high, and bring the pan to the boil. As soon as it starts boiling, clamp on the lid, turn the heat down to very low, and cook for 20 minutes, by which time the rice should be cooked, and all the stock absorbed. Turn off the heat, remove the lid, cover the pan with a clean tea towel, replace the lid and leave for at least 40 minutes and up to 1 hour. This step is essential to ensure the rice is fluffy rather than puddingy.

5. All that remains to be done are the crispy bits. You can fry the garlic and shallots now, or you can wait and do it towards the end of the rice's standing time. Either way, you may as well prepare them now. So, peel the garlic, and cut each clove into long thin slices. Then peel the shallots, and cut each one into fine circles, separating them with your fingers into a mound of fine, pink-edged hoops.

6. When you're ready to fry, cover three plates with a double layer of kitchen paper, and place them near the hob, though not so close they're in danger of catching alight. Heat the oil in a small frying pan, and fry the garlic slivers until golden. This doesn't take very long, so be ready to whip them out onto one of your paper-lined plates quickly. Now fry the delicate shallot rings, in two batches if need be (you don't want to crowd the pan) until they are a deep golden brown, and transfer them to another paper-lined plate.

7. Warm a large shallow bowl for the rice. When you are moments away from serving up, fry the cashews until golden, and duly transfer them to the third plate. Reserve the oil for future, fragrant use.

8. Thrash the rice with a large fork to break it up. Add half your fried garlic, shallots and cashew nuts and fork them through to mix, fluffing the rice up as you do so. Tip into your warmed bowl, and sprinkle with the remaining cashews and crispy shallots and garlic.

CHOCOLATE PEANUT BUTTER CAKE

Much as I love baking, pudding is just not a feature of everyday dinner in my house. I certainly make one if I have people over, but it's not a habit I've ever got into for family supper. Really the only time dinner ends with dessert in my house is on birthdays or other family celebrations. Over the years, I've made many different cakes for my children's birthdays, but for some time now this has been the chosen one, the cake of cakes, elected to grace many special occasions, and with good reason.

The cake itself is dark, damp and divinely chocolatey, but it's the icing that truly makes it, as my daughter says, 'the cake of dreams'; even my son, who is not a peanut butter fan, adores it. I've yet to find anyone who doesn't. And those whose issue with peanut butter is its claggy and, as the American writer Nicholson Baker describes it, 'glotally claustrophic' consistency, will find this a particular revelation. I don't, you see, keep it just for family consumption. When something tastes as good as this, it's only right to share it far and wide.

And what's more, it's wonderfully easy to make. The cake is a straight-forward melt-everything-in-a-pan number, and the icing a simple buttercream. What turns the simple into spectacular is the amount of time you spend whipping the icing and the addition of double cream. But it does have to be made with normal commercial, mass-produced peanut butter; the health-store varieties, with their dense heft, will not do here, I'm afraid.

Now I know I have often been somewhat sneery about many-tiered cakes, declaring them better suited for being photographed than sliced, but I recently cracked, and ordered a set of four ultra-shallow tins to aid the baking of those multi-layered cakes I disdain. I pretended (to myself) I was doing it for the children. (And yes, I do still call them children, even though they're both older than my first book, which was published in 1998.) If you wish to do likewise, you will be able to fill these improbably thin tins with the amount of batter here, though you'll need to double the buttercream quantities.

This cake has a certain gorgeous elegance with the icing left unadorned, but I love the contrast of a crunchy sprinkling of roughly chopped, dry roasted peanuts.

GIVES 8–12 slices

FOR THE CAKE

200g unsalted butter, plus more for
  greasing

250ml hot water from a just-boiled kettle

50g cocoa

100g soft dark brown sugar

125g caster sugar

2 teaspoons vanilla extract

225g plain flour

1 teaspoon baking powder

½ teaspoon bicarbonate soda

2 large eggs, at room temperature

FOR THE ICING
(double the quantities below if making a
four-tier cake)

300g icing sugar

150g soft unsalted butter

200g smooth peanut butter (see recipe
  intro)

1 teaspoon vanilla extract

¼ teaspoon fine sea salt

4 x 15ml tablespoons (60ml) double
  cream

TO DECORATE

4 x 15ml tablespoons (30g) chopped dry
  roasted peanuts

CHOCOLATE
PEANUT BUTTER
CAKE

For make-ahead, store and/or freeze notes, see p.335

1. Heat the oven to 180°C/160°C Fan. Butter two 20cm sandwich tins
(or four tier-cake tins) and line them with baking parchment. Don't use
loose-bottomed tins as this is a runny batter.

2. Cut the butter lengthways into four pieces (just to aid melting) and put
into a heavy-based fairly wide saucepan – I use one of 22cm diameter
– and set over gentle heat. Add the just-boiled water, and whisk in the
cocoa and both brown and white sugars, and keep on low heat, whisking
gently, until the butter has melted, and you have a smooth, amalgamated
mixture. Remove from the heat, and stir in the vanilla extract. Let stand
for 5 minutes.

3. Measure out the flour in a bowl, add the baking powder and bicarb
and fork to mix. Whisk the eggs together in a small jug.

4. Pour the eggs gradually into the pan, whisking all the while, until they
are completely absorbed.

5. Finally, whisk in the flour slowly and gently until you have a smooth
batter, and pour and scrape evenly into your waiting tins.

6. Bake in the oven for 18–20 minutes (or approx. 7 minutes for the
ultra-shallow tins), by which time the cakes will be beginning to shrink
away at the edges, and a cake tester will come out cleanish; it is a damp
cake, though, so it's fine if a few crumbs cling to the cake tester.

7. Leave the cakes to cool for 10–15 minutes on a rack; they can be
turned out once the tins are not so hot that you'd need to use oven gloves.
Or you can leave them in their tins until cold. I always do this if making
the four-tier variant.

8. To make the buttercream, you must first sift the icing sugar into a bowl. This is one of the few jobs in the kitchen I hate, so I wouldn't tell you to do it if it weren't necessary.

9. In another – large – bowl (or the bowl of a freestanding mixer that you've fitted with the whisk), beat the butter and peanut butter together very thoroughly; that's to say, for 3 minutes if you're using a mixer, or 5 minutes with a handheld electric whisk, by which time you should have a light and fluffy creamy mixture. Beat in the vanilla extract and salt.

10. Still beating, but now at a slightly lower speed, patiently add the sifted icing sugar a spoonful at a time until you've used half of it, then beat in the rest in 3 batches. Once it's all in, turn up the mixer a little and carry on beating for 2 minutes, or for 3 with a handheld electric whisk. Scrape down the sides, to incorporate any icing sugar clinging to the bowl, and beat again for 30 seconds to 1 minute.

11. Still beating, add the cream a tablespoonful at a time and, when it's all in, carry on beating for 4 minutes (or for 6 minutes with a handheld electric whisk) until you have a soft, aerated and moussily light mixture.

12. Peel away the lining papers from the cakes and place one of the layers, flat-side up, on a cake stand or plate. If this is a 2-layer cake, spread – armed, ideally, with a bendy spatula and a small offset spatula – about a third of the icing evenly onto the waiting cake layer, taking it right out to the very edges of the circle; this will bulge out a bit when you place the other cake on top, which will make it easier for you to ice the sides. And if this is a 4-layer cake, just think in terms of spreading the icing 1cm thick.

13. Top with your second cake, placing it domed-side up, so that the two flat sides are meeting. Then spread another third of the icing over the top. And if making a 4-layer cake, create your tower, spreading 1cm thickness of icing between each layer, and on the top.

14. Use the bendy spatula to get a dollop of buttercream onto the side of the cake, then spread it gently to cover and smooth, ideally with a small offset spatula, and carry on like this, with your two tools, until the cake is covered all the way round. Then run the offset spatula on top and all round the cake again to smooth the buttercream. Leave plain or decorate with the chopped peanuts or as your heart desires.

CHERRY AND ALMOND CRUMBLE

I do so love a crumble. I don't just mean to eat, but also to make. When I stand at the kitchen counter, with my hands immersed in cool flour, fluttering my fingers against the cold cubes of butter to turn these two disparate ingredients into one light pile of soft and sandy flakes, I feel, at one and the same time, that I'm not only repeating a process but reliving the memory of all the times I've done so before, and yet utterly immersed in the present, alive only to the sensation of flour and butter in my fingers, as they scutter about the bowl.

This is not, of course, to say you can't use a processor or mixer to make the crumble topping; and I often do. We are all open to living lyrically more on some days than others. And a crumble embraces either approach, a stout, no-nonsense kind of a pudding that offers a taste of the sublime.

I'd been hankering after a cherry crumble for some time, and a couple of summers ago, extravagantly bought a kilo of cherries and, with this great mound in front of me, set to with a cherry-stoner (which I, in Lucille Ball mode, first used upside down, shooting myself in the forehead with a bloodied kernel) only to find that the crumble was best made not with fresh cherries, but frozen.

And here it is, the crumble I needed: sweet-sharp cherries oozing fruitily into the sour pulp of butter-softened Bramleys and bubbling up brightly around the edges of its crisp but still yielding golden topping. I've added almonds, and in many manifestations – extract, ground, flaked – but their presence is a delicate one. I like to think they're there to evoke the flavour of the stones I never had to bother with.

If you want custard with this, you will certainly get no argument from me; indeed, there's a recipe you can turn to on p.135. But hold on just for a minute. Consider, please, an easy No-Churn Cheesecake Ice Cream. And when I say easy, I mean you just stir 175g (half a can) of condensed milk into 250ml of double cream and whisk until aerated and voluminous, then carry on whisking as you add 1½ tablespoons each of lemon and lime juice and – wait for it – 3 tablespoons of advocaat. Fill a couple of 500ml tubs with this heavenly mixture (which, I dare say, you could serve like this in its own right) and place in the freezer until firm. Remember to take it out of the freezer 10–20 minutes before serving.

And if you have a stash of frozen cherries, you could also turn them into that retro classic Cherries Jubilee, which would also be fabulous with the cheesecake-flavoured ice cream. For a 400g packet of frozen cherries, you need 50g of caster sugar and 3 tablespoons of lemon juice. Put all three ingredients (you don't need to thaw the cherries first) in a wide heavy-based saucepan, and give them 3 minutes over medium to low heat with the lid on, then remove the lid, and carry on cooking gently until the cherries are hot, and have exuded a pool of glossy deep red juice. Now for a spot of flambéing if you're up for it. Strictly speaking you should be using kirsch, but cherry brandy, regular brandy or rum would all do. Turn off the flame under the pan, measure out 60ml (you can use an American ¼ cup measure) of your chosen liqueur and then put the bottle safely away from the hob. Throw the kirsch or whatever you're using into the pan and, quickly, with a long candle lighter or fireplace match, and standing at arm's length, set fire to the surface where you've just added the alcohol, and give the pan a bit of a swirl. It will flame only briefly, but when the last of the fire has flickered out, pour the cherries and their ruby juices into a heatproof bowl, and let people spoon this over ice cream; this amount is plenty for an ice-cream topping for four. And of course you can leave the cherries alcohol- and flame-free if, for whatever reason, you would prefer to. In which case, taste before serving to see if you need to add an extra spritz of lemon juice. And I have plans to make this with Seville orange juice instead of lemon when they're next in season.

If you would like to make the crumble topping in advance and freeze it to have on standby, do. You don't need to thaw it before sprinkling it over the fruit later. Or you can make it a couple of days before you need it, and leave it in the fridge. I don't generally cook the apples and cherries that much in advance, but I do prefer to do so before I start on the meal proper, so that they are ready and waiting in the pie dish.

SERVES 4–6

FOR THE CRUMBLE TOPPING
150g plain flour (or gluten-free plain flour)
50g ground almonds
1 teaspoon baking powder (gluten-free if necessary)
⅛ teaspoon of fine sea salt
125g cold unsalted butter
50g granulated sugar
30g flaked almonds

FOR THE FILLING
375g Bramley apples
35g unsalted butter
1 x 15ml tablespoon (12g) caster sugar
800g frozen sweet pitted cherries
1 teaspoon vanilla extract
¼ teaspoon almond extract

CHERRY AND
ALMOND CRUMBL

For make-ahead, store and/or freeze notes, see p.335

1. To make the crumble topping, put the flour, ground almonds, baking powder and salt into a bowl and mix together.

2. Cut the butter into approx. 1cm cubes, add to the bowl, and blend into the flour using your fingertips – fluttering the soft pad of your thumb against the soft pads of your fingers – or use a mixer or

processor, until you have a mixture that looks like rough pale oatmeal, with a few flattened pea-sized lumps of floury butter still visible. Add the sugar and use a fork to mix. You can now chill or freeze until needed.

3. To make the filling, peel the apples, then quarter and core them. Cut into approx. 4cm chunks. I don't advise using apples other than Bramleys here – no other apple gives that sour fluff – but in an emergency you could use Granny Smiths, though you'd have to cut them half the size, be prepared to cook them for longer, and purée a quarter of them.

4. So, melt the butter in a wide, heavy-based saucepan (that comes with a lid) over lowish heat, stir in the sugar and add the apples. Give a good stir to mix, then cover the pan, and let the apples cook, still on fairly low heat, for 5–10 minutes, until they are soft and beginning to break down a little.

5. Turn up the heat to medium-high and add the frozen cherries, stirring them into the apples and cook, covered, for 3 minutes only, or the cherries will make too much liquid. Remove the lid, and cook for a further 2 minutes by which time the apples will have been absorbed into their redness. It doesn't matter if the cherries are not completely thawed at this stage.

6. Switch off the heat, stir in the vanilla and almond extracts, and turn the fruit into a 23cm round pie dish, or whichever ovenproof dish you plan on using.

7. You can let the fruit stand in the dish for up to 3 hours or leave it in the fridge for up to 5 days. When you want to bake the crumble, heat the oven to 190°C/170°C Fan. Top with the crumble mixture just before cooking. Try and scatter the crumble evenly over the fruit, without pressing down on it, and make sure you go right to the edges.

8. Sprinkle the flaked almonds on top and cook for 30 minutes by which time the filling will have bubbled up beautifully around the edges, the topping will be golden, and the flaked almonds toasted.

9. Let the crumble stand for 15 minutes or so, and then serve with cream, custard or ice cream, as you wish.

RICE PUDDING CAKE

This is every bit as wonderful as it sounds: an Italian *torta di riso*, refracted through the prism of someone who loves a bowl of very British rice pudding. The Italians like to stud their rice cake with candied peel, bake it in a tin lined with breadcrumbs or crushed amaretti, and eat it cold; I sprinkle mine with nutmeg, and serve it warm, most frequently with a jewel-bright jam sauce made by heating 200g of seedless raspberry jam with 2 tablespoons of lemon juice. And you might well consider adding a splosh of Chambord, too. But I love it equally paired with a rhubarb compote (see p.127) or drizzled with the blood orange syrup that drips brightly over the pavlova on p.242.

The rice pudding cake itself is time-consuming to make, but not difficult – the one is often confused for the other – and it more than repays the hour or so spent in the kitchen, and the number of bowls you'll get through.

You could make it with pudding rice, but I prefer not to: the larger grains of Arborio lend it a far better texture.

I'm very happy to eat leftovers cold, should I be lucky enough to get them (very much recommended for breakfast) but first time out, I feel, it must be warm, by which I mean to indicate a gentle warmth, rather nearer room temperature than hot. This means the cake is still quite tender, so I should caution you against trying to remove it from its base. I'm afraid this is not always advice I take myself: aesthetic considerations lead me to risk ruination by slipping my comedy cake lifter – which is like a ping-pong bat fashioned into a kitchen utensil – under it so that I can it transfer it to a serving plate with nothing to mar its simple beauty.

GIVES 8–12 slices

150g Arborio rice

700ml full-fat milk

¼ teaspoon fine sea salt

1 lemon

75g soft unsalted butter, plus more
  for greasing tin

3 large eggs, at room temperature

75g caster sugar

2 teaspoons vanilla extract

Nutmeg, for grating

For make-ahead, store and/or freeze notes, see p.335

1. Put the rice, milk and salt into a heavy-based saucepan – I use one of 18cm diameter – and finely grate the zest of the lemon into it. Over high heat, and stirring regularly, bring to the point where it looks like it's just about to boil, though do not let it actually boil. Turn the heat down to low, and continue to cook the milk and rice for about 30 minutes, stirring every now and then, until the rice is cooked and the milk is absorbed. Keep an eye on it, as you don't want the milk to start boiling, nor do you want the rice to stick to the bottom of the pan.

2. Take the pan off the heat, and stir in the 75g of butter until melted. Scrape the contents of the pan into a bowl large enough to take all the remaining ingredients. Leave for about 1 hour to cool. Once it's at room temperature, you can move on, so heat the oven to 160°C/140°C Fan, and butter a 20cm springform cake tin.

3. Separate the eggs, letting the whites fall into a large grease-free bowl (which could be the bowl of a freestanding mixer) and drop the yolks into a wide measuring jug (or a bowl). Whisk the whites until stiff, and set aside for a moment. Add the sugar to the yolks, and whisk – I use a balloon whisk with vigour, rather than an electric one here – until pale and moussy.

4. Add the vanilla extract and 2 teaspoons of juice from the zested lemon to the yolks and sugar, and then pour gradually into the cooled rice, folding it in well as you go.

5. Dollop a large spoonful of the stiffly whisked whites into the rice bowl and stir briskly to lighten the mixture, and then fold in a third of the remaining whites gently but thoroughly, then another third, and when that's incorporated, fold in the rest. Pour and scrape this mixture gently into the prepared tin.

6. Grate nutmeg over generously and bake for 45 minutes; by then the top will have set, with no hint of wobble underneath.

7. Sit on a wire rack for about 1 hour, until it's just slightly warm. To ease the unmoulding, slip a small spatula all around the edges, unclip the tin, and transfer the cake, still on its base (unless, like me, you don't mind risking damage trying to remove it), to a flat plate.

8. Serve each slice drizzled with a little of the glistening sauce mentioned in the recipe intro, or with the rhubarb compote on p.127 when in season.

BLOOD ORANGE AND PASSIONFRUIT PAVLOVA

If you're offered pudding in my house, there is a very high probability that it will be a pavlova. I am always ready to whisk up egg whites and bake them into crisp-edged, tender-bellied meringue, to be topped with softly whipped cream and sharp fruit.

I will, on occasion, forgo the fruit – for example in my cappuccino pavlova, where I add coffee to the meringue, and just a dusting of cocoa to the cream, or my lemon pavlova, which calls for curd, cream and toasted flaked almonds – but if added, it's vital that it balances the sweetness of the meringue base. Thus, I advise you, when blood oranges are not in season, against using ordinary eating oranges, which are too sweet to convey that crucial contrast. Instead, just double the amount of passionfruit, to make the pure perfect pavlova that made me fall in love with this pudding in the first place; though a grapefruit might indeed be a fierce enough substitute.

A quick note on the syrup: you don't absolutely need to add the orange zest to the juice, since you strain it out, but it seems a pointless waste not to. It boosts the flavour and deserves more than to end up in the bin. (If you're going for grapefruit, though, omit it.) It is a glorious concoction: if you don't have time or energy to make a pavlova, know that it is wonderful simply drizzled over good shop-bought vanilla or chocolate ice cream or, indeed, the No-Churn Cheesecake Ice Cream on p.235.

Known in my house as the Petite Pavlova, this is perfect when there's only two of you. It will certainly stretch to four without disappointment, but is a divine dessert when you're dining à deux.

And with the two egg yolks that this leaves you with, you can make a Crème Caramel (or indeed Crème Brûlée) for one (see p.87).

SERVES 2–4

FOR THE BASE

2 large egg whites, at room
 temperature

A pinch of fine sea salt

125g caster sugar

1 teaspoon cornflour

½ teaspoon white wine vinegar

FOR THE SYRUP

3–4 blood oranges

50g caster sugar

FOR THE TOPPING

2–3 blood oranges

150ml double cream

1–2 passionfruit to give about
 50ml (pulp and seeds)

For make-ahead, store and/or freeze notes, see p.335

1. Heat the oven to 180°C/160°C Fan. With a pencil, draw a
15cm diameter circle on a piece of baking parchment. Use the
parchment to line a baking sheet, putting it pencil-side down.

2. Whisk the egg whites and salt in a grease-free bowl until satiny
peaks form, and then beat in the sugar a spoonful at a time until
the meringue is stiff and shiny. The trick to getting the meringue
properly thick but still smooth and shiny is to whisk fast and
furiously but add the sugar slowly and serenely. Sprinkle over the
cornflour and the vinegar. Then gently fold them in.

3. Mound the meringue mixture onto the baking sheet inside the
outline of your circle, and smooth it patiently to the edges until you
have a thick, straight-sided, flat-topped disc, rather like the crown
of a boater.

4. Place in the oven, then immediately turn the temperature
down to 150°C/130°C Fan and cook for 40 minutes. Leave the
pavlova to cool in the switched-off oven, with the door ajar to
let out the residual heat. If you take the pavlova out too soon
the base will crack and collapse, so it's best to apply this gentler
cooling-down method.

5. To make the syrup, finely grate the zest from 2 of the blood
oranges into a small saucepan – I use one of 14cm diameter.
Squeeze the 3–4 oranges until you have 150ml juice, and add to
the saucepan, along with the sugar. Give everything a good stir,
then heat the pan until boiling, and let it boil for 5 minutes.
Strain the syrup into a small heatproof measuring jug, and I
implore you not to throw this zest away but eat it, just with a teaspoon; it tastes like fresh essence of marmalade. Pour the syrup
back into the pan, keeping the jug to hand, and continue boiling for about another 6 minutes or so until it has thickened and

reduced to about half the volume, leaving you with 75ml. Leave to cool in the measuring jug.

6. Now prepare the topping. With a small serrated knife, slice off the top and bottom of 2–3 blood oranges so that they sit flat on a board, then working from top to bottom, cut the peel and pith away from the rounded sides to reveal the flesh. Turn each orange on its side and slice into circles, and then cut some of those circles into smaller segments so you have a mixture of flower and petal shapes. Put the orange pieces in a bowl, or if you're not eating the pavlova the same day, seal in an airtight container.

7. When you're ready to eat and the pavlova base is cold, turn it onto a flat plate with the underside uppermost; this is so the tender marshmallow belly of the meringue melds with the soft topping.

8. Whip the cream until thick and airy but still soft, and spread on top of the pav base in a swirly mound, working the cream all the way to the edges so that it is evenly covered.

9. Halve the passionfruit and scoop the pulp onto the cream, then spoon over the orange pieces, letting the juice from both fill the swirls and dribble a little down the sides of the pav. Give the syrup a good stir and then drizzle a little over the top, pouring the rest into a dolls'-house-sized jug to serve alongside. If you don't have a jug small enough, pour it into an espresso cup with a coffee spoon on the saucer.

SUMMER PUDDING

This is the only pudding my mother ever made, and I think of her as I make mine, my hands stained quite as blue by the berries as hers always were. Of all of our traditional puddings, this is neither as well known abroad nor as frequently made at home as it really should be. It's true, I admit, that a dessert of compacted berries encased in bread is not an appealing proposition for those who haven't grown up on this seasonal treat, but all it takes is a mouthful to convince. Having fed it to various French and Italian friends over the years, I know this to be the case.

I should, however, say that my version is not the traditional one, which uses one part redcurrants to three parts raspberries. Not that I've ever eaten it in that duo-fruited red incarnation. My mother used any berry (excepting strawberry) she could get her hands on, and I do, too. In fact, I go further, adding cherries, which I am more than happy to pit for this. I have left blackcurrants in my list of ingredients, although they are sadly all but impossible to come by unless you grow your own (which I don't) since they are nearly all destined for cordial these days. But you can get lucky at greengrocers and farmers' markets.

Essentially, though, just bear in mind that you need 850g of berries for the 1.1 litre pudding basin (a 2 pint one, in old money) that I use here. Talking of which, I am also untraditional in my approach to this, forsaking the china pudding basin my mother used in favour of a bendy plastic one which makes unmoulding the pudding very much easier. I don't have any of the pâté weights she used to exert compacting pressure on the pud, so I balance a diminutive but still hefty cast-iron frying pan on top of mine, and on top of that a small (but very heavy) brass and marble pestle and mortar. I don't expect you to have the same accoutrements, and I'm not sure they are ideal in the first place, so try and find a plate that will fit as exactly as possible inside the rim of the basin on top of the pudding and then find the heaviest thing you've got to sit on it.

And for all that this is a summer pudding, I am peculiarly drawn to the idea of a Christmas variant, using frozen berries – a sprig of holly on top – in place of the Christmas Pudding. You'll need the same total weight of frozen summer berries, which come ready-mixed; though if the packets are 400g each, just get two, as the extra 50g is neither here nor there. The only difference between using fresh or frozen berries, in terms of the preparation, is that with frozen it'll take about 10 minutes to get them up to a simmer in the pan, with your stirring frequently to dislodge and mix the berries in the scant liquid. (You can see a picture of this wintry beauty on p.260.)

All that remains to be discussed is the bread. There is a time and a place for white-sliced: this is not it. Unfortunately, it just goes slimy rather than sodden though if you're eating it just a day after making it, it's manageable. And it's better than no Summer Pudding at all. I prefer to use a white tin loaf that has been put through the slicer in the bakery or supermarket. Unless you're good with a knife (which I am very much not) it is almost impossible to cut the bread into 12 evenly matched thin slices. Having said that, I know that the Old-Fashioned Sandwich Loaf on p.43 would be perfect here.

This is one of those puddings that absolutely has to be made at least a day ahead.

SERVES 4–6

250g redcurrants

100g blackcurrants (if unavailable,
  increase the quantity of raspberries or
  blackberries by this amount)

200g cherries (or replace with an extra
  150g of raspberries or blackberries)

200g blackberries

200g raspberries

75g caster sugar

125ml cold water

Approx. 12 thinnish (around 1cm) slices
  cut from a large loaf of white bread

TO SERVE

Fresh mint (optional)

Double cream (very much not)

For make-ahead, store and/or freeze notes, see p.335

1. Set aside a couple of clusters of redcurrants for serving. Strip the rest of the currants off their stalks and drop them into a large saucepan that comes with a lid. If you're are going to follow me down the untraditional route and use cherries, pit them over the pan so that you don't waste their wonderful juices. Add the rest of the berries, along with the sugar and water.

2. Bring the pan to a bubble over medium heat, which will take around 5 minutes (or twice that long for frozen berries). Once it begins to bubble, put on the lid, turn the heat to low and cook the fruit gently for 3–4 minutes; this is just to encourage them to exude their juices.

3. Cut the crusts off 10 slices of bread, and line the sides of a 2 pint (1.1 litre) plastic pudding basin with as many of the slices as you need, cutting others in half to fill in the triangular gaps.

4. Use a glass that has a diameter just a little bigger than the flat base of your dish to cut out a circle of bread for the base and press it down to sit inside the other slices of bread. And cut the crusts off the other 2 slices, ready for the top.

5. Take all the bread out of the basin and form a pattern or layout on your work surface in the order you lined the basin. And if you're not using a flexible plastic basin, you can line a china one with a generous overhang of clingfilm to aid umoulding later.

6. Put a ladleful of juice from the berry pan into a shallow dish and then take each slice in turn, beginning with the big pieces, and dip one side only of each slice into the juice, just to colour it. Line the bowl, purply-red side outwards.

7. Ladle out more juice as you need it: you don't want to wet the bread through, just to colour it on one side. Finish with the round bit of bread for the base, and have the slices for the top ready but not dipped yet.

8. Ladle in the fruit and juice from the pan to fill the basin. Let the mixture sit in the bread-lined basin for about 5 minutes, and then you'll be able to top up a little more.

9. Cut the reserved slices so that they will fit neatly on top, and dip them into a little of the remaining juice, before pressing them down on top, coloured side outwards, to make a lid. You'll have a little juice left, but you'll need it later.

10. Once the bread top is on the pudding, cover with food wrap, and sit a plate that fits neatly on it just inside the rim of the bowl, and put something heavy on top to weigh it down as it stands. Leave it out on the counter to cool.

11. Strain the leftover juices into a cup, cover and put in the fridge. The best thing to do with the fruit pulp in the sieve is eat it with cream now.

12. Put the cooled, weighted pudding in the fridge overnight or for up to 2 days, remembering to take it out in time to come to room temperature before serving.

13. Remove the weights, plate and food wrap, and if you're using a plastic basin, give it a gentle squeeze to help the pudding slip out shortly. It may help, too, to slide a small palette knife around the edges of the pudding at the top. Ready? Place your serving plate on top of the basin and then quickly and firmly flip it all, putting the plate on the work surface, with the upturned pudding basin on top. Give the basin another little squeeze and shake and then lift the basin up and off. If the circle of bread that was on the bottom of the basin does stick, gently remove it and place it on top of the turned-out pudding.

14. Using a silicon pastry brush, paint any patches of bread that have stayed white with the reserved juice, and decorate the top with the redcurrants you have set aside for this very purpose and, if you have it, a small sprig or two of fresh mint.

15. Slice into wedges rather like a cake, making sure everyone gets enough fruit, and serve with double cream in a jug.

BASQUE BURNT CHEESECAKE

I just can't stop making this. A lover of all cheesecakes, in every one of their manifestations, I had – I must admit – neither eaten nor heard of this until a few years ago. It was created, in fact, about three decades ago, by Santiago Rivera of La Viña in San Sebastian, and has for a while been the most modish of desserts in restaurants, as far as I can see, around the world, introduced here by Tomos Parry of Brat in East London.

This is my version, and while I don't have the wood-fired stove it was cooked in when I had my first taste of it, a hot oven at home creates it beautifully enough.

It is, I should say, very easy to make. There's no crust, it's just a wodge of tangy cheesecake that, although burnt on top, is only barely set in the middle. The hard thing is learning to take it out of the oven when it feels undercooked. At 45 minutes, in my oven at least, it is a disappointing pale gold; another 5 minutes, it appears suddenly, miraculously, burnished. But shake the tin and the centre of the cheesecake jiggles all over the place. It's supposed to: despite your doubts and fears, take it out of the oven now; don't give it a cautious further few minutes or it'll set too firm and compact when it's cold. I know you won't believe me, and the first time you make it, you'll overcook it. And I know that, because it's exactly what I did.

And, unlike most cheesecakes, this doesn't need to stand in the fridge overnight before you eat it. In fact, it very much mustn't, although you can sit it in there briefly, no more than 30 minutes, before you eat it. We're so used to eating cheesecake set and chilled over here that the texture of it at room temperature, or even slightly above, can seem strange at first. Naturally, you will have to keep any leftovers in the fridge, but for its grand unveiling, do try and preserve the tenderness of its texture. Half an hour in the fridge seems a respectful compromise, although in the cold of winter, even that won't be necessary. So choose a day when you're able to make it in the afternoon for the same day's supper.

I always used to eat this plain, with a glass of excellent sherry or, when in season, a rhubarb compote (p.127), but I recently had the version from Sabor in London, where the sublime Basque chef Nieves Barragán Mohacho serves it with a savagely intense, darkly glinting liquorice sauce, and there's no turning back. She very kindly told me how she made it. Quite rightly, Nieves uses Spanish liquorice pastillas, but it's much easier to find the Italian hard pure liquorice pellets over here. The amounts in the recipe below may give you more sauce than you need for the cheesecake, given that there are strange people who recoil from liquorice, but it lasts well and is just as thrilling over

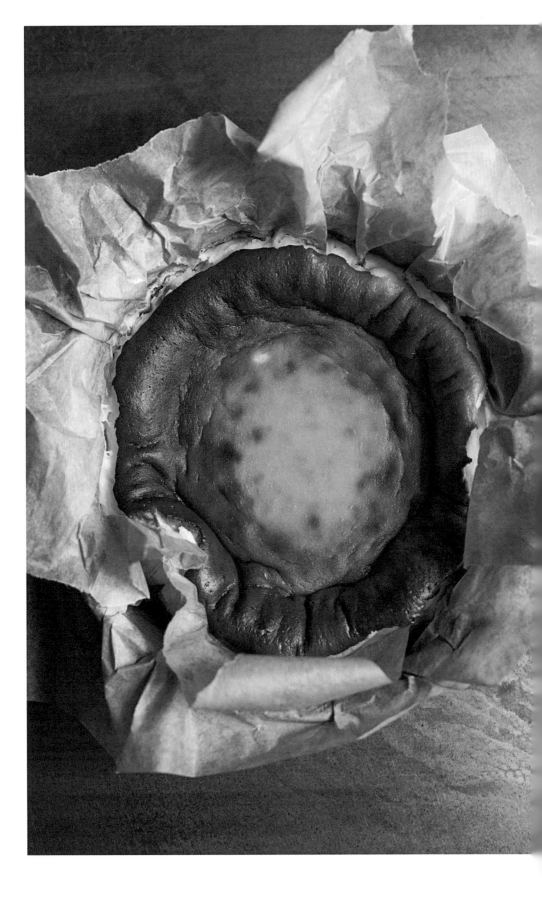

the No-Churn Cheesecake Ice Cream (p.235). I also feel moved to make the pavlova base from the recipe on p.244, topping it with softly whipped cream, blackberries and a shiny black liquorice zigzag of sauce.

BASQUE BURNT CHEESECAKE

GIVES 8–12 slices

FOR THE CHEESECAKE

600g full-fat cream cheese, at room
   temperature

175g caster sugar

3 large eggs, at room temperature

300ml sour cream, at room
   temperature

¼ teaspoon fine sea salt

25g cornflour

FOR THE SAUCE

15g hard pure liquorice pellets

90g caster sugar

300ml water

A pinch of fine sea salt (optional)

TO SERVE

Blackberries or other berries of your
   choice

For make-ahead, store and/or freeze notes, see p.335

1. Heat the oven to 200°C/180°C Fan. Get out a 20cm springform tin and a roll of baking parchment. Unfurl a long piece from the roll, and when it looks like you've got enough to line the tin with an overhang of 5–7cm, tear it off and press it into the tin, and down into the edges at the bottom. Now do the same again with a second piece, placing it perpendicular to the first so that the tin is entirely lined. Push this piece down, too, and don't worry about any pleats, creases and wrinkles; this is The Look. Sit something heavy in the tin to keep the paper in place while you get on with the cheesecake mixture.

2. I use a freestanding mixer fitted with the flat paddle for this, but you could easily use a large mixing bowl, wooden spoon and elbow grease. First beat the cream cheese with the sugar until light and smooth; I beat for quite a long time, certainly not under 2 minutes, and it would be at least 5 minutes by hand. It is absolutely essential – and I'm sorry to repeat myself – that the cream cheese is at room temperature before you start.

3. Beat in the eggs, one at a time, waiting for each one to be incorporated before adding the next, and when they're all mixed in, you can – beating all the while – pour in the sour cream.

4. Once that is also incorporated, you can slow down the mixer a little (or risk getting cornflour all over yourself) and then beat in the salt, followed by the cornflour, one teaspoon at a time. Remove

the bowl from the mixer, scrape down the sides with a silicon spatula, and give everything a good stir.

5. Pour into the lined tin (removing whatever's been sitting in it, obviously), making sure no cheesecake mix is left in the bowl, and then rap the filled tin on the work surface about five times to get rid of any air bubbles.

6. Place in the oven and bake for 50 minutes, by which time the cheesecake will be a burnished bronze on top, even chestnut brown in places, and it'll have risen, like a dense soufflé. It will, however, still be very jiggly. It's meant to be. You'll think it's undercooked, but it will carry on cooking as it cools, and it should have a soft set, anyway.

7. Remove the tin to a wire rack and leave to cool. It will sink in the middle a little, but that too is part of its traditional appearance. I reckon it's cool enough to eat after 3 hours, although you may need to leave it for a little longer. If you want to chill it in the fridge, do, but not for more than 30 minutes.

8. Make the liquorice sauce once the cheesecake is out of the oven. If you have a bullet blender, you can pulverise the liquorice pastilles first, but whether whole or powder, put in a small sauce-pan with the 300ml of water. Stir in the sugar, then put on a lowish flame until the liquorice has all but dissolved, stirring to give it a bit of a nudge every now and again to help it melt. Then turn up the heat and let bubble away until reduced to 150ml – turning the heat down a bit if it looks like it's boiling over. In a 14cm diameter pan, I find this can take up to 20 minutes. Keep checking – you'll need a small heatproof measuring jug by your side. Stir in a pinch of salt, if wished, and leave to cool, when it will have the texture of a syrup, which in effect, it is.

9. Before serving, unclip and lift the sides of the tin up and away, and then lift the cheesecake up with the edges of the parchment. Place this on a board, and peel the paper back, and take it like that, rustically beautiful, to the table, along with your blackberries and even blacker liquorice syrup. Just drizzle a little over the slices of cheesecake as you hand them out, allowing hardcore liquorice lovers to spoon more over as they eat.

VEGAN LEMON POLENTA CAKE

I'd been trying for a while to come up with a vegan version of my Lemon Polenta Cake, an old and particular favourite, as I've had so many requests from people who love it as much as I do, but who can no longer eat the original, with its butter and eggs, or have children who are vegan.

My experiments were successful, in that I had a recipe that worked, but not good enough in terms of recreating its glorious texture, that cornmeal-grainy custardiness, that makes it taste like lemon curd solidified – but only just – into cake.

As it so happens, the stars aligned, and just as I was about to give up, I saw, posted, a photograph of just such a vegan version by Katy Morgan, author of the Oat Milk & Cookies blog and who often posts with the hashtag #veganisingnigella. I asked her how she'd adapted it, she told me, I tried it and loved it. So here, with much gratitude, and only a little tinkering, it is. This is the story of the cross-pollination and creative collaboration that underpins cooking and the evolution of recipes.

You can never have too many lemon cakes in my book – which, after all, this is – and this one must surely be a near-universal pleaser, being dairy-free, egg-free and gluten-free; I dare say those who must also exclude nuts (what a cruel world this is) could replace the ground almonds with rice flour. If you need the cake to be gluten-free then do check that all of the ingredients are labelled gluten-free – brands can vary.

I should also say that I haven't had much success with it when I've used purer plant-based yogurts, delicious though they are; a standard commercial type seems to be necessary for the cake's structure. Soya milk is the one foodstuff I truly cannot get on with but its flavour is not detectable in the cake with the almond-soy yogurt I propose here.

I daresay you could replace the syrup with the lemon and elderflower drizzle on p.76, if you felt so minded.

GIVES 8–12 slices

150g ground almonds

150g fine polenta (not instant)

2 teaspoons baking powder

½ teaspoon bicarbonate of soda
(gluten-free if necessary)

¼ teaspoon fine sea salt

100ml light olive oil, plus a little extra
for greasing the tin

200g caster sugar

2 large lemons, at room temperature

250ml almond-milk plain soy yogurt, at
room temperature

75g icing sugar

TO SERVE (OPTIONAL)

Berries of your choice

For make-ahead, store and/or freeze notes, see p.335

1. Heat the oven to 180°C/160°C Fan, and line and lightly grease the sides of a 20cm springform cake tin. Measure the ground almonds and polenta into a bowl, add the baking powder, bicarb, and salt, and fork to mix.

2. Pour the oil into a wide-necked large measuring jug, add the sugar and finely grate the zest of the 2 lemons on top. Stir together for a minute, then beat in the yogurt until completely incorporated. Then simply pour your jug of wet ingredients into your bowl of dry ingredients, making sure everything is completely mixed.

3. Scrape into the prepared tin, and bake in the oven for about 40 minutes, until the cake is beginning to nudge away from the sides of the tin, and a cake tester comes out clean. Make the syrup, though, as soon as the cake goes in the oven.

4. Put the icing sugar into a small saucepan and add 75ml of juice from your zested lemons. Heat, whisking gently to beat out any lumps, just until the sugar's dissolved into the juice, and pour straightaway into a little jug to cool.

5. When the cake's cooked, transfer it to a wire rack and, with your cake tester, prick it all over, going in deep, to help the syrup run down into the cake. Pour or spoon the syrup over, trying to be patient, so the syrup doesn't just make a large pond on top.

6. Leave the cake, drenched with its syrup, to cool and, before unclipping, run a slim palette knife round the edges to help dislodge it where the syrup has stuck it to the tin. If you don't feel confident of getting the cake off the base in one piece, don't worry. Serve the cake plain, or with berries of your choice.

CHRISTMAS COMFORTS

Whether you see the words 'cook, eat, repeat' as a reassuring reminder of a routine that provides solace and structure, anchoring us in what truly matters in life, or as a draining encapsulation of the drudgery of cooking, you will find much at Christmastime to confirm your views. Even those of us vehemently in the former camp cannot deny the encroaching exhaustion so dreaded by the latter. In truth, I exult in the cooking, but I can get worn down by all the planning and the never-ending clearing up. And yet, at the time of writing, under lockdown and unsure of how expansive Christmas celebrations might actually be in 2020, I feel a wistful pang for those frenziedly mapped-out schedules and shopping lists, those cluttered surfaces, messy tables, even those ever-full kitchen sinks and roasting pans on perma-soak.

But even curtailed Christmas celebrations in my house will, I know, rely on repetition and, what's more, we'll luxuriate in it. We human beings need ritual; for me, at Christmas that need is met in cooking and at the table. All families create their own traditions. They're the ones that make you wake early in overexcitement as a child, the ones you feel stifled by in your adolescence, that you remember either in horror or in the glow of nostalgia as you get older. And then there are the ones you create yourself, allowing the cycle to start up all over again.

This is not only about the food, of course. It's about the same jokes and the same rows; about when you put up the tree, and which decorations you hang on it; what time you open presents, and the film you watch after lunch (*The Sound of Music*). It all matters.

This year there will be some changes: the tree may well go up earlier than usual, for longer wallowing in the season, and there will be more fairy lights and candles everywhere. Some things cannot change: I will never renounce my traditional Christmas lunch menu; that is Untouchable. But I've written about it so much over the years, I scarcely feel the need to replay it here now, for all that the title of this book would seem to invite it. Anyway, the truth is, as long as I have my children around my table, I could eat gruel and be happy.

Ritual is important, but we cannot always rely on the past to give meaning to the present. Life has to be about making new memories, too. So my celebrations this year will centre around a Christmas Eve feast, a dinner that is at the heart of this chapter. I suspect that my customary cocktail, Poinsettia (a bottle of Prosecco or Cava mixed with 125ml of Cointreau or Grand Marnier and 500ml of cranberry juice), will come into play on the 25th, so for festivities the evening before, Pomegranate Fizz it is.

Along with a pitcher of this bubbling, blush-coloured cocktail, dinner will kick off by the fire with black bread and smoked salmon and a fairly restrained plateful of Black Treacle Sausages, to make way, once at the table, for the Norwegian Pork Ribs, Roast Quinces, Pickled Red Cabbage, Scandi Cucumber Salad, my House Special Slow-Cooked Peas, and the Parmesan version of Jansson's Temptation.

And for pudding, I plan a bonanza, the triple treat of the winter version of the Summer Pudding (the explanation for which I'll come to later) that, in this festive guise, illustrates the opening of this very chapter, the candlelit Black Forest Brownies and an absurdly Christmassy platter of Linzer Cookies.

It's such an easy menu: the bread, quinces, pickled cabbage, cucumber salad and peas can all be made – and the Jansson's Temptation assembled and ready to bake – ahead of time.

But no matter the menu itself, what is essential for me at Christmas (although it is always a rewarding and important factor in the way I cook and eat) is a particular expression of the rule of repetition that so many decry: I'm talking leftovers. I'm made happy by unwrapping ever-more crunkled foil packages; like my mother before me, I measure out the days by decanting food into ever smaller bowls and tubs. A festive fridge forage is a particular joy: this time of year is for me a hallowed time for sandwiches.

This is partly the reason my Fermented Hot Sauce features in this chapter. Yes, I need this to splodge searingly in sandwiches (and to enliven leftovers) but it also happens to make the perfect Christmas present. I'd always rather spend an evening in my kitchen than brave the shops, this year especially so. Just remember to get fermenting two weeks (or longer, if that's easier) before you plan to hand over the flame-filled jars to friends who, I am willing to bet, will thenceforth request it becomes an annual tradition.

And while you have only to see the Ruby Noodles to understand how spectacularly they fit into any festive menu, they are here, too, for the same reason the Tuscan Bean Soup is: even committed carnivores can find the festive *Fleischfest* a little heavy-going without the odd meatless meal. Besides, this soup warms you when you're cold, and bolsters you when you're fragile; I consider

it a seasonal necessity, no less than I do the Luscious Vegan Gingerbread (especially good with the Pomegranate-Poached Quinces) and Christmas Bread and Butter Pudding. And, as the season ends, I joyously propose the new year be celebrated with doughnuts, a Dutch tradition I am all-too-eager to adopt. And by the way, I haven't given page references to any recipes that are in this chapter as you can find them easily by flicking through the following pages.

I cannot – even with the prospect of small-scale celebrations this year – say that my entire Christmas menu will be contained in the recipes that follow. As well as reaching back to the past, I also have plans for food from other chapters in this book, taking in – but not limited to – the Beef Cheeks with Port and Chestnuts (p.112); the beetroot soup from p.152, only with cranberries standing in for the rhubarb; the Roast Red Peppers with Pomegranate Molasses (p.202); Spiced Bulgur Wheat with Roast Vegetables (p.181); Roast Cauliflower with Apricot Harissa and Spinach (p.216); Celeriac Remoulade and Caesar Mayo (p.23 and p.16); the Burnt Onion and Aubergine Dip (p.96), repurposed as the most divine sandwich spread; the Brown Butter Colcannon from p.209, which I hope will yield, too, cheesy patties for a late breakfast or an even-later night-time fry-up; the snowy-spiked Toasted Marshmallow and Rhubarb Cake (p.144); and, of course, but of course, the Rhubarb and Custard Trifle from p.138, also to be considered (as mooted in the intro to that recipe) with frozen berries or cherries, should rhubarb either elude or unfathomably fail to enchant you. And, while we're on frozen berries and cherries, if it sounds odd (to all but those in the southern hemisphere) for me to be suggesting you make the Summer Pudding from p.246, I have never forgotten Jane Grigson writing in her *Fruit Book* that friends of hers always made summer pudding with frozen fruit at Christmas, and I cannot think of a better suggestion. A little bit of holly on top – though no setting alight – and this would be fabulously festive, and a light and bright alternative for Christmas Pudding haters, and for many of the rest of us besides. Should you want something even easier, then I have no hesitation in sending you urgently towards the No-Churn Cheesecake Ice Cream and the Cherries Jubilee, both to be found on p.235. What better way to celebrate, sweetly and simply, this time of fire and ice?

NORWEGIAN PORK RIBS

You are in for such a treat. This recipe has utterly changed the way I customarily cook pork belly now. In truth, I had come across this Norwegian pork rib roast before, as I spent quite a lot of time in Norway when I was a young child, but I had no idea then how it was cooked and had long since forgotten about it. Actually, it is not just the cooking that is radically different, but also its preparation, and for this you will need to ask the butcher for pork belly on the bone – so far so unremarkable – and for them to saw through the bones in two lines lengthways, as if about to divide the pork into three equal, long strips; however, you do not want them to go so far, they just need to cut through the bones, but not deep into the meat. On serving, you simply and so easily cut the belly into chunky slabs of ribs. You also need them to score the rind, and if possible not in the customary narrow diamond pattern, but to make small squares: in other words, you want them to score the rind into lines 2cm apart both vertically and horizontally. Or, if you fancy a bit of light surgery later, you can do that bit yourself: it'll be easy enough when you come to it, I promise. And I speak as the most cack-handed of cooks.

This is the cut of pork eaten on Christmas Eve in Norway; I plan to follow suit in London this year and, I rather think, for every year of grace I'm granted. There, it is generally seasoned with no more than salt and pepper; I have added garlic, juniper berries and dill, which keeps us in Nordic territory. But this cut has application far outside those borders: I'm thinking sage, shallots and English mustard powder; cumin, coriander, chilli and ginger; miso, soy and garlic; thyme, lemon and Dijon; even just a rich, red massage of gochujang, the Korean fermented red chilli paste, would be wonderful.

With dill and juniper berries scenting the meat for the roast, I have planned my menu around it. I'm not a starter person, but I do like a pre-drink, stomach-lining slice or two of the No-Knead Black Bread (p.305), spread with horseradish-spiked cream cheese and smoked salmon draped silkily on top. If you want a proper sit-down starter, you could serve the Beetroot, Rhubarb and Ginger Soup, seasonally substituting the rhubarb with cranberries (see the recipe intro on p.152). With these pork ribs themselves, you need do no more than the Pickled Red Cabbage (p.281), Scandi Cucumber Salad (p.283), the Roast Quinces (p.278), and some plain boiled or steamed potatoes with lots of butter, white pepper and dill, and quite possibly, even probably, the Fennel Gratin from p.214. It is a feast, but a simple one, celebrating what's important and keeping seasonal stress at bay.

Of course, you could always lean across to Norway's neighbour and serve the Swedish Jansson's Temptation (p.275) alongside. And I cannot deny that the Root Vegetable Mash (p.206) would be glorious here, too. But either of these additions keep matters manageable: both of them can be made in advance.

It is not out of a desire to cut corners that I say this, but I do not want gravy here. This pork rib roast really doesn't need it, and I'm not sure it suits it. I much prefer the softly lapping cream sauce from the Fennel Gratin or indeed from the Jansson's Temptation, known in my house as Chip Gratin. You could also put a bowl of rhubarb sauce (the recipe for which is on p.135) on the table, and I rather favour a concoction comprising equal parts of redcurrant jelly and wholegrain mustard mixed together.

I reckon on a 3kg joint being enough, generously, for four to six good eaters, with essential leftovers. And just so you know, the 3kg piece I go for measures around 28 x 20–22cm (it won't be a neat oblong), so the size of the roasting tin you have will also dictate how big a piece you can get.

One last thing: if the pork you get from the butcher is wrapped not in paper but plastic, remove it, and wrap in baking parchment before putting it into the fridge.

SERVES 4–6 with leftovers

2.5–3kg bone-in belly pork, prepared
  as per instructions in recipe intro

3 fat cloves of garlic

3 x 15ml tablespoons sea salt flakes
  (or 1½ x 15ml tablespoons fine
  sea salt)

1 teaspoon juniper berries

A large bunch (or 2 x 20g
  supermarket packets) of dill

2 onions

250ml hot water from a just-boiled
  kettle

For make-ahead, store and/or freeze notes, see p.335

1. You need to take the pork out of the fridge about an hour
before you cook it so factor that into your timetable, adding it to
the 3 hours, give or take, that the pork will be in the oven. For now,
unwrap it and lay it rind-side down on a large chopping board.

2. Peel the garlic cloves and drop them into the mortar part of a
pestle and mortar, or into a bowl you can use with a stick blender.
Add 2 tablespoons of the sea salt flakes (or 1 tablespoon of fine
sea salt), the juniper berries and the stalks from your dill, and start
either bashing, grinding and crushing or whizzing, as you prefer,
until you have an aromatic green paste. It's harder work with a
pestle and mortar, but I adore making it this way: it makes my
kitchen smell, rather invigoratingly, like a Nordic spa.

3. Take this mixture over to the pork, and where the butcher has
sawn through the bones, you will have two long troughs to tuck the
paste into. Run a knife through them if you need to open up the cut
area a little more. Press the mixture evenly between them.

4. Push as many of the dill fronds into the paste as you can fit. Turn
the pork rind side up. Rub the rind and sides of the pork with the
remaining 1 tablespoon of sea salt flakes, (or 1½ teaspoons of fine
sea salt).

5. Get out a large roasting tin – I use one measuring 34 x 37 x 5cm.
Peel the onions, then cut each of them into 3 thick slices; you need
these as a flavour platform, to prop up the pork. One end must
be slightly higher than the other, so that any liquid pours off and
doesn't pool on the rind, so place the pork, rind-side up, on the
onions, arranging the slices as you feel best achieves that.

6. Leave the pork in the tin for about 1 hour to lose its fridge chill
and, when you're not long off, heat the oven to 220°C/200°C Fan.

7. Pour the 250ml of just-boiled water into the roasting tin, cover
the top tightly with foil, and cook in the hot oven for 45 minutes.

It's counter-intuitive, I know, but softening the rind now makes it crisp up unimaginably later.

8. When it's had its 45 minutes, take the pork out of the oven and remove the foil; the rind should have softened and puffed up a little. Use a large sharp knife to define the squares on the rind, cutting a little deeper into the original scoring marks. Or if you didn't get it done by the butcher, do your own scoring at this point, cutting the softened rind into 2cm squares; it's a curiously pleasant sensation.

9. Turn the oven down to 170°C/150°C Fan. Put the pork back into the oven without the foil, but make sure first that it's still perched, one end higher than the other, on the slices of onion.

10. Give the pork 2 ½ hours at this temperature, by which time much of the fat should have rendered down, melting lusciously into the meat, and less lusciously into the tin, and the rind will be beginning to crackle. But if, when you poke the tip of a knife into the pork, it doesn't feel tender yet, leave it in for another 30 minutes.

11. Turn the oven back up to 220°C/200°C Fan, and give the pork around 15 minutes – or a little longer if needed, but keep watch to make sure the rind doesn't go too far and burn – until the crackling is deep gold and crunchy, and some of the little squares may have popped up.

12. Take the pork out of the oven and remove carefully to a carving board. Cut through both sides of each rib, down to where the butcher cut through the bones, to get a chunky rib section for each person. The crackling on the pork may make this tricky, so you can use poultry shears or kitchen scissors to cut through it – the splintering noise is rather splendid – before slicing down into the meat. This way each rib section gets a proper piece of crackling. Because the meat has to be so heavily salted to boost juiciness and flavour, most of the onions will be far too salty to serve. One or two will be perfect though, and divinely sticky with pork fat; you can share these out meagrely now, eat them yourself, or save them for sandwiches later.

I build leftovers into my portion plan (a notional rather than meticulously devised strategic document) any time I'm deciding what to cook, and thus to shop for, but at Christmas this is the very linchpin of functional family life.

Perhaps my love of having the same meal all over again so soon after eating it the first time is idiosyncratic, but I – in the first instance – gladly reheat the pork and a quince slice or two, bring the pickled cabbage and cucumber salad out of the fridge, and perhaps ring the changes by baking a potato. Of course, you can microwave a portion or so of the pork at a time, but I prefer to put a piece or two in a small tin, splash in some water, to which I may add some sake, soy sauce and chilli (sauce or flakes), then put in a fierce oven (220°C/200°C Fan), until the meat is hot all the way through (the liquid in the base of the tin will make sure it's tender and succulent) and the crackling will be crunchy. To be fair, it stands up well in the microwave, too. If you're reheating more than one portion in a proper oven, then I'd cover with foil for the first 10 minutes.

But a sandwich is what I always look forward to most. I want thick, soft white bread cut from a sandwich loaf (p.43) or taken from a packet of ready-sliced; the bread should be spread with mayo mixed with the leftover redcurrant and mustard sauce (or mango chutney) and some Fermented Hot Sauce (p.300); the pork must be hot; if there are any cooked and cold potatoes lying around, they will be reheated and mashed up with a fork with butter, a spritz of lime and some hastily chopped coriander, and wodged in too, although I'm also in favour of a cold wedge or two of roasted quince instead of the reheated potatoes; the only other filling the sandwich needs before you clamp on the top slice of bread is some of the cucumber salad (well drained) and pickled cabbage, but were you to have any pink-pickled onions about the place (and see p.61), then I'd recommend squeezing them in, too. And a soft bun is perfectly acceptable in place of the bread.

It's only a short shift sideways to turn this sandwich into truly wonderful tacos. I shred the pork and put it in a small frying pan – you don't need any oil as the pork has enough lovely fat as it is – and toss it about over high-ish heat until it's very hot, golden brown and gorgeously crisp in places. Then I turn the heat down a little and stir in some minced garlic, sweet smoked paprika and a pinch of cumin, and squeeze over lime juice and a spritz of orange or, indeed, clementine or satsuma juice; I tend to eat the crackling cold as I linger languidly stoveside, but you could certainly give it a nuke in the microwave and drop or crumble it on top of the pork when you're assembling your taco. Talking of which, what I want in mine is some coriander, avocado, Pickled Red Cabbage (p.281), pink-pickled onions or chopped spring onions, my hot sauce and some shredded iceberg; if you have any pineapple (fresh or tinned) in the house, you could do worse than toss some small cubes of it with chilli flakes, grated ginger, salt and lime, and invite it to the party, too. Heat a few tortillas in a hot, dry pan, and feast with joy in your heart.

Or you can reheat the pork as for the taco, then roll it up in its tortilla – adding cooked rice, coriander, pickled jalapeños, black beans, avocado, and salsa or hot sauce – to make a burrito.

The pork – shredded and reheated in a pan with a little water, sake, fish sauce and soy – is also wonderful with noodles. I prefer rice noodles, but any will do. Prepare them as directed on the packet, then stir-fry some garlic, chilli and spring onions in a wok, throwing in a handful of sliced mushrooms if you have any. Add the soaked or cooked noodles, then pour over some miso which you've mixed with water, grated ginger, a little rice vinegar and a drop of sesame oil, toss well and quickly, and add the pork, toss again, and sprinkle with chopped coriander.

And then there is stir-fried rice, friend equally to the hungover and the leftover. Stir-fry spring onions, garlic and ginger in a hot wok, add shredded pork, whatever vegetables you need to use up (if you have any sprouts left over from Christmas lunch, halve them and bung them in) and toss in the pan until hot. Add cold cooked rice (and, as suggested earlier for the tacos, some pineapple if you have some, and the idea appeals) and stir-fry until piping hot. Sprinkle in some soy sauce and, if you've got any kimchi, roughly chop as much or as little as you feel like, add it to the pan, then pour in some of the kimchi juice. If you haven't got any kimchi, and have made the Fermented Hot Sauce, just dilute it with a little water, add that to your wok and toss to mix, along with chopped chives and coriander. Though you can just splodge the hot sauce – and this goes for any hot sauce of your choice – over the rice as you eat. Top with a fried or poached egg as your head or heart desires.

JANSSON'S TEMPTATION

What with this and the Norwegian Pork Ribs (p.265) and Scandi Cucumber Salad (p.283), there is certainly a pronounced if modest Nordic element to my proposals for your Christmas menu; this influence takes in the Pickled Red Cabbage (p.281) as well, which is as much part of our home-grown repertoire.

Jansson's Temptation – *Janssons Frestelse*, to give it its correct name (and the Jansson is pronounced Yonnson) – is very much the taste of Christmas for Swedes, and I have enthusiastically incorporated it into my own festive eating schedule. In Sweden it would be part of the *julbord*, coming after (among other dishes) the smoked salmon and pickled herring, the cold ham, liver pâté, creamy beetroot salad and cheese, and to be eaten alongside meatballs, sausages, pork ribs and cabbage.

And while I do, indeed, serve it with the Norwegian Pork Ribs, it is so addictively good, I am happy to make a main meal out of it, with no more than a salad or two on the side. The Scandi Cucumber Salad and Pickled Red Cabbage are obvious contenders. But any bitter leaves – the pale jade of escarole, rubied radicchio – would be perfect. It may seem odd that I suggest what is give or take a potato gratin for a main course. But I convince myself that since it contains sprats, it is not so very dissimilar to a fish pie, only with the fish element rather reduced.

Talking of the fish, you may have come across Jansson's Temptation described as a potato and anchovy dish. But in fact, the Swedish *ansjovis* are sprats rather than anchovies, not a completely different kettle of, but different enough. Significantly, they are less salty and intense, having a lighter, sweeter cure than anchovies; it might be more accurate to describe them as pickled. I get mine from my usual online supermarket but otherwise you can get them from specialist Scandinavian food websites.

Most Swedes add the liquid from the cans of fish to the dish as well; I prefer not to, letting the flavour of the *ansjovis* punctuate the sweetness of the potatoes, cream and onions rather than merge with it. I apologise to any Swede who disapproves of this omission. And I should say that I am very grateful to Ingrid Soläng, who answered my queries, steered me right, and was even under-standing (I think) of my decision to temper the fishy force of this dreamy dish.

And if you are surrounded by fishphobes, as I often am, you can actually leave the sprats out altogether, though you'd need to season well in their absence; I also add 3 tablespoons (20g) of grated Parmesan to the cream. It will, of course, no longer be Jansson's Temptation, but a very fine potato gratin, which is nothing to apologise for in and of itself, though I suggest you never ever serve it like that to a Swede.

SERVES 4–6

2 large onions (approx. 400g)

4 x 15ml tablespoons (60g) butter,
plus more for greasing

A good grinding of pepper

2 x 125g tins of Swedish *ansjovis*
(see recipe intro)

300ml full-fat milk

2 teaspoons sea salt flakes, plus
½ teaspoon (or 1 teaspoon fine sea
salt, plus ¼ teaspoon)

1.25kg potatoes

300ml double cream

2–3 x 15ml tablespoons breadcrumbs
(optional)

For make-ahead, store and/or freeze notes, see p.335

1. Peel the onions and slice into fine half-moons, and melt
3 tablespoons of the butter in a large frying pan; I use a non-stick
one of 28cm diameter. Add the onions to the pan, sprinkle with the
½ teaspoon of sea salt flakes (or ¼ teaspoon of fine sea salt) and
stir for a few minutes over medium-high heat. Once they start to
lose their raw look, turn the heat down to low and cook very gently
for 15–20 minutes. Keep an eye on them, and stir regularly: they
should be soft and pale gold. If you think they are beginning to
catch, you can sprinkle a very little water into the pan, or simply
add more butter. Once they're ready, use a bendy spatula to scrape
them and their buttery juices into a bowl to stop them burning in
the hot pan.

2. Meanwhile, heat the oven to 200°C/180°C Fan. Butter an oven
dish of about 2½ litres capacity; I use one (an old friend that you
may have seen in a few of my books) of 34 x 20 x 6cm.

3. Peel the potatoes, cut them into narrow strips rather like French
fries, then mound them into three roughly equal piles.

4. Put a third of the potatoes into the bottom of the buttered dish.
Season with 1 teaspoon of sea salt flakes (or ½ teaspoon of fine sea
salt) and a good grinding of pepper.

5. Spread half the soft onions over the potato strips, followed by
one tin of *ansjovis*; it is up to you whether you add the liquid in the
tin or not (see recipe intro).

6. And now layer up again: so, the second third of potatoes, salt
and pepper as before, followed by the rest of the onions and the
second tin of *ansjovis*.

7. Top with the final third of potatoes, then mix together the milk
and cream in a jug and pour it over, although it won't cover the
potatoes completely. Push any that are poking up down into the

creamy milk, just so that they're lightly covered, but don't worry if they pop up again.

8. Sprinkle over the breadcrumbs if using (I confess I forgot to add them for the photo on p.274) and dot over the remaining tablespoon of butter, then bake in the oven for 1 hour, making sure you check at 45 minutes; push a fork in, and if it meets with no resistance, the potatoes are cooked. They'll certainly be golden on top, but it's essential they're soft underneath.

9. The gratin will stand for a while until needed, and tastes just as good, if not better, warm rather than hot. Leftovers are easily reheated for repeated rapture. For many Swedes – and those of us who are not Swedish – it is these reheated leftovers that are the real Christmas treat.

ROAST QUINCES

I am always happy when I have quinces in my kitchen: their heady, honeyed perfume, mixed with a floral citrusiness that prevents its becoming cloying, is better than the most expensive scented candle in the world. They used to be hard to come by if you didn't have a quince tree in your garden, but now they seem to come proudly to the shops in November and December, and you should make the most of them.

This recipe is where I propose you start. It could scarcely be simpler. I've been cooking with quinces for decades now, but only recently have I done this little to them to such great effect. It is hardly a recipe: all I am suggesting you do is cut these pregnant pears, as the writer Bee Wilson describes them, into long wedges and roast them with some olive oil in a hot oven. I often roast them in duck fat (and they are also utterly wonderful with duck itself, as they are with lamb, too), but here, with the pork, I reach for the oil.

The last time I cooked these, I was trying to explain what they were to someone who'd never come across a quince before, and I said he should think of them as a cross between a parsnip and a pear. This makes no sense botanically, but it conjures up the sweet graininess of their flesh, even if it misses the sharpness that is just as much an essential part of what they bring. Indeed, you could so easily roast quinces in place of the traditional parsnips to go with your Christmas turkey.

But should you not be able to get quinces, then do roast some parsnips to go with the pork. In which case, I suggest that you use 750g of parsnips, peel them, cut them into familiar chunks, and arrange them on a baking tray. Now – and this is my new go-to – mix together 2 teaspoons of the Apricot Harissa from p.218 (or use harissa from a jar) with 3 tablespoons of olive oil and pour this over the parsnips, turning them well to coat. Sprinkle with salt, and roast them in an oven at 200°C/180°C Fan for 30–45 minutes, depending on their size. Once they're ready, drizzle over 2 teaspoons of honey and pop them back into the oven for a final 5–10 minutes. Should you at any time over Christmas be passing round a plate of Black Treacle Sausages (p.290), make these Harissa Parsnips for any vegetarians or vegans present. I can eat a plateful all by myself.

The quinces need no spicing, however: they are poetically perfect just as they are. I roast them the day before I'm doing the pork, as then all I have to do is reheat them for 15 minutes or so in their tray on a shelf below the pork when it's having its final blast. And you could do exactly the same if you are parsnipping rather than quincing.

Once you have made these simple roast beauties, it may be time for you to move on to the Pomegranate-Poached Quinces on p.319.

4 x 15ml tablespoons (60ml) olive oil
(or other fat of your choice)

For make-ahead, store and/or freeze notes, see p.335

1. If you have small quinces, quarter them; if large, cut them into eighths. I neither peel nor core them, though if they're covered in fuzz, wipe or wash it off, depending on how you feel about such matters. Go carefully as you take a knife to them: they are brutes to cut into.

2. Heat the oven to 200°C/180°C Fan, and pour the oil into a lipped baking sheet. If you're using duck fat, or anything else that's solid, then pop the tray into the oven so the fat can melt.

3. Schmoosh the quince wedges in the oil, and then leave flat on the tray and roast for about 45 minutes (though they are more likely to need an hour), turning them after they've had 30 minutes. It's very difficult to say exactly how long they'll take, as they vary enormously; the colour they turn as they cook can differ wildly, too. But when they're ready, they should be gloriously burnished, and feel tender if you pierce one with a fork.

PICKLED RED CABBAGE

Soft, soused, slow-braised red cabbage has been part of my Christmas table forever. I haven't completely forsaken it, but – and I'm only going to whisper it – I think this pickle has now become quite my favourite way of eating red cabbage. It's barely any work to make and is so much better than the pickled red cabbage that you buy from a shop.

I do think it makes a difference using the raw, unfiltered vinegar, which is labelled rather tautologically 'apple cider vinegar', but if all you have is regular cider vinegar, go ahead; indeed, any vinegar would work here. I pair the cider vinegar with actual cider but should you not want to use cider itself, then replace it with apple juice.

This doesn't make a huge amount, but it is a condiment rather than a vegetable accompaniment, and it will give you enough to go with the pork and any leftovers you may be wanting to zhuzh. Besides, you will soon find yourself making up batches of this ludicrously purple pickle in regular rotation.

You need to make this 2 days (or up to 3 weeks) before you eat it.

FILLS 1 x 750ml jar

500g red cabbage

35g fine sea salt

200ml medium dry cider (or apple juice)

400ml raw, unfiltered apple cider vinegar

2 x 15ml tablespoons (25g) caster sugar

2 teaspoons peppercorns

2 teaspoons juniper berries

1 teaspoon mustard seeds

½ teaspoon dried thyme

2 fat cloves of garlic

25g fresh ginger

For make-ahead, store and/or freeze notes, see p.335

1. Sterilise a 750ml (although a 1 litre one will be fine) preserving jar. I consider a jar sterilised if it's come straight out of the dishwasher and not so much as a finger has touched the inside of it. But you can just hand wash the jar in soapy liquid, rinse it well, and dry it in a 140°C/120°C Fan oven. Leave to cool before filling.

2. Remove the core, then slice the red cabbage finely and put into a colander. Sprinkle over the salt and gently toss the cabbage to get it all coated, then leave over a bowl for 3 hours. Do not be tempted to leave out this step. It makes all the difference.

3. Make the pickling liquid as soon as the cabbage is in the colander. Put the cider and vinegar into a saucepan, and add the sugar, peppercorns, juniper berries, mustard seeds and thyme.

4. Peel both the garlic and ginger, cut them into thinnish slices, and add them to the saucepan. Give everything a good stir, bring gently to the boil, then turn up the heat, and let it bubble away for 2 minutes, switch the heat off and leave everything in the pan to cool.

5. When the cabbage has had its 3 hours, get out a large chopping board and lay a tea towel you don't mind staining on top of it. Take the colander to the sink and rinse the cabbage really well under the cold tap. Squeeze as much water as you can out of it, then spread it out on the tea towel and wrap it and pat it dry.

6. Put the cabbage into your sterilised jar, pushing it down so that it is tightly packed. Strain the pickling liquid into a jug, using a fine-mesh sieve so nothing drops through, and pour over the cabbage, then press down on the cabbage to submerge it all.

7. Put it into the fridge and leave for at least 2 days before eating it. In theory, it will keep happily for 3 weeks, but it is unlikely that you will have any left by then. Always remember to take it out of the fridge in time to get the chill off it before eating.

SCANDI CUCUMBER SALAD

My maternal grandmother had an enduring love affair for all things Scandinavian, and I rather think she passed it on to me. This salad is very like the one that adorned her table, though a bit less sweet, and it makes me smile inwardly as I both prepare and eat it: family memories are so evocatively conveyed through food; a connection we carry with us always.

SERVES 4–6 or fills 1 x 750ml jar

300ml raw, unfiltered apple cider vinegar

2 x 15ml tablespoons (25g) caster sugar

2 x 15ml tablespoons (10g)
 coriander seeds

1 teaspoon peppercorns

A small bunch of fresh dill (approx. 20g)

2 cucumbers (approx. 700g)

2 teaspoons fine sea salt

For make-ahead, store and/or freeze notes, see p.336

1. Sterilise a 750ml (although a 1 litre one will be fine) preserving jar either by putting it through the dishwasher, or by washing it in soapy water, rinsing it and then drying it in a 140°C/120°C Fan oven. Either way, let it cool before filling.

2. Put the vinegar into a saucepan with the sugar, coriander seeds and peppercorns. Tear the leaves from your bunch of dill, and drop the stalks into the pan, reserving the fronds. Give the vinegar a good stir, then gently bring to the boil, and let it bubble – but not too vociferously – for 2 minutes. Switch off the heat, and let everything cool down in the pan.

3. You don't need to peel the cucumbers, but you do need to slice them very thinly. I use a mandolin for this; if you want to do likewise, I must insist you wear a cut-resistant glove as you do so. Or don't go down to the very end of the cucumber.

4. Put the finely sliced cucumber into a very large mixing bowl and, with your hand just above the bowl, sprinkle in the salt. Toss gently together, before leaving to stand for 30 minutes. When the time's up, finely chop enough of the reserved dill to give you about 3 tablespoons' worth.

5. Squeeze the cucumber slices in your hands over the bowl to get rid of excess water, leaving a dazzlingly vibrant green pond at the bottom of the bowl. Do not throw this precious liquid away, but turn

to p.286 at your earliest convenience. Transfer the slices to another bowl – sorry for the extra washing up – and toss gently with the chopped dill.

6. Pack into your cold, sterilised jar. Strain the now cold pickling liquid into a jug, and pour over the cucumber slices, so that they are just covered, and leave to stand for 30 minutes before serving. Or place straight in the fridge, where it'll last for a week: it'll look a bit faded after a few days, but still be good to eat. And you must take it out in time to lose the fridge chill. I like to serve it, as I do the Pickled Red Cabbage, in its jar, with a fork in it, but if you want to serve it in a bowl, sprinkle a little more freshly chopped dill over it as you take it to the table.

GREEN, MEAN, DIRTY MARTINI

I can't say that this cocktail, in itself, particularly conjures up Christmas. In fact, it would be perfect on hot summer days (for those in the southern hemisphere, of course, the two are combined) but it incontestably belongs here, as it is an emanation of the Scandi Cucumber Salad, the previous recipe in this chapter and a crucial part of my Christmas Eve supper.

I have Caz Hildebrand, who has been the Art Director on all my books, to thank for this, as for so much over the years. It is she, who, on tasting the vivid green juice left behind in the bowl after the cucumber had been salted for the salad, suggested I make a dirty martini with it. Could a person be more right? This salty viridescent liquid is not merely an excellent substitute for the olive-tin brine in a dirty martini, but – I am most agreeably convinced – a superior one.

You may, of course, use vodka or gin in it, but the obvious choice would be, were you to have it in your drinks cupboard, a gin that is distilled itself with cucumber. And should you have a bottle lurking about somewhere, you could always use aquavit instead to enhance the Scandinavian flavour of the evening. Or, maybe better, keep the martini as it is, and have an icy shot or two of the aquavit – when it becomes *snaps* – with the No-Knead Black Bread (p.305) and smoked salmon.

MAKES 1 martini

4 x 15ml tablespoons (60ml) gin or vodka

1 x 15ml tablespoon dry white vermouth

2 x 15ml tablespoons liquid leftover after salting cucumbers (see p.283)

Ice cubes, for shaking

1. Put a martini glass in the fridge or freezer to get good and cold.

2. Pour the gin (or vodka), dry white vermouth and the salty cucumber liquid into a cocktail shaker, along with a generous tumble of ice cubes. Shake it vigorously and then strain into your chilled martini glass. *Skål!*

POMEGRANATE FIZZ

This is a twist on an old favourite from The River Cafe in West London, which consists simply of delicately and grapily aromatic Moscato d'Asti, its sweetness all but swallowed up by the fierce sourness of limes. At home, you do not need to reach for the most exquisite of wines; a bottle of Asti Spumante or any sweet, sparkling Muscat you can find, will do just fine. Added to it, most seasonally, is freshly squeezed pomegranate juice along with the lime, offering its own fragrant sweet-sharpness. Yes, you can get pomegranate juice in a bottle, but this tastes very much better if you halve those beautiful, jewel-seeded crimson and coral coronated globes and squeeze them yourself. It's hardly laborious to do, even with a manual citrus press, and you need get only 100ml of juice from both pomegranate and lime.

While these are the proportions I like, it may well be that you want to vary them to your taste, so go slowly as you add juice to fizz, sipping a little after each addition. It's always hard to say exactly how much juice each fruit will yield, so to be on the safe side I have assumed that both the pomegranates and limes will be relatively unjuicy specimens. While it's important that the fruits are both at room temperature – if you juice them from the fridge, you'll get much less out of them – you should chill both juices before mixing the cocktail. If you can fit the jug for the cocktail itself in the fridge, too, so much the better. I mean, you want a relatively small pitcher or jug – you need it to hold no more than a whisper under a litre – but I know that fridge space is at a premium at Christmas.

MAKES approx. 950ml

4–5 limes, to yield 100ml juice, or more as needed

1–1½ pomegranates, to yield 100ml juice

1 x 75cl bottle of sweet fizzy Muscat wine, chilled

1. Juice the limes, pouring into a small measuring jug as you go, and stop when you get to 100ml. Cover and place in the fridge.

2. Now juice the pomegranate, bearing down on top and against the sides of the halved pomegranate so that the seeds really come into contact with the citrus press, and after each half is done, squeeze the juiced half with your hands to get out any more drops you can. When you have 100ml, duly strain this into a cup, glass or little jug, and place this in the fridge, too. If you have room, put the serving jug into the fridge at the same time.

3. When it's drinks time, open the fizzy Muscat and pour it slowly into your serving jug, so as not to let it froth up too much. Once the bubbles have quietened down, add the pomegranate juice, give the gentlest of stirs, then add half the lime juice, give another gentle stir, and spoon a little out into a shot glass to taste, then slowly – sipping after each addition, but steady now – pouring in as much of the remaining lime juice as you need to make it exactly as you like it.

BLACK TREACLE SAUSAGES

Over the years I have categorically insisted that there can be no party without cocktail sausages. With heavy-duty entertaining no doubt off the cards this year, I had thought not to include them in my seasonal eating schedule, but find I cannot do without them. I now realise that the parties were just an excuse for having the cocktail sausages.

The black treacle in these gives them a dark, deep, rich savouriness, edging on bitter, aided and abetted by the marmalade. I have given the choice of ginger conserve – often, itself, called ginger marmalade – as its peppery fire partners the molasses-rich treacle and fat of the plump juicy sausages just as rewardingly. And it is for that same pepperiness that I use, for preference, cold-pressed rapeseed oil here, but its contribution is a minor one. You may replace it with olive or other vegetable oil, without undue concern.

You certainly don't need a dip to go with these, but should you want one, I must tell you that these sausages are wonderful dunked in a sauce made with equal parts grain mustard and crème fraîche (or sour cream), with or without some finely grated ginger stirred in as well.

MAKES 30, which should be enough for 4–6

3 x 15ml tablespoons cold-pressed rapeseed oil (or other oil of your choice)

1 x 15ml tablespoon black treacle

1 x 15ml tablespoon dark, bitter marmalade or ginger conserve

½ teaspoon fine sea salt

30 cocktail sausages

For make-ahead, store and/or freeze notes, see p.336

1. Heat the oven to 170°C/150°C Fan.

2. Mix together 2 tablespoons of the oil, 1 tablespoon each of black treacle and marmalade (removing the shreds or bits, which I do, most efficiently, by eating them) and the salt in a small bowl.

3. Separate the cocktail sausages, and arrange them on a lipped baking sheet, preferably one that is light-coloured and non-stick (otherwise line with baking parchment). Give the treacle mixture a good stir and spoon half of it out on top of the sausages and turn everything together well so that the sausages are very lightly coated all over. Drizzle over the remaining tablespoon of oil, and give everything another schmoosh, before taking to the oven and cooking for 30 minutes.

4. Remove the tray of sausages and, with a bendy spatula, scrape out every last bit of the remaining half of the treacle mixture on top of the sausages, and gently turn everything together in the tray. Put back in the oven to cook for a further 10 minutes, by which time the sausages should be cooked – though do check – and a deep, glistening brown. Remove the tray from the oven, and let stand for about 5 minutes, then turn once again in the sticky tin to coat the sausages, allowing yourself the cook's treat of eating one (or two) before transferring to a plate which you can then proffer generously.

RUBY NOODLES

These are, quite simply, a seasonal showstopper.

I first came across pasta cooked in beetroot juice in Felicity Cloake's wonderful *A–Z of Eating* (she in turn had found it in an American food magazine) and knew I had to make it. I did, and continue doing, although my recipe is rather different. Hers is a plate of hot pink spaghetti, tossed with toasted walnuts and wilted baby kale, and dotted with soft goat's cheese; I prefer mine cold (yes, really), spiky with garlic, ginger and chilli, the intense and earthy sweetness of the beetroot tempered with lime. Of course, there's nothing to stop you eating these spicy, sweet and sour noodles hot, but even if you're unconvinced by the idea, I implore you to try them cold.

It makes for a spectacular store-cupboard supper as the beetroot juice comes in cartons and, what's more, has a long shelf life. And while I always need an infusion of chilli and ginger and zingy sourness over Christmas, which these ruby noodles gloriously provide, there is something beautifully festive, too, about a bowl of stickily scarlet spaghetti, tossed in olive oil, and dill, with a salty snow of feta on top. To cook the pasta for this, follow the first three steps of the recipe below, but leave the ginger out of the beetroot juice, halve the garlic and chilli, and replace the lime with 2 teaspoons of lemon juice. Serve with as much chopped dill and crumbled feta as you like, and eat immediately.

But when I make the cold gingery noodles, I always like to have enough left over to keep boxed up in the fridge for another day. They will absorb their dressing, but you can bring back their glisten by adding a little sesame oil, a splash or two of soy and a spritz of lime.

SERVES 4

450ml beetroot juice

2 limes

2 fat cloves of garlic

2 teaspoons grated fresh ginger

2 teaspoons sea salt flakes (or 1 teaspoon fine sea salt)

½ teaspoon dried chilli flakes

350g spaghetti

2 teaspoons toasted sesame oil, plus 2 teaspoons more

3 teaspoons fish sauce

1 teaspoon plus 1 x 15ml tablespoon brown rice vinegar

4 teaspoons soy sauce

4 x 15ml tablespoons roughly chopped coriander

2 x 15ml tablespoons finely chopped chives

For make-ahead, store and/or freeze notes, see p.336

1. Put water on to boil for the spaghetti, adding salt as usual when it comes to the boil.

2. Pour the beetroot juice into another pan, also large enough for the pasta later, and add the juice of one of the limes. Peel and mince or grate in the garlic, then stir in (I'd advise against using a wooden spoon, unless you don't mind its getting stained) the grated ginger, salt and chilli flakes. Once you put the pasta in to cook, bring this pan to a simmer over low heat.

3. Cook the spaghetti in the salted boiling water for 5 minutes, then drain, add to the simmering beetroot juice pan, turn up the heat so that the beetroot juice bubbles more robustly, and cook it until the pasta is al dente. This can take up to 8 minutes, but check at 5. It really depends on the spaghetti you are using but I find it cooks more slowly in the beetroot juice. At any rate, you will need to hover over the pan a bit, tossing it around with a pasta fork every now and again to make sure it doesn't stick. When the spaghetti's cooked, it will have absorbed all the bubbling beetroot juice, except for a scant, shiny scarlet syrup. If the spaghetti has absorbed all the beetroot juice before it has cooked, add in a little hot water from a just-boiled kettle, very slowly, and in gradual increments, as needed.

4. Once the pasta is cooked, take the pan off the heat and add 2 teaspoons of the sesame oil, 2 teaspoons of the fish sauce, 1 teaspoon of the brown rice vinegar and 2 teaspoons of the soy sauce, toss well, and decant into a shallow bowl to cool.

5. It will be quite sticky when cold, but don't panic. In a little jug, mix together the juice of half a lime, the remaining 2 teaspoons of sesame oil, the tablespoon of brown rice vinegar, the last teaspoon of fish sauce, and the last 2 teaspoons of soy sauce, pour over the noodles and toss to combine. Taste for seasoning and sprightliness; you may want more lime juice or salt. Add the chopped herbs, toss to mix, and devour.

TUSCAN BEAN SOUP

This is a real rib-sticker of a soup, warming and filling, and just what you need on a cold night when you've been eating a lot of meat. It's my version of the Tuscan *ribollita* and, strictly speaking, the beans in question should be cannellini. I much prefer borlotti, as I find their more tender skins help them to cook into a soft fuzziness, losing their intrusive pebbliness so much faster. I'm sure it's not the case in Tuscany, but the dried cannellini sold in the UK seem nearly always to have an impenetrably tough skin. But I'm not entirely regionally incorrect: I do use cavolo nero, which is also called Tuscan kale. You could just as easily use regular curly kale. But this is really a soup built around whatever ingredients you have to hand, so make the most of its generosity; what's in your vegetable drawer will no doubt dictate your choices: I have made a wonderful version using celeriac in place of the potatoes.

Primarily, of course, it's there to use up stale bread, and although I don't believe my black bread would be a good choice, any sourdough or country-style loaf would do. You can always do what I do, and bag up stale bread whenever you have it, stash it in the freezer and dig it out when you want to make this. Similarly, you can soak your beans and freeze them, ready to be made into soup, without having to plan for it the night before. It's not for me to forbid you to use beans out of a can, but I don't, unless in an emergency: I never get a canned bean to melt creamily into the soup in quite the right way. But if you do have to use them, I'd suggest two tins and that you add them to the pan with the cavolo nero. Should you have an old Parmesan rind knocking about (and yes, I do stash these in the freezer as well, since you ask), do add it to the soup along with the water.

The vegetably goodness of this soup, combined with its fortifying double-carb action, makes it ideal when you may be feeling festively frail. In which case, may I suggest you add a splodge of the Fermented Hot Sauce (p.300)?

I have marked the fennel seeds as optional, purely because I am so used to having to leave them out when I cook this for certain members of my family (said with a sigh) who fail to appreciate anything in the aniseed arena.

I make this routinely even if I don't have six people to eat it, turning the leftovers into a savoury bread pudding. Fill an ovenproof dish with the solidified soup, top lavishly with grated cheese and bake in a 200°C/180°C Fan oven for about 30 minutes or until piping hot and bubbling under the melted cheese.

It is only fair to warn you that, unless you have already-soaked beans put away in your freezer, you will have to embark on this soup the day before you want to eat it.

SERVES 6

250g dried borlotti beans

250g onions

3 x 15ml tablespoons olive oil

1 stick of celery

1 large or 2 smaller carrots
  (approx. 200g)

3 fat cloves of garlic

500g potatoes

1½ teaspoons finely chopped
  rosemary needles

3 x 15ml tablespoons freshly
  chopped flat-leaf parsley

1 teaspoon fennel seeds (optional)

¼ teaspoon dried chilli flakes

2 x 15ml tablespoons tomato purée

2 litres cold water

2 teaspoons sea salt flakes (or
  1 teaspoon fine sea salt)

3 fresh bay leaves

Approx. 500g cavolo nero

2 thick slices of stale sourdough or
  other robust bread

TO SERVE, AS WISHED

Freshly grated Parmesan

Hot sauce

For make-ahead, store and/or freeze notes, see p.336

1. Soak the borlotti beans in copious amounts of cold water overnight, or for at least 8 hours.

2. Peel and chop the onions. Get out a large heavy-based pan or casserole (I use one of 26cm diameter) and warm the oil in it. Add the chopped onions, and cook for 5 minutes over medium heat, and then another 5 on low. They won't soften in that time, but should have turned translucent and lost their raw look.

3. Finely slice the celery, and peel and finely chop the carrot. Add to the pan, give a good stir, and continue to cook for another 5 minutes.

4. Peel the garlic and mince or grate into the pan, and peel the potatoes, chop into 2cm cubes and stir into the vegetables in the pan, followed by the rosemary, parsley, fennel seeds (if using) and chilli flakes.

5. Spoon in the tomato purée, giving a good stir to mix it in. Drain the beans, add them to the pot, and pour in the 2 litres of water. Add the salt and bay leaves, and bring to the boil over high heat.

6. Once it's come to a good rolling boil, turn the heat down, put the lid on at a jaunty angle, so that the pan is partially covered, and cook for about 45 minutes at a robust simmer.

7. Check to see if the beans are cooked through. They may well be, or then again, they may need up to 30 minutes more, in which case put the lid on fully, so you don't lose any more liquid.

8. Once the beans and potato cubes are soft, tear the leaves off the stalks of cavolo nero and add to the pan before clamping on the lid and cooking for 10 minutes.

9. When the greens are cooked, take the pan off the heat. Tear the bread into chunks and stir into the pot. Put the lid back on and leave for 5–10 minutes for the bread to swell and soften in the soup. Serve immediately with Parmesan and hot sauce as wished. By the time you get to second helpings, it will be solid – which tastes so much better than it sounds.

FERMENTED HOT SAUCE

Christmas eating may hinge on sandwiches, but I feel that chiefly, Christmas is all about the condiments. The two are not unconnected, of course. The choice of condiments is an intensely personal one, as anyone who has ever been brought fruitlessly into an argument about whether it should be ketchup or brown sauce in a bacon sandwich can attest. (And for me, it's neither of those, by the way: all I require is that the bread be dunked in the bacon fat and then smeared with English mustard.) The list of my must-have condiments would run too long to fit in here, but at the top would be the aforementioned mustard, Chilli Crisp oil, Crispy Anchovy Chilli, hot lime pickle and mango chutney, this last essential for a turkey sandwich.

And then there is this. If you are a hot sauce and sriracha eater, this is for you: the hottest of hot sauces, full of fire from the chillies and deep, peppery heat from the ginger. But it's the ferment that gives the sauce its addictive pull, creating a funky, complex sourness that you can never quite have enough of.

Please don't let the talk of ferment make you feel that this is a complicated exercise. You simply mix up the chillies, ginger, garlic and salt as instructed below, put in a jar, leave for a couple of weeks, burping it daily, before blending and bottling. We get through so much of this sauce in my house, I always have a batch on the go, and keep a daily alarm on my phone instructing me to 'burp sauce'. All this means is that you unclip the jar it's fermenting in, hold it up, and lightly pat its bottom, helping the carbon dioxide bubbles to rise to the surface.

Chillies differ enormously in heat, even those that are ostensibly the same variety, and so the amount of sugar and vinegar you add when you blend the sauce after it's fermented will vary. You should also know that the sauce breathes the most fire when it is just blitzed and bottled. The longer it hangs around – which may not be very long – the more forcefully the tang develops and the heat mellows, if only slightly.

I know that 'red chillies' is not the most precise descriptor, but that is baldly how they are customarily sold in the UK. The ones labelled as long red chillies are also fine here. I caution in the strongest terms imaginable against using either Scotch bonnet or bird's-eye chillies.

For once, I am going to say that you must not treat the quantities below as approximate. As instructed by a long-time fermenter, I work on the principle that the amount of salt needed is 2% of the weight of the food you are fermenting (though obviously people have been fermenting food long before they had weighing scales). This is the required amount to allow the bacteria you want to develop, and also to destroy the bacteria you most definitely don't want.

300g red chillies

50g cloves of garlic

150g fresh ginger

10g fine sea salt

1–2 x 15ml tablespoons (12–25g)
 caster sugar

1–2 teaspoons sea salt flakes (or
 ½–1 teaspoon fine sea salt)

For make-ahead, store and/or freeze notes, see p.336

1. Wash a 900ml preserving jar (or a 1 litre one would be fine), rinse thoroughly and let it drain and dry naturally, that's to say, without using a cloth.

2. Remove the stalks from the chillies, and peel the garlic. Scrape the skin from the ginger, using the tip of a teaspoon.

3. You can either chop them all by hand – somewhere between roughly and finely – then mix in a large bowl with the salt, or use a processor. If so, process them briefly, with the salt, then pulse until chopped but not reduced to mush.

4. Spoon this mixture into your clean (and now cold) preserving jar. Press it down with a spatula, then get a resealable freezer bag with a zip and sit it on top of the patted-down contents, with its mouth open, so that its seal sticks out slightly higher than the top of the jar. Of course, if you have fermenting weights, do use one instead, but this is my favoured method.

5. Carefully fill the freezer bag with cold water and don't let any spill down the inside of the jar. In other words, run the tap slowly. Close the zip on the bag, expelling any air as you do so, and then screw or clip on the lid. The weight of the water-filled bag keeps the ingredients underneath the brine that they make as they ferment.

6. I stash the jar on a bookshelf, as I feel this protects it from too much cold or too much heat. With the jar thus protected, I haven't found enormous variation on fermenting times through summer and winter, though obviously heat will speed up the process and cold will retard it. Still, it's hard to be precise: a lot depends on just how fermented you want your hot sauce to be. For me 14 days seems to be the sweet – or sour – spot, but you will have to develop your own relationship with both process and sauce to work out what suits you.

7. With the proviso above, let us work on a 14-day fermentation period. You will need to burp your sauce every day. In other words, unclip or remove the lid, lift the water-filled bag up a little, though you can keep it in the jar, and gently pat the bottom of the jar. This prevents any gassy build-up, but it won't matter if you miss the odd day. I find this a very bonding exercise. It also allows you to smell the development of the ferment.

8. You will be able to decide for yourself whether you want to ferment the sauce for a shorter or longer time the more you make it, but for now let's say that once the 14 days are up, wash and dry naturally (as before) a 500ml jar. When it's cold, tip the chopped chillies, garlic and ginger and their funky brine into a bowl you can use with a stick blender. Scrape the jar with a bendy spatula to make sure you don't leave even a fleck of chilli behind.

9. I prefer this sauce smooth, like a vicious ketchup, so I blend it thoroughly; you can obviously have it as chunky as you want. Once it's the desired consistency, add 1 tablespoon of sugar and 1 teaspoon of sea salt flakes (or ½ teaspoon of fine sea salt). Stir it in and taste to see if you want to add the remaining sugar and salt. How much you'll want depends on the fermentation, the heat of the chillies to start off with, and, of course, your own taste. And if you grow to love this sauce as much as I do, as soon as you're blending one jar, you will be chopping up your chillies and so forth for the next.

10. Once you have blitzed your sauce, keep it in the fridge if you don't want it to ferment further, although I'm happy to leave mine out as we all whip through it so fast. While I am obliged to tell you officially that it should only be kept at room temperature for 1 week, I must confess that I do not follow the guidance I must give. At any rate, it's best to keep it in a cool place in the kitchen. If you get through your sauce more slowly than I do, unclip it and burp it regularly. But the risk is yours to take, so keep it in the fridge if you feel happier that way.

NO-KNEAD BLACK BREAD

Sometimes I can get so fixated on a recipe that I find it hard to step away when, even after repeated testing and retesting, what I'm looking for continues to elude me. I'm glad that I persisted here, where more reasonable people would long since have given up, as I have finally created the dark, treacly bread I had hitherto only imagined and obsessed over.

The thing that made me persist is that I had got the taste right straight-away; the properly dense and chewy – but not too dense or too chewy – texture of the crumb took longer to achieve. It was the crust that nearly defeated me: it was either too dry, or too hard, or just split cavernously in the oven. But it was so nearly right so often: that small gap between what I was baking and what I knew it should be became a torment.

Early iterations of this bread relied on a traditional kneading method, but things looked up once I applied what I'd learned from Jim Lahey's life-changing No-Knead Bread (see p.39). But the loaf still held out on me. I knew I needed some expert input. So I spoke to the great baker Dan Lepard. He told me to make fewer additions to the dough (something I couldn't quite bring myself to do, as I knew I wanted to hold on to the flavour) and to try adding an egg. I did. That got me closer. The solution turned out to lie in using just the white of the egg, with the yolk reserved to wash the top of the loaf before it went into the oven.

Although it tastes like traditional Eastern European black bread, I have to concede that the stout in the loaf – its ferrous tang partnered by black treacle and mellowed by dark muscovado sugar – is a louche aberration. And nigella seeds are certainly not *echt*. In fact, I can't claim authenticity – that suspect and contentious entity – for much of it. And nor do I care.

I love this bread with smoked salmon, smoked trout, any smoked fish: so far so traditional. And this is indeed how I suggest you serve it as a first course, if one is wanted, before the Norwegian Pork Ribs (p.265). But I also have to say, it is quite spectacular with taramasalata. And it's spirit-liftingly glorious when spread with the almost fluorescently pink Beetroot and Chick-pea Dip (p.199), topped (though it's not compulsory) with slices of avocado, with its tender green flesh, and a few fronds of dill. And although I could stay listing ways you could eat it forever, I won't. But I have to mention curd or cream cheese with some fresh horseradish stirred into it.

I find it hard to imagine anyone wouldn't love this, but I know there are those who regard anything aniseedy with antagonism. And while I cannot understand this antipathy, I accept it exists. If it's one you share, this bread may not be for you. I'm sorry. Don't worry about the fact that there is cocoa in the bread: it doesn't give it a chocolatey taste at all; it just gives a touch of bitterness and helps deliver that delicious darkness. You may come across black cocoa and think this would be perfect to use here. It wouldn't. It seems (rather like coconut flour, which I have yet to be convinced is actually edible) to suck every bit of moisture out of anything it touches. You can, however, if you feel so inclined, add 1 teaspoon of activated charcoal powder to deepen the colour, as I have here.

Should you be making this for vegan company, then replace the egg white with 1 teaspoon of vegan egg-replacer powder mixed in along with the other dry ingredients, and instead of the yolk wash, glaze the loaf with 1 teaspoon of maple syrup stirred into 2 teaspoons of almond milk, although you won't get the high shine of the egg wash.

I should really tell you that any leftover bread can be turned in the processor into fabulous black breadcrumbs. I keep them in the freezer to use whenever I want to add an aniseed crunch. They are particularly good sprinkled over a tomato salad.

And, finally, a warning: you need to get started on this bread the day before you want to eat it; this is not because it is elaborate in any way to make, but just because it needs an overnight rise.

MAKES 1 large loaf

1 x 500ml bottle of Guinness or other dry dark stout, opened in advance if possible

1 large egg, at room temperature

2 x 15ml tablespoons (30g) dark muscovado sugar

2 x 15ml tablespoons extra-virgin olive oil

2 x 15ml tablespoons black treacle

300g dark rye flour

300g strong white bread flour

4 x 15ml tablespoons (25g) cocoa

1 teaspoon activated charcoal (optional; see recipe intro)

4 teaspoons nigella seeds, plus ½ teaspoon for the top of the loaf later

4 teaspoons caraway seeds

4 teaspoons fennel seeds

¼ teaspoon (1g, but it's hard to get it to register on the scales) fast-action dried yeast

1¼ teaspoons fine sea salt

Oil, for greasing the loaf tin

NO-KNEAD
BLACK BREAD

For make-ahead, store and/or freeze notes, see p.336

1. Pour the stout into a measuring jug to come up to 400ml; this will take a bit of time, as you need to wait for the frothing to subside. If you think about it ahead of time, it might be wise to open the bottle a bit earlier. Don't drink the remaining 100ml yet, as you may need some of it shortly. When the beer's calmed down enough to be measured clearly, add the white of the egg (reserving the egg yolk in a little covered bowl in the fridge for the egg wash the next day), followed by the sugar, the oil, and then the treacle. Stir or whisk gently to mix, as it may fizz up a bit.

2. Mix the flours, cocoa, activated charcoal (should you be using it), seeds, yeast and salt in a large bowl. As with the standard No-Knead Bread (p.39), I like a Danish dough whisk for this, but you can use your hands or any stirrer of choice.

3. Give your jug of dark liquid another stir, then pour a third into the bowl and mix. Repeat until all the liquid is used up. By this stage you may still need to use more liquid, so slowly stir in as much of the remaining 100ml of stout as you need to form a stiff, sticky mixture. It won't look very dark: until it's baked, it has the rich buff colour of cookie dough, unless you're adding activated charcoal, in which case it will be cowpat brown. Cover with food wrap (or a shower cap) and leave it in the kitchen for 16–20 hours, until it has increased in volume, has a slightly spongy texture and is bubbly on top.

4. Grease a sturdy 2lb (900g) loaf tin, line the base with baking parchment, and scrape the bread dough into it, smoothing it very, very gently out to the edges and on top. Drape a clean tea towel over the tin and leave for 2 hours. It will rise a little, but not much. Heat the oven to 220°C/200°C Fan towards the end of this time.

5. Add a teaspoon of cold water to the reserved egg yolk and use a little whisk or just a fork to loosen it, then dab a pastry brush into the yellow goo, and lightly paint the surface of the bread. I can't honestly say you use much of this yolk; if, like me, you find waste difficult, then just keep it to add to a couple of eggs for scrambling. Sprinkle the 1½ teaspoons of nigella seeds on top and put the tin into the oven, straightaway turning the heat down to 200°C/180°C Fan. Bake for 40 minutes, then (wearing oven gloves, and perhaps giving a nudge around the edges first with a small palette knife) slip it out of its tin. It will feel almost cooked, but it is a dense, weighty loaf: don't expect white-bread lightness; even when fully cooked, this loaf feels as heavy as a brick.

6. Give the loaf a knock underneath: it probably won't sound hollow, but register the sound. Put it, out of its tin now, back into the oven directly on the shelf, for 10–15 minutes, by which time it will feel firm, but still with a bit of give at the sides and, when you knock it underneath, it will sound, if not exactly hollow, then hollower than it did before. Allow to cool completely on a wire rack before even thinking of cutting into it. To keep the loaf fresh for as long as possible, store in a bread bin. The next best method is to wrap it in a tea towel.

LINZER COOKIES

In its wildest dreams, a jammy dodger could never aspire to the melting tenderness and celestial lightness of the Linzer cookie. The idea is the same: two biscuits, sandwiched together with jam, a hole or small shape cut out of the top one, so that the jam glints beckoningly through. But the Linzer cookie is the extravagant Austrian Christmas version, the dough rich and short with ground toasted hazelnuts.

I buy skinned hazelnuts that have already been toasted, but it's easy enough to find blanched or skinned hazelnuts and not enormously hard work to toast them on a lipped baking sheet in a 180°C/160°C Fan oven for 10–15 minutes. But you must make sure they're completely cold before you grind them to dust. Of course, you could change tack altogether and replace the hazelnuts with 100g of ready-ground almonds.

You'll need a 6cm round cookie cutter (smooth, not crinkle-edged) to make these and, ideally, a set of mini Christmas cutters, though you could always use the sharp end of a piping nozzle. I do feel the investment in the mini cutters is worthwhile, however, as I foresee many batches of these in your future.

MAKES 28 sandwich cookies, with ruthless re-rolling

100g skinned toasted hazelnuts (see recipe intro)

125g caster sugar

300g plain flour, plus more for rolling out

200g unsalted butter (cold if using a processor, soft if making by hand)

¼ teaspoon ground cinnamon

⅛ teaspoon fine sea salt

1 large egg, at room temperature

1 large egg yolk, at room temperature

Icing sugar, to dust the cookies

Approx. 4 x 15ml tablespoons redcurrant jelly

Approx. 4 x 15ml tablespoons seedless raspberry jam

For make-ahead, store and/or freeze notes, see p.336

1. For the processor method: tip the toasted hazelnuts and sugar into the bowl of the processor and blitz until you have fine sand, then add the flour. Cut the cold butter into 1cm dice and add to the processor, along with the cinnamon, salt, whole egg and egg yolk. Run the processor until the contents start to cohere and form a dough; this won't happen instantly, so be patient.

2. If you don't have a processor but have a bullet blender, you can grind the hazelnuts in that. Or if you have neither, simply use ready-ground almonds. And to make the cookies by hand, mix the ground nuts with the flour, cinnamon and salt and set aside for a moment. Cream the butter and sugar together. Whisk together the whole egg and egg yolk in a jug then beat them very gradually into the butter mixture. Add the dry ingredients, a little at a time, and beat in until the mixture forms a soft dough.

3. Whether you've mixed the dough by hand or in a processor, divide evenly into 4. Roll each quarter into a ball, then gently squash to form fat patties. Cover tightly in food wrap and put in the fridge for 1 hour. You can, in fact, leave them in the fridge for up to 3 days.

4. Once your dough has rested, take two of the discs out of the fridge and let them stand for about 15 minutes, or longer if either your fridge is very cold or the dough's been sitting in it for a long time, heating the oven to 180°C/160°C Fan while you wait. Get out a couple of cookie sheets and cut two pieces of baking parchment to exactly the same size as the sheets.

5. Put one piece of parchment directly on the counter and when the dough feels ready to roll – firm, but not too cold – roll out one of the discs thinly (2–3mm thick) on it. If you find your dough is very sticky, you can roll it out between two pieces of parchment.

6. Using a 6cm round cookie cutter, dipped first in flour, cut 6 circles out of the rolled dough. You don't have to leave a huge gap between the cookies, as the dough doesn't really spread much. Lift away the excess dough, leaving your circles on the parchment. Carefully place this parchment on one of your cookie sheets. Form a ball with this excess dough to add to the remainder of the other 3 discs later.

7. Repeat the process with the next disc, only this time you're making the top half of the cookie, so you will need to choose your mini cutters, dip them in flour and then cut out your shapes – a small hole, heart, Christmas tree, snowflake, angel or star – and if the shape you're stamping out doesn't come out with the cutter, use a cocktail stick to help. Add the offcuts to the other scraps of dough, ready for re-rolling. If your kitchen is warm it can really help to put these cookies in the fridge on their parchment-lined cookie sheet for 10 minutes or so, as it will help the cut-out shapes keep a very clean edge.

8. Bake the cookies for 9–10 minutes, until they're only just beginning to turn a very light gold at the edges; they will, overall, still be pale. Transfer straightaway to a cooling rack or, if you'd feel safer, gently slide the loaded parchment on to the rack instead.

9. Repeat the process with the 2 remaining discs and all the squidged-together offcuts, making sure the cookie sheets have cooled down before you load them up.

10. When the cookies are completely cold, they are ready to be sandwiched. Dust the biscuits you've cut a shape out of with icing sugar and leave on the wire rack for now. Mix the jelly and jam together until smooth, and spread ½ teaspoon of this mixture over one non-dusted cookie half, leaving a pale frame around the edge. Pick up a sugar-dusted cookie, carefully holding the edges only, and place it on top of the jam-loaded cookie, feeling justifiably proud of yourself and your beautiful Christmassy creation. And carry on with the rest of the cookies, your festive sense of bliss increasing giddily as you go.

LUSCIOUS VEGAN GINGERBREAD

I am preposterously proud of this squidgy gingerbread, and I don't mind who knows it. It's everything you want out of a gingerbread – sticky, spicy, deeply aromatic – and you would never miss the butter or eggs.

Eat darkly on its own, or with the glow of the Pomegranate-Poached Quinces (p.319) and some oat-milk crème fraîche.

Warning: ideally you need to make this at least a day before you plan to eat it. Harsh, I know.

GIVES 12 slabs but could easily be cut into 18

150ml vegetable oil

200g golden syrup

200g black treacle

125g dark muscovado sugar

75g pitted soft prunes (about 8 in number)

30g fresh ginger

2 teaspoons ground cinnamon

2 teaspoons ground ginger

1 teaspoon ground allspice

⅛ teaspoon ground cloves

¼ teaspoon ready-ground black pepper

¼ teaspoon fine sea salt

250ml oat milk

300g plain flour

1 teaspoon bicarbonate of soda

2 x 15ml tablespoons warm water

2 teaspoons regular cider vinegar

For make-ahead, store and/or freeze notes, see p.336

1. Heat the oven to 170°C/150°C Fan. Line a 23cm square tin with a sheet of baking parchment, so that it covers the bottom and comes up the sides of the tin. Leave something heavy on it to keep it down while you melt everything together.

2. Measure the oil in a jug, and pour it into a fairly wide, heavy-based saucepan; I use one of 22cm diameter. Measure the syrup and treacle using the oily jug, as this will stop them sticking and help them pour out easily into the saucepan.

3. Tip the sugar into the pan, and chop the prunes finely before adding them. Peel the ginger with the tip of a teaspoon and grate it finely into the pan. Sprinkle in the spices and salt and warm over gentle heat, whisking to combine. But don't whisk too much: you do not want to get a lot of air in the mixture.

4. Once everything's melted and mixed, take the pan off the heat; it should be warm at this stage, rather than boiling hot. Add the oat milk, whisking gently to make sure it's incorporated.

5. Whisk in the flour in 3 or 4 batches, getting rid of any lumps patiently as you go. This will take a few minutes; the only lumps you should see are the little bits of prune, although they will melt into the gingerbread as it bakes.

6. Dissolve the bicarb in the warm water in a bigger cup than you think it needs, then add the vinegar and quickly whisk the fizzing mixture into the pan.

7. Pour the gingerbread batter into the lined tin carefully and bake for 50–55 minutes, though start checking at 45. It may look cooked at 45 minutes, but as it's so damp, a cake tester won't help enormously – you'd expect some crumbs to stick to it – so take it out of the oven and touch the top quickly; if cooked, it should bounce back a bit under your fingers.

8. Leave to cool in its tin on a rack, although I'm afraid I'm going to caution you against eating it the minute it's cold. To taste this at its best, wrap the tin first in baking parchment and then in foil, and leave for a day or two before cutting into it.

BLACK FOREST BROWNIES

I don't need much of an excuse to bake a brownie, and I've rather started to feel that I am not alone in this. They are, quite simply, the quickest route to a delectable dessert or anytime treat I know.

And these Black Forest Brownies are particularly fabulous: softly studded with kirsch-soaked cherries, with a few toasted hazelnuts for crunch, and a little freshly chopped rosemary for bosky redolence.

I have long made a stack of brownies, each pronged with a cake candle, for birthdays, and I propose you pile these up, dust them with icing sugar and stud with birthday candles, to flicker in the festive spirit.

If you can't find hazelnuts that are ready-toasted, toast them on a lipped baking sheet for about 10–15 minutes in a 180°C/160°C Fan oven, then tip them into a shallow bowl to cool while you get on with the brownie batter. And if you don't have kirsch or would rather not use alcohol, then simply soak the dried cherries in orange juice.

The dried fruit, alcohol and rosemary don't make these particularly child-friendly but why should they have all the fun?

MAKES 16 brownies

150g dried cherries

75ml kirsch (or orange juice)

200g dark chocolate (70% cocoa solids), preferably labelled 'for cooking'

200g unsalted butter

100g dark muscovado sugar

225g caster sugar

¼ teaspoon fine sea salt

25g cocoa

4 large eggs, at room temperature

100g toasted hazelnuts

150g plain flour (or gluten-free plain flour)

1 teaspoon finely chopped rosemary needles

Icing sugar, for dusting

For make-ahead, store and/or freeze notes, see p.336

1. Heat the oven to 180°C/160°C Fan. Line a 23cm square tin with baking parchment. Leave something heavy on it to keep it down while you make the brownies.

2. Put the dried cherries into the smallest saucepan you have, pour over the kirsch (or orange juice) and bring to the boil, stirring frequently to make sure all the cherries get turned in the liquid. Once it comes to the boil, let it bubble for a minute, then take the pan off the heat, leaving the cherries to cool a little, and soak up the liqueur or juice.

3. Chop up the chocolate and cut the butter into slices to help it melt. Put these slices into a wide-ish saucepan – I use one of 22cm diameter – and melt over very low heat. Add the chopped chocolate, and when it is all but melted into the butter, take the pan off the heat, stir gently with a spatula, add the sugars, salt and cocoa, stir gently again, and take off the heat and leave to cool a little.

4. Crack your eggs into a jug, and whisk to combine. Put the hazelnuts into a bag, and bash with a rolling pin to break them up a bit. Rather satisfyingly, most of the hazelnuts spring apart in two perfect halves.

5. Gradually whisk the beaten eggs into the pan of melted chocolate and, when they're incorporated into the batter, slowly whisk in the flour, until you can't see it any more. Tip the steeped cherries, bashed hazelnuts and chopped rosemary into the pan, and fold to mix, then scrape into your lined tin.

6. Bake in the oven for 25–30 minutes. When the brownies are cooked, the top will look a little dry, and the edges will be beginning to come away from the sides of the tin. A cake tester should come out with a few damp crumbs attached, but no raw batter. They will, however, be delectably gungy inside.

7. Leave to cool in their tin on a wire rack, even though they are gorgeous warm; they won't hold their shape until they're cold, though. Dust with icing sugar on serving. And if you put any leftovers (I know) in the fridge, you will be rewarded: fridge-cold, these brownies taste like the most glorious fudge.

POMEGRANATE-POACHED QUINCES

There is something magical about these poached quinces, with their soft, scented terracotta-tinted flesh and glowing pomegranate-perfumed syrup. While I eagerly make them from November onwards, as soon as the quinces come into season, they are so fabulously festive cooked like this, decoratively and decorously demanding a place at your Christmas table.

Don't get misled by the fact that they're fruit: this may seem like a light dessert, but in fact it is headily intense. Three quinces are more than enough for six people and, if you're lucky, will provide you with leftovers. I use these up greedily, either making a crumble with them (and see the recipe for the topping on p.235, though you may well need to halve it, as you're unlikely to have enough to fill a big dish) or fashioning them into a quick-assemble plate trifle. By this, I simply mean I line a small plate with slices of loaf cake – you can use the Marzipan Loaf Cake on p.70, the Lemon and Elderflower Drizzle Cake on p.75 or just use a lemon or vanilla shop-bought one – then dampen with Marsala or sherry, top with some softly whipped cream, the left-over quinces and a scattering of pomegranate seeds and toasted flaked almonds.

Should quinces elude you, you can make Pomegranate-Poached Pears. Make the syrup as for the quinces, reducing the sugar to 250g. Peel 6 firm pears – I suggest Williams, and you don't want them very ripe, which is probably just as well, as most pears are sold unripe – keeping the stalk intact. Cut a little off the bottom of each pear, so that it will be able to stand up on a plate later, and chisel out the core from the underneath. Try to remove it, and the seeds if you can, without damaging the rest of the pear. If you feel that's too fiddly, ignore me and just peel and poach. They won't need as long as the quinces; 45 minutes should do it, but do check them regularly while they cook.

SERVES 6

700ml pure pomegranate juice (from a bottle is fine)

300ml cold water

350g caster sugar

3 fresh bay leaves

1 teaspoon pink peppercorns

A few sprigs of fresh thyme, plus more to decorate

3 quinces

2–3 x 15ml tablespoons pomegranate seeds, to sprinkle over

For make-ahead, store and/or freeze notes, see p.336

1. Heat the oven to 160°C/140°C Fan. Get out a large, heavy-based casserole that has a lid, and into it pour the pomegranate juice and water, and add the sugar, watching it mesmerised as the white sugar is engulfed by the rubied liquid. Well, you don't have to watch, but I do.

2. Stir well, add the bay leaves, pink peppercorns and a few sprigs of thyme, leaving the daintier sprigs for later, then stir again and set over low heat. You can leave it warming while you get the quinces ready.

3. Peel and quarter the quinces and then, carefully, core them. I sometimes, out of exhaustion or laziness, leave the cores in; the almost ethereal aroma of quinces never quite prepares one for their stony solidity. Unless you happen to have small quinces, cut the cored quarters in half lengthways. Add the prepared quinces to the pan as you go, as they'll brown quickly when exposed to the air.

4. When all the quinces are in the pan, turn the heat up. Once it starts boiling, scrunch up a piece of baking parchment slightly bigger than the diameter of the pan, unscrunch it again, and press it down on top of the quinces, tucking it in and up the sides of the pan. Clamp on the lid, and stagger over to the oven.

5. Cook for 1½–2 hours, until the quinces feel tender when you prong a few with the tines of a small fork. Remove the lid and the baking parchment, and, with a couple of spoons, turn the quinces over in their red liquid before leaving them to cool. I often make these a couple of days in advance and just leave the quinces in the pomegranate syrup, darkening ruddily as they sit.

6. Not long before you're ready to serve them, remove 150ml of the syrup (use a heat-resistant glass measuring jug) and pour into a small saucepan. Set the pan over high-ish heat, bring to a bubble and keep it bubbling, watching over it the whole time, until it has reduced by half. I keep the glass measuring jug right by the hob so that I can keep checking. When the garnet-glinting syrup is viscous and reduced, and you have 75ml of it, leave it to cool. If you have space in your freezer, you can strain the rest of the poaching liquid, bag or tub it up and keep it for repeat performances. Or strain it, reduce it by half and keep it to pour over ice cream, or to scent pears or apples for pies or crumbles, or indeed, add to cocktails as you wish.

7. Using a slotted spoon, convey the quinces to a shallow bowl or plate with a slight lip, shaking your cargo gently over the pan as you go, so that you don't get too much liquid into your dish. Drizzle over the syrup, and scatter with pomegranate seeds and fresh thyme sprigs. Serve with real crème fraîche or oat-milk crème fraîche.

CHRISTMAS BREAD AND BUTTER PUDDING

I love the Christmas ritual of endless cold cuts. For me, that's an essential part of the season. But I know there are those who can grow restive when they see that poor old bird brought out for the third time. However, any grumbling over the cold comfort of what seems the constant reappearance of Christmas lunch leftovers can be soothingly silenced, the mutiny dispelled, by a hot pudding straight from the oven.

A bread and butter pudding is pretty effortless to make, and this special Christmas edition doesn't require anything fancy: you simply sandwich the slices of bread with mincemeat or fig jam. The former may call to those in particular who have an open jar of mincemeat knocking about in the kitchen; for those who shudder at the very idea of dried fruit, and feel a bit beleaguered on that front at this time of year anyway, the latter offers sweet salvation. Besides, after a mincemeat bread and butter pudding, what could be more seasonally suitable than a Figgy Bread and Butter Pudding?

When I came back from my last visit to Australia, I brought with me six jars of the darkest, treacliest Burnt Fig Jam and, eking out my last pot, I mixed it, half and half, with a less hard-hitting fig jam for this. But you can create that same fireside smokiness by making the caramel part of the Crème Caramel on p.87, and quickly whisking or forking it into your jam, already spooned out safely in a heatproof bowl. It will turn into solid splinters at this stage, but all will come good in the oven later. However, it's a high-stress activity for this time of year, and is only to be considered if you like cooking on the edge.

Finally, I use ready-sliced bread, but if the idea appals you, then by all means cut the slices yourself from a more distinguished loaf.

SERVES 4–6

6 slices of white bread

6 x 15ml tablespoons (90g) soft
unsalted butter, plus more to
grease dish

6 x 15ml tablespoons fig jam or
mincemeat

3 large eggs, at room temperature

2 x 15ml tablespoons (25g) caster
sugar

½ teaspoon ground cinnamon

300ml double cream, at room
temperature

300ml full-fat milk, at room
temperature

FOR THE TOPPING

1½ teaspoons demerara sugar

Icing sugar, for dusting

For make-ahead, store and/or freeze notes, see p.336

1. A couple of hours before you plan to make the bread and butter pudding, take the bread slices out of the packet (or slice the bread if you're not using ready-sliced) and lay them out to stale slightly.

2. Butter a pie dish with about a 1½ litre capacity; I use an oval one 28cm long, and measuring 20cm across at its widest point.

3. Butter the slices of bread generously, spread half of them with the jam or mincemeat, make sandwiches with the three remaining buttered slices, and cut each sandwich into 4 small triangles. Arrange these in your dish, overlapping each other in as orderly or higgledy-piggledy fashion as you like; you can tell which camp I'm in.

4. In a batter jug or similar, whisk the eggs with the caster sugar and the ½ teaspoon of cinnamon, and then gradually whisk in the cream and milk. Pour this over the sandwiches in the dish, making sure the crusts get wet, and leave to stand for at least 30 minutes, or up to 2 hours. Spoon the custardy mixture over the slices now and then during this time, paying particular attention to the crusts.

5. Heat the oven to 180°C/160°C Fan. When it reaches temperature, sprinkle the demerara sugar over the top of the pudding, then bake for 35–40 minutes, until crisp and golden on top, with the custard around the bread puffy and softly set. But then, aren't we all at this time of year? Let stand for 10–20 minutes and then dust lightly with icing sugar, letting a little seasonal snow fall on the golden pudding. Take to the table with a jug of double cream for people to pour over their bowls as they eat. It is Christmas, after all.

NEW YEAR DOUGHNUTS

I am not one for New Year's Eve parties at the best of times – the combination of enforced jollity and large crowds makes what's left of my soul shrivel – but I rather suspect that even those who are less curmudgeonly and more gregarious than I am might not find themselves out carousing this New Year's Eve.

But there are other ways of celebrating, and I propose we go Dutch. In the Netherlands, it is customary to see in the New Year with doughnuts; all of the kingdom, it is said, smells of frying and icing sugar on New Year's Eve. This is a tradition I am more than ready to adopt.

The Dutch doughnuts in question (and, indeed, often called just that in America) are *oliebollen* (pronounced ollybollen), which with wonderful literalness, just means "oil balls". True, if you buy them from one of the many kiosks lining the streets in Holland from November onwards, you might see just why they got their name, though these little ones I have for you are anything but greasy. They need only 5 minutes' frying, by which time the outside is good and crisp, and the inside bouncy and soft. And while they are indeed supposed to be ball-shaped, I love it when the dough drips a little as they go into the pan, making super-crunchy spikes in the hot oil.

To be truly traditional, you should add raisins and currants to the *oliebollen* dough, but I much prefer mine plain. It's not unheard of to eat them without the dried fruit in Holland, either, though it's more usual to find both fruited and unfruited versions served together. Should you want the raisins and currants in your *oliebollen*, then soak about 2 tablespoons of each in rum or orange juice overnight the day before you plan to make them. Or put the dried fruit into a small pan, cover with the liquid, whether rum or orange juice, and bring to the boil, and let everything bubble for a minute. Then switch off the heat and leave your currants and raisins to steep until cold. Either way, fold the plumped-up fruit into the dough once it's mixed up and ready to prove.

I can't leave it there. Nor do many Dutch. For *oliebollen* have a partner in crime, and their name – thrillingly – is *appelflappen* (which you pronounce much as you'd think you would) and although they are not actually doughnuts, but peeled and cored apple slices in the lightest of batters, they do look like miniature ring doughnuts. I think they might even be my favourite of the two, for I do love a fritter. They are also known as *appelbeignets* and, indeed, for many Dutch *appelflappen* refer rather to deep-fried apple turnovers. But I've always known these deep-fried apple rings as *appelflappen*; what name they go by largely depends on which part of the Netherlands you're in. Moreover, it seems in practice, the two words are used interchangeably; and I know which one I prefer.

What's crucial here is the variety of apple you use: it needs to be able to soften in the few minutes the fritter batter takes to cook. Cox's Orange Pippins would be my first choice, though I often use the much-disdained Golden Delicious which – although they lack the Cox's slightly sharp edge and fragrance – slice well and cook to wonderful juiciness very fast. You may well find another apple you prefer; if Egremont Russets were in season over the New Year, I would definitely choose them. Whatever you do, though, don't use Granny Smiths, however much you like eating them: they stay too crunchy and seem almost to dry out as they fry.

Now, deep-frying is never an entirely stress-free exercise, but should you be in possession of an electric deep-fat fryer (and I confess I eagerly bought one as an early Christmas present to myself) you will find it a relatively breezy undertaking. You can, of course, deep-fry the *oliebollen* and *appelflappen* in a saucepan, but then you will need a digital or jam thermometer so that you can monitor the heat and keep the oil at the right temperature. It's not enough just to drop in a cube of bread and know it's the right temperature if it bubbles up immediately, for it's a long game, and the trick is to keep the heat constant.

All doughnuts are best eaten immediately, but should you have any left over, you can heat them up on a baking sheet in a 180°C/160°C Fan oven for about 5 minutes, dust them with icing sugar when out, and give yourself a rather fabulous New Year's Day breakfast.

OLIEBOLLEN

MAKES approx. 30

250g plain flour

A pinch of salt

2 x 15ml tablespoons (25g) caster sugar

2½ teaspoons (7g) or 1 sachet fast-action dried yeast

250ml full-fat milk

An exuberant grating of nutmeg

1 lemon

1 teaspoon vanilla extract

2 x 15ml tablespoons (30g) soft unsalted butter

1 large egg, at room temperature

Sunflower oil for frying; depending on what you're frying in, approx. 4 litres in a deep-fat fryer, and approx. 1.5 litres in a 22cm diameter pan

Icing sugar, for dusting

For make-ahead, store and/or freeze notes, see p.336

1. Mix the flour, salt, sugar and yeast in a large bowl.

2. Pour the milk into a saucepan or, if you have a microwave, a measuring jug. Either way, finely grate in a generous amount of nutmeg, followed by the zest of the lemon, add the vanilla and butter and heat until lukewarm; I just give the milk 45 seconds in the microwave at top whack, which for me means 900W. And it doesn't matter, by the way, if the butter doesn't melt entirely.

3. If you've heated the milk in a pan, pour it into a jug. Crack the egg into the jug, quickly whisk it in, then pour the lukewarm, lemon-scented, nutmeggy, buttery and eggy milk into the dry ingredients, beating vigorously with a wooden spoon or a little hand whisk until you have a smooth dough. Well, I say 'dough' since you're making doughnuts with it, but actually it has more the consistency of thick cake batter.

4. Cover the bowl with food wrap or a slightly dampened tea towel, and leave in a warm place for about 1¼ hours, until the dough has puffed up voluminously and the surface is a mass of large bubbles. When I was young, the airing cupboard was always the place where dough would be left to prove, but times change, and I put the bowl on a shelf up above all the computer bits and pieces and their flashing lights, aka Mission Control. A warm and steamy kitchen will do fine, though. (And if you wanted to make the dough in advance, you could instead stash the bowl, covered with food wrap, in the fridge to rise slowly overnight or for up to 24 hours, in which case, let it come to room temperature before proceeding to step 5.)

5. Using, for ease, a bendy spatula, scrape down the sides, which will deflate the dough. It will start bubbling up again as you wait for the oil to heat.

6. If you're going to make your *oliebollen* in an electric deep-fat fryer – which is very much easier – pour in sunflower oil until it reaches the minimum mark. Otherwise, use a heavy-based saucepan at least 12cm deep and no less than 22cm in diameter – pour in enough oil to come up about 3½cm. Heat the oil to 180°C. Don't leave the oil unattended while it heats up, but you can potter about nearby, getting yourself a rounded metal tablespoon measure and a teaspoon to shape the doughnuts (though you could just use a couple of dessert spoons) and some tongs to turn them as they fry and to retrieve them once they're cooked. You'll also need to line a couple of large plates with kitchen paper (replacing as necessary) and fill a small bowl with cold oil for you to dip your spoons in while cooking.

7. Once the oil is at 180°C (and if you're frying them in a saucepan, you really do need to use a digital or jam thermometer) carefully dip your rounded tablespoon measure and teaspoon (or pair of dessert spoons) into the cold oil, then scoop up a tablespoon of dough, using the teaspoon to help mould it and then release it gently into the hot oil, then do the same to make a second one and

fry them about 2½–3 minutes a side, so that they are a deep golden brown all over, and the dough is cooked all the way through. And the only way to find out is to eat these first two, allowing them to cool for a few minutes and dusting each with icing sugar before you bite in.

8. Once you're happy with the timings, repeat the process (without necessarily eating them all) to fill your pan without overcrowding it; I don't like to fry more than four or five at the same time.

9. Transfer them as they're ready to the paper-lined plates to blot the excess oil. Leave them on the kitchen paper for 3–5 minutes; the icing sugar will melt if it's sprinkled on them when they're piping hot. Then arrange on a few plates, and dust generously with icing sugar. Eat immediately.

MAKES approx. 28

75g plain flour

25g cornflour plus ½ teaspoon per apple

¼ teaspoon (1g, but it's hard to get it to register on the scales) fast-action yeast

100ml full-fat milk

1 x 15ml tablespoon (15g) soft unsalted butter

1 large egg, at room temperature

1 x 15ml tablespoon (12g) caster sugar per apple

½ teaspoon ground cinnamon per apple

6 Cox's Orange Pippins (or 4 Golden Delicious) apples

Sunflower oil for frying; depending on what you're frying in, approx. 4 litres in a deep-fat fryer, and approx. 1.5 litres in a 22cm diameter pan

Icing sugar, for dusting

For make-ahead, store and/or freeze notes, see p.336

1. Mix the flour, the 25g of cornflour and ¼ teaspoon of yeast together in a medium-sized mixing bowl; it needs to be a wide one for ease of dunking later.

2. Either in a saucepan or, if using a microwave, a measuring jug, heat the milk and butter until just lukewarm; I give it 20 seconds on high (which for me means 900W) in the microwave.

3. If you've warmed the milk in a pan, pour it into a jug. Crack the egg into the jug of buttery milk, and immediately mix it in with a little hand whisk, with an end a bit like a bearded loop.

4. Pour the eggy, buttery milk into the dry ingredients, whisking vigorously and patiently until smooth, and with the consistency of pancake batter. Cover, either with food wrap or a slightly

dampened tea towel, and leave in a warm place (and see step 4 of the previous recipe) for about 1¼ hours, by which time it will be dotted with tiny bubbles, many no bigger than pinpricks. Place the bowl of batter as near to your frying station as you safely can.

5. If you're going to make your *appelflappen* in an electric deep-fat fryer – which is very much easier – pour in sunflower oil until it reaches the minimum mark. Otherwise, use a heavy-based sauce-pan at least 12cm deep and no less than 22cm diameter – pour in enough oil to come up about 3½cm. Heat the oil to 180°C, and though you must stay near the pan as you wait, you can look away briefly to prepare the apples, but – unless you're using an electric deep-fat fryer – do keep breaking away from that to check back on the oil.

6. I prefer to do the apples 2 at a time, using a shallow dish for each. I'm sorry about the extra washing up, but – as my late husband John used to say – throw the cat another canary. You're going to be washing up a greasy pan or deep-fat fryer later on: another bowl or plate is neither here nor there. So, get two shallow dishes out and, in each, stir together 1 tablespoon of caster sugar and ½ teaspoon each of cornflour and cinnamon. And line a large plate with a double layer of kitchen paper. Keep the roll handy, as you'll need to replace it over the course of your frying.

7. Peel and core 2 apples and cut each one into slices about ½cm thick. I reckon on getting 8 or 9 rings out of each Golden Delicious and 6 or 7 out of each Cox, though my record is far from seamless; one bad cut, and you've lost a ring. Besides, it may be wiser to get fewer slices out of each apple and not risk cutting yourself. At any rate, add the rings from each apple to its designated dish, and turn them, one by one, in the sugar, cornflour and cinnamon.

8. When the oil is at temperature – and you will need to have a digital or jam thermometer handy if you're frying the *appelflappen* in a saucepan – take a cinnamony apple ring from its dish, and lower it into the batter, turning it a few times (don't worry about the batter getting cinnamony). Lift it out by hooking your index finger through the hole, hold it over the batter bowl for a moment, before carefully and very gently releasing it into the oil and fry for about 3 minutes a side, until the batter is golden brown and crisp and the apple within juicy and soft.

9. Using tongs, but taking care not to break the thin, crisp coating, transfer the *appelflap* to your paper-lined plate and leave it there for a couple of minutes before dusting it with icing sugar and eating it to make sure you're happy with the timings. If you are, proceed as before, this time frying 4 apple rings at a time. And I always set the timer once the fourth ring has gone in. Repeat the process with the remaining apple slices.

10. Wipe out the dishes with kitchen paper before mixing up your sugar, cornflour and cinnamon again. Turn the heat off under the pan while you prepare the apples for the next batch. Make sure the oil comes back up to temperature, and skim out any strands of batter left behind (crunch on them privately – cook's treat), before you fry, fry, and fry again.

11. Leave the slices on the kitchen paper for 3–5 minutes; the icing sugar will melt if it's sprinkled on them when they're piping hot. Then arrange on a few plates, and spoon icing sugar into a fine-mesh sieve or tea strainer and push against it with the back of a tea-spoon to dust the *appelflappen* with icing sugar. Serve immediately. They will get a bit soggy if left standing about. But that's unlikely to happen: they disappear fast.

MAKE-AHEAD, STORE AND FREEZE NOTES

If there are no make-ahead, store or freeze notes for a recipe below, that is because it is not recommended. Once cooked, all food must be cooled, covered and stored in the fridge as quickly as possible, and within 1–2 hours of making. Reheat leftovers only once. When reheating, follow the instructions given and check that all food is piping hot all the way through to the centre.

p.18 **Spaghetti with Chard, Chilli and Anchovies**
Make Ahead – Prepare chard a day ahead. Store, covered, in fridge.
Store – Refrigerate leftovers, covered, for up to 3 days. Reheat in microwave or saucepan over medium heat, adding a little water if needed, until piping hot. Or eat cold.

p.22 **Celeriac and Anchovy Gratin**
Make Ahead – Assemble gratin up to 2 days ahead, press food wrap onto surface to submerge celeriac and refrigerate. To cook, add extra liquid if needed, dot with butter and then bake, allowing an extra 20 minutes or so until piping hot.
Store – Refrigerate leftovers, covered, for up to 2 days. Reheat in a microwave or transfer to ovenproof dish, cover with foil and heat in 180°C/160°C Fan oven until piping hot.
Freeze – Freeze leftovers in airtight container for up to 3 months. Defrost overnight in fridge. Reheat as above.

p.26 **Anchovy Elixir**
Make Ahead/Store – Store in airtight container in fridge for up to 2 weeks. Shake well before use.

p.39. **No-Knead Bread**
Store – Store in airtight container or wrapped in clean tea towel in cool place for 3–5 days.
Freeze – Freeze loaf or slices in freezer bags, removing as much air as possible, for up to 3 months. Defrost at room temperature. Layer slices with baking parchment or food wrap if using individually. Slices can be toasted from frozen.

p.43 **Old-Fashioned Sandwich Loaf**
Store – Store in airtight container or wrapped in clean tea towel in cool place for 4–5 days.
Freeze – Freeze loaf or slices in freezer bags, removing as much air as possible, for up to 3 months. Defrost at room temperature. Layer slices with baking parchment or food wrap if using individually. Slices can be toasted from frozen.

p.52 **Crab Mac 'n' Cheese**
Make Ahead – Prepare cheese sauce (without crab) up to 1 day ahead. Press baking parchment onto surface and refrigerate. Reheat in saucepan over low heat until piping hot, cook the pasta and continue as directed in recipe. Eat when freshly made.

p.57 **Wide Noodles with Lamb Shank in Aromatic Broth**
Make Ahead – Prepare lamb shank to end of step 4 up to 3 days ahead. Store lamb and broth together, covered, in fridge. Reheat as directed in recipe.
Store – Refrigerate leftovers and use within 24 hours. Heat in saucepan over medium heat, stirring, adding extra liquid if needed, until piping hot. Noodles will soften on reheating.
Freeze – Freeze lamb (fat removed and meat shredded) covered with broth in airtight container for up to 3 months. Defrost overnight in fridge.

p.60 **Fish Finger Bhorta**
Store – Refrigerate leftovers, covered, for up to 3 days. Reheat in microwave until piping hot. Or eat cold.

p.63 **Smoky Squid and Beans**
Store – Refrigerate leftovers, covered, and use within 24 hours. Eat cold.

p.67 **Fried Chicken Sandwich**
Make Ahead – Marinate chicken up to 2 days ahead. Refrigerate, covered, then cook as directed in recipe.

p.70 **Marzipan Loaf Cake**
Store – Store in airtight container cool place for up to 7 days.
Freeze – Tightly wrap whole loaf slices in double layer of food wra then wrap loaf in layer of foil or slices in airtight container. Freez for up to 3 months (loaf) or 1 mo (slices). Unwrap and defrost on rack at room temperature.

p.75 **Lemon and Elderflower Drizzle Cake**
Store – Store in airtight contain in cool place for up to 5 days.
Freeze – Tightly wrap whole loaf its tin) or slices in double layer o food wrap, then wrap tin in layer foil or put slices in airtight cont Freeze for up to 3 months (loaf) 1 month (slices). Unwrap and de on wire rack at room temperatur

p.78 **Gluten-Free Banana Bread Chocolate and Walnuts**
Store– Store in airtight containe in cool place for 4–5 days.
Freeze – Tightly wrap whole loaf its tin) or slices in double layer food wrap, then wrap tin in laye foil or put slices in airtight cont Freeze for up to 3 months (loaf) 1 month (slices). Unwrap and de on wire rack at room temperatu

p.80 **Chocolate, Tahini and Ban Two Ways**
Store – Store banana bread in a container in cool place for up to 5 days. Refrigerate pudding left covered, for up to 5 days. Can b reheated in microwave.
Freeze – Tightly wrap whole loa slices in double layer of food wr then wrap loaf in layer of foil or slices in airtight container. Free for up to 3 months (loaf) or 1 m (slices). Unwrap and defrost on rack at room temperature.

p.84 **Mine-all-Mine Sweet and Salty Cookies**
Make Ahead – Prepare dough c up to 5 days ahead, cover and refrigerate. Bake as directed in allowing an extra 1–2 minutes.
Store – Store in airtight contai for up to 1 day. Warm gently in

owave at 70% power (600W) for
econds. Do not reheat gluten-
cookies.
ze – Freeze uncooked dough
s on lined baking sheet until
, transfer to airtight container
reeze for up to 3 months. Bake
frozen as directed in recipe,
ing an extra 2–3 minutes.
dually wrap baked cookies when
place in airtight container and
e for up to 3 months. Unwrap
efrost at room temperature.
n same day.

Crème Caramel for One
e Ahead – Prepare up to 3 days
d, cover and refrigerate.
ove from fridge 30 minutes
e serving.

Burnt Onion and Aubergine Dip
e Ahead – Prepare up to 5 days
d, cover and refrigerate.
ove from fridge 1 hour before
ng.
e – Freeze in airtight container
o to 3 months. Defrost
ight in fridge.

Soupy Rice with Celeriac
Chestnuts
– Leftovers can be stored in
dge, covered, for up to 2 days.
at gently in saucepan, stirring,
g extra liquid if needed, until
hot.
e – Freeze in airtight container
o to 3 months. Defrost
ight in fridge. Reheat as above.

Short Rib Stew for Two
Ahead – Prepare up to 3 days
. Refrigerate, covered, and
t as directed in recipe until
hot.
– Refrigerate leftovers and
thin 24 hours. Reheat until
hot.
e – Freeze in airtight container
to 3 months. Defrost
ight in fridge. Transfer to
ole dish and reheat as
ed in recipe.

Marrowbone Mince
Ahead – Prepare up to 3 days
, cover and refrigerate.
reading on toast, reheat
cepan over medium heat
iping hot. For serving with
ings, reheat in casserole over
m heat until piping hot, add
ings, transfer to preheated
nd cook as directed in recipe.

Store – Refrigerate leftovers and
use within 24 hours. Reheat until
piping hot.
Freeze – Freeze in airtight container
for up to 3 months. Defrost
overnight in fridge and reheat
as above.

p.112 Beef Cheeks with Port and
Chestnuts
Make Ahead – Prepare up to 3 days
ahead. Refrigerate, covered, and
reheat as directed in recipe until
piping hot.
Store – Refrigerate leftovers and
use within 24 hours. Reheat until
piping hot.
Freeze – Freeze in airtight container
for up to 3 months. Defrost
overnight in fridge. Transfer to
casserole dish and reheat as
directed in recipe.

p.116 Oxtail Bourguignon
Make Ahead – Prepare up to 3 days
ahead. Refrigerate, covered, and
reheat as directed in recipe until
piping hot.
Store – Refrigerate leftovers and
use within 24 hours. Reheat until
piping hot.
Freeze – Freeze in airtight container
for up to 3 months. Defrost
overnight in the fridge. Transfer
to casserole dish and reheat as
directed in recipe.

p.122 Black Pudding Meatballs
Make Ahead – Prepare sauce up to
3 days ahead, cover and refrigerate
or freeze as below. Form meatballs
up to 1 day ahead using mince
and black pudding straight from
fridge. Refrigerate on baking sheets,
covered loosely with food wrap.
Remove from fridge 1 hour before
cooking. Reheat sauce in large
saucepan until just boiling, reduce
to a simmer and add meatballs.
Store – Refrigerate leftovers,
covered, for up to 3 days. Reheat
gently in saucepan until piping hot.
Freeze – Freeze leftover cooked
meatballs in sauce in airtight
container for up to 3 months.
Defrost overnight in fridge and
reheat as above. Freeze sauce only
in airtight container for up to 3
months. Defrost overnight in fridge.

p.138 Rhubarb and Custard Trifle
Make Ahead – Prepare trifle
(without cream layer) up to
1 day ahead, cover and refrigerate.
Remove from fridge 1–2 hours

before serving, then top with
whipped cream.
Store – Refrigerate leftovers,
covered, for up to 2 days.

p.144 Toasted Marshmallow and
Rhubarb Cake
Make Ahead – Bake sponges up to
1 month ahead. Once cold, wrap
each sponge in double layer of food
wrap. Freeze on baking sheet until
solid, remove from baking sheet,
wrap in layer of foil and freeze until
needed. Freeze egg whites in grease-
free, airtight container for up to
1 month. Defrost egg whites
overnight in fridge and bring to room
temperature before making frosting.
To assemble cake, make frosting as
directed in recipe. Remove sponges
from freezer and assemble cake
while the sponges are still frozen
and frosting is slightly warm. Toast
frosting then let cake stand for 1–2
hours before slicing. The cake with
frosting is best on day it is made.
Store – Refrigerate leftovers,
covered, for up to 1 day. Frosting
will soften slightly in fridge.

p.150 Pickled Rhubarb
Make Ahead/Store – Seal in
sterilised jar and refrigerate as
soon as cool for up to 4 weeks.
If processed in a water bath, store
in a cool, dark, dry place for up to
1 year. Once opened, refrigerate and
use within 1 month.

p.152 Beetroot, Rhubarb and
Ginger Soup
Make Ahead/Store – Prepare up to
5 days ahead, cover and refrigerate.
Reheat gently in saucepan, stirring,
until piping hot. Or eat chilled.
Freeze – Freeze in airtight container
for up to 3 months. Defrost overnight
in fridge and reheat as above. Or eat
chilled.

p.161 Chicken in a Pot with Lemon
and Orzo
Store – Refrigerate leftovers,
covered, for up to 3 days. Reheat in
microwave or saucepan over medium
heat, stirring and adding extra water
if needed, until piping hot. Pasta will
soften on reheating.
Freeze – Freeze leftovers in airtight
container for up to 3 months. Defrost
overnight in fridge. Reheat as above.

p.164 Chicken with Garlic
Cream Sauce
Make Ahead – Prepare sauce to

end of step 5 up to 1 day ahead, cover and refrigerate. Reheat in saucepan, stirring, until piping hot, then add chicken juices.

Store – Refrigerate chicken and sauce leftovers, covered, for up to 3 days. Reheat sauce in saucepan until piping hot. Reheat chicken in microwave or transfer to ovenproof dish, cover with foil and heat in 180°C/160°C Fan oven until piping hot. Or eat cold.

Freeze – Freeze leftover chicken only in airtight container for up to 3 months. Defrost overnight in fridge. Reheat as above.

p.168 **One-Pan Chicken with Apricot Harissa and Sweet Potatoes**
Store – Refrigerate leftovers, covered, for up to 3 days. Reheat in microwave or transfer to ovenproof dish, cover with foil and heat in 180°C/160°C Fan oven until piping hot. Leftovers can also be used to make soup.

Freeze – Freeze leftovers in airtight container for up to 3 months. Defrost overnight in fridge. Reheat as above.

p.171 **Lasagne of Love**
Make Ahead – Prepare meat sauce up to 3 days ahead, cover and refrigerate until needed. Assemble lasagne (without cheese topping) up to 2 days ahead, cover and refrigerate until needed. Add cheese and bake as directed in recipe.

Store – Refrigerate leftovers, covered, for up to 2 days. Reheat in microwave or cover with foil and heat in 180°C/160°C Fan oven until piping hot.

Freeze – Freeze assembled lasagne (without cheese topping) for up to 3 months. Tightly wrap dish in double layer of food wrap and layer of foil. Defrost for 24 hours in fridge. Add cheese and bake as directed in recipe. Freeze leftovers in airtight container for up to 3 months. Defrost overnight in fridge and reheat as above.

p.177 **Pappardelle with Cavolo Nero and 'Nduja**
Store – Refrigerate leftovers, covered, for up to 3 days. Reheat in microwave or saucepan, adding extra water if needed, until piping hot. Pasta will soften on reheating.

p.181 **Spiced Bulgur Wheat with Roast Vegetables**
Store – Refrigerate leftovers, covered, for up to 5 days. Reheat in microwave

or transfer to ovenproof dish, cover with foil and heat in a 180°C/160°C Fan oven until piping hot. Or eat cold.

p.184 **Fear-Free Fish Stew**
Make Ahead – Prepare sauce up to 5 days ahead, cover and refrigerate until needed. Place in saucepan, bring to boil and then reduce to simmer and continue as directed in recipe.

Store – Refrigerate leftovers, covered, for up to 1 day. Reheat in microwave or saucepan, adding extra water if needed, until piping hot. Fish will be flakes rather than pieces on reheating.

Freeze – Freeze sauce only in airtight container for up to 3 months. Defrost overnight in fridge before using. Freezing stew with fish is not recommended.

p.199 **Beetroot and Chickpea Dip**
Make Ahead – Roast beetroots up to 2 days ahead, refrigerate until needed.

Store – Refrigerate leftovers, covered, for up to 3 days.

Freeze – Freeze in airtight container for up to 1 month. Defrost overnight in fridge and use within 24 hours. If dip separates on defrosting, blitz again in food processor.

p.202 **Roast Red Peppers with Pomegranate Molasses and Dukkah**
Make Ahead – Roast peppers up to 2 days ahead, cover and refrigerate. Bring to room temperature before serving. Prepare dukkah and store in airtight container in a cool place for up to 1 month or in fridge for up to 3 months.

Store – Refrigerate leftover peppers, covered, for an extra 3 days. Bring to room temperature before serving. Refrigerate dressing, stored in jar, for up to 1 week. Warm as directed in recipe before serving.

Freeze – Freeze dukkah in airtight container for up to 6 months. Defrost for 1 hour before using. Or sprinkle direct from frozen.

p.206 **Root Vegetable Mash**
Make Ahead – Prepare up to 5 days ahead, cover and refrigerate. Reheat as directed in recipe intro until piping hot.

Store – Refrigerate leftovers,

covered, but do not exceed 5 day storage time from point of cooki Reheat as directed in recipe intr until piping hot.

Freeze – Freeze mash in airtight container for up to 3 months. Defrost overnight in fridge. Rehe as directed in recipe.

p.209 **Brown Butter Colcannon**
Make Ahead – Prepare brown b up to 2 weeks ahead, cover and refrigerate until needed.

Store – Refrigerate leftovers, covered, for up to 3 days. Rehea in microwave or transfer to ovenproof dish, cover with foil a heat in 180°C/160°C Fan oven u piping hot. Or use to make patti

Freeze – Freeze brown butter or in airtight container for up to 3 months. Defrost overnight in fridge.

p.214 **Fennel Gratin**
Make Ahead – Assemble dish tc end of step 5 up to 2 days aheac press food wrap onto surface to submerge fennel and refrigerate Bake, allowing an extra 15 minu until piping hot.

Store – Refrigerate leftovers, covered, for up to 1 day. Reheat in microwave or transfer to ovenproof dish, cover with foil a heat in a 180°C/160°C Fan oven until piping hot.

Freeze – Freeze leftovers in airt container for up to 3 months. Defrost overnight in fridge. Reh as above.

p.216 **Roast Cauliflower with Apricot Harissa and Spinach**
Make Ahead/Store – Prepare a harissa up to 2 weeks ahead, cc and refrigerate.

Store – Refrigerate cauliflower leftovers, covered, for up to 5 d Reheat in microwave or transfe ovenproof dish, cover with foil heat in 180°C/160°C Fan oven piping hot. Or eat cold.

Freeze – Freeze apricot harissa in portions in ice cube trays. Once frozen, transfer cubes to airtight container. Defrost for 1 hour at room temperature an use immediately.

p.220 **Crisp and Creamy Artichoke Hearts**
Store – Refrigerate leftovers, covered, for up to 5 days. Eat c

extra shaved Parmesan or
rino Romano, if wished.

**Butternut with Beetroot, Chilli
Ginger Sauce**
e Ahead – Butternut squash can
epared and coated with oil and
es up to 2 hours ahead. Cover and
e in cool place until needed. Or
t up to 3 hours ahead and leave
om temperature until needed.
t beetroot up to 2 days ahead and
are sauce up to 1 day ahead. Cool,
r and refrigerate until needed.
e – Refrigerate leftover butternut
sh, covered, for up to 5 days.
at in 200°C/180°C Fan oven
) minutes or let come to room
erature before serving. Refrigerate
er sauce, covered,
p to an extra 4 days.

**Spice-Studded Rice with
y Shallots, Garlic and
ew Nuts**
e Ahead – Fry garlic, shallots and
ew nuts up to 2 hours ahead.
fer to fresh kitchen paper and
at room temperature for up to
rs. Can transfer to baking
and warm for 5–10 minutes
)°C/80°C Fan oven before adding
e.
– Refrigerate leftovers,
ed, for up to 2 days. Rice must be
erated within 2 hours of making.
ts, garlic and nuts soften when
d. Reheat in microwave until
g hot and serve immediately.

Chocolate Peanut Butter Cake
Ahead – Prepare frosting
but cream) up to 1 day ahead.
and store in cool place. Whisk
ng briefly then whisk in cream
e using.
– Store leftovers in airtight
iner in cool place for up to
s.
e – Freeze sponge layers,
dually wrapped in double layer
d wrap and layer of foil, for up
nonths. Unwrap and defrost at
temperature for 2–3 hours.

Cherry and Almond Crumble
Ahead – Prepare crumble
ng up to 1 week ahead. Cover
frigerate until needed or freeze
ow. Prepare fruit ahead and
erate, covered, as directed in
. Bake crumble up to 1 hour
. Leave in warm place before
g.

Store – Refrigerate leftovers,
covered, for up to 5 days. Reheat
in microwave or transfer to
ovenproof dish, cover with foil and
heat in a 180°C/160°C Fan oven until
warmed through. Remove foil for
last 5 minutes to let topping crisp
up a little. Or eat cold.
Freeze – Freeze crumble topping
(without flaked almonds) in freezer
bag or airtight container for up to
3 months. Use direct from frozen.
Freeze individual portions of leftovers
in airtight container for up to
1 month. Defrost overnight in fridge.
Reheat as above. Or eat cold.

p.238 Rice Pudding Cake
Store – Refrigerate leftovers,
covered, for up to 3 days. Must be
refrigerated within 2 hours of baking.
Eat cold.

**p.243 Blood Orange and Passionfruit
Pavlova**
Make Ahead – Prepare meringue
up to 1 day ahead. Store in airtight
container until needed. Prepare
orange segments up to 2 hours
ahead and leave at room
temperature or up to 1 day ahead
and refrigerate overnight. Prepare
orange syrup up to 1 month ahead,
cover and refrigerate. If refrigerated,
allow orange segments and syrup
to come to room temperature
before serving.
Store – Refrigerate leftovers, loosely
covered. Eat within 24 hours.
Meringue will soften slightly
in fridge.
Freeze – Freeze orange syrup
only in airtight container for up
to 6 months.

p.246 Summer Pudding
Make Ahead – Prepare pudding up
to 3 days ahead. Leave in basin and
refrigerate until needed.
Store – Refrigerate leftovers,
covered, for up to 2 days. Bread will
soften the longer it is stored.

p.251 Basque Burnt Cheesecake
Make Ahead – Prepare liquorice
sauce up to 1 week ahead. Cover
and refrigerate until needed.
Allow sauce to come to room
temperature before serving.
Store – Refrigerate cheesecake
leftovers, covered, for up to 3 days.
Refrigerate sauce leftovers, covered,
for up to 3 months.

Freeze – Freeze cheesecake
leftovers in airtight container for
up to 1 month. Defrost overnight
in fridge and eat within 24 hours.
Sauce leftovers can be frozen in
airtight container for up to 6 months.
Defrost overnight in fridge.

p.257 Vegan Lemon Polenta Cake
Store – Store in airtight container
in cool place for up to 7 days.
Freeze – Tightly wrap cake (on base
of tin) or slices in double layer of
food wrap, then wrap whole cake
in layer of foil or put slices in airtight
container. Freeze for up to 3 months
(cake) or 1 month (slices). Unwrap
and defrost on wire rack at room
temperature.

p.265 Norwegian Pork Ribs
Store – Refrigerate leftovers,
covered, for up to 3 days. Reheat as
directed in recipe until piping hot.

p.275 Jansson's Temptation
Make Ahead – Assemble dish
(without breadcrumbs) up to
2 days in advance, press food wrap
onto surface to submerge potatoes
and refrigerate. Add breadcrumbs
and bake as directed in recipe,
allowing an extra 15–20 minutes,
until piping hot.
Store – Refrigerate leftovers,
covered, for up to 2 days. Reheat
in microwave or transfer to
ovenproof dish, cover with foil
and heat in 180°C/160°C Fan oven
until piping hot.
Freeze – Freeze leftovers only in
airtight container for up to
3 months. Defrost overnight in
fridge. Reheat as above.

p.278 Roast Quinces
Make Ahead – Roast quinces up to
3 days ahead, cover and refrigerate.
Reheat as directed in recipe intro
or in 190°C/170°C Fan oven for
15–20 minutes until piping hot.
Store – Refrigerate leftovers,
covered, and use within 24 hours.
Transfer to baking sheet, drizzle with
a little olive oil and reheat as above.
Or eat cold.
Freeze – Freeze quinces in airtight
container for up to 1 month.
Defrost overnight in fridge and
reheat as above.

p.281 Pickled Red Cabbage
Store – Seal in sterilised jar and
refrigerate for up to 3 weeks.

p.283 Scandi Cucumber Salad
Store – Seal in sterilised jar and refrigerate for up to 1 week. Cucumbers will discolour slightly after 4 days but remain good to eat.

p.290 Black Treacle Sausages
Store – Refrigerate leftovers, covered, for up to 3 days. Reheat in microwave until piping hot. Or eat cold.

p.292 Ruby Noodles
Store – Refrigerate leftovers, covered, for up to 5 days. Eat cold.

p.296 Tuscan Bread, Bean and Kale Soup
Make Ahead – Prepare soup (without bread) up to 3 days ahead. Reheat in saucepan over medium heat, stirring, until just boiling, remove from heat and add cubes of bread.
Store – Refrigerate leftovers, covered, for up to 2 days but do not exceed 3 days from original cooking. Reheat in saucepan over medium heat, stirring and adding extra liquid as needed, until piping hot. Or make savoury bread pudding.
Freeze – Freeze soup (without bread) in an airtight container for up to 3 months. Defrost overnight in fridge. Reheat as above.

p.300 Fermented Hot Sauce
Make Ahead/Store – Store sauce at room temperature for 1 week. Burp sauce if not used regularly, as it continues to ferment. Refrigerate for up to 1 year, but do not seal jar tightly and burp sauce occasionally if not used regularly, as it continues to ferment a little, even when stored in cold conditions.

p.305 No-Knead Black Bread
Store – Store in airtight container or wrapped in clean tea towel in cool place for up to 7 days.
Freeze – Freeze loaf or slices in freezer bags, removing as much air as possible, for up to 3 months. Layer slices with baking parchment or food wrap if using individually. Defrost at room temperature. Slices can be toasted from frozen.

p.309 Linzer Cookies
Make Ahead – Bake cookies up to 3 days ahead. Store, unfilled, in airtight container until needed. Once filled, cookies are best eaten on same

day as they will soften over time.
Freeze – Freeze uncooked dough discs tightly wrapped and in airtight container for up to 3 months. Defrost overnight in fridge. Freeze baked but unfilled cookies in airtight container for up to 1 month. Defrost at room temperature. Fill cookies as directed in recipe.

p.312 Luscious Vegan Gingerbread
Store – Store, wrapped in baking parchment and foil or in airtight container, in cool place for up to 5 days.
Freeze – Tightly wrap whole cake left on baking parchment or slices in double layer of food wrap, then wrap whole cake in layer of foil or put slices in airtight container. Freeze for up to 3 months (cake) or 1 month (slices). Unwrap and defrost on wire rack at room temperature.

p.315 Black Forest Brownies
Store – Store in airtight container in cool place for up to 5 days or in fridge for 1 week.
Freeze – Wrap brownies individually or layer with baking parchment in airtight container. Freeze for up to 1 month. Defrost at room temperature or overnight in fridge.

p.319 Pomegranate-Poached Quinces
Make Ahead – Poach quinces up to 2 days ahead, cover and refrigerate.
Store – Refrigerate leftovers quinces, covered, for up to 3 days. Reduced syrup only keeps for an extra week, covered, in the fridge.
Freeze – Freeze poached quinces in syrup or reduced syrup only in an airtight container for up to 3 months. Defrost overnight in fridge.

p.321 Christmas Bread and Butter Pudding
Make Ahead – Assemble pudding (without topping) up to 24 hours ahead, then cover and refrigerate. Allow to come to room temperature and sprinkle with sugar before baking.
Store – Refrigerate leftovers, covered, for up to 3 days. Reheat in microwave or transfer to ovenproof dish, cover with foil and heat in 180°C/160°C Fan oven until piping hot.

p.326 New Year Doughnuts: Oliebollen
Make Ahead – Prepare dough up 1 day ahead, cover and refrigera Allow to come to room temperat before frying.
Store – Transfer cold leftovers to paper-lined plates and cover loo with more kitchen paper. Store in airtight container at cool roo temperature for up to 1 day. Reh in 180°C/160°C Fan oven on bak sheets for 5 minutes or until cris up and hot throughout. Allow to cool slightly then serve as direct in recipe.
Freeze – When oliebollen are completely cold, put in airtight container and freeze for up to 3 months. Defrost at room temperature and reheat as direc above. Or reheat direct from fro increasing reheating time to 10–12 minutes, until hot throug

p.328 New Year Doughnuts: Appelflappen
Make Ahead – Prepare batter u 1 day ahead, cover and refrigera Allow to come to room tempera before frying.
Store – Transfer cold leftovers t paper-lined plates and cover loosely with more kitchen pape Refrigerate for up to 1 day. Reh in 180°C/160°C Fan oven on win rack set over baking sheet for 5–10 minutes or until crisped u and hot throughout. Allow to co slightly then serve as directed in recipe.

NOTE
The following recipes contain raw or lightly cooked eggs, and are not suitable for people with compromised or weak immune systems, such as younger child the elderly, or pregnant women

p.16   Caesar Mayo
p.144   Toasted Marshmallow a
        Rhubarb Cake

ACKNOWLEDGEMENTS

Writing is necessarily a solitary occupation; this year especially so. And yet the making of a book relies on the support and hard work of so many others, and I am glad to be able to thank those who have indefatigably provided it. First, Mark Hutchinson who, on reading a piece I had written for my website on asparagus, told me it was the beginning of a book. As always (even if that actual piece didn't find its way into the preceding pages) he turned out to be right. My sister Horatia brilliantly supplied the title, for which I am enduringly grateful.

These have been strange conditions in which to midwife a cookbook and, even if we have all had to work together remotely, the care and attention I have received have been anything but distant. Clara Farmer and Lisa Pendreigh, my editors at Chatto & Windus, Zoe Wales, my first reader, and eagle-eyed editorial assistant, have shown a dedication that verges on the devotional.

On the food front, I am, as ever, indebted to Hettie Potter, my longtime consœur, Yasmin Othman and Caroline Stearns. And I wouldn't have even got the food I write about without Rex Goldsmith of The Chelsea Fishmonger, HG Walter, Peter Hannan (aka Meatpeter) of Hannan Meats, and Panzer's Delicatessen and Greengrocer's, where Dale Middleton, the general manager, has helped me out of many an ingredient impasse.

I am more grateful than I can say to Caz Hildebrand, my designer and art director, who once again has turned my writing and recipes into a beautiful book, aided and abetted by Jonathan Lovekin, whose painterly photographs – taken under novel conditions – illuminate these pages which, in turn, owe so much to the efficiency and hard work of Shabana Cho and Julie Martin.

While I don't use a food stylist, I cannot provide all the bowls, plates and so on needed for a book shoot, so can't thank Roya Fraser enough for hunting them down for me. I hope I never have to do another book without her. And I am so very grateful for the generosity of Summerill & Bishop and Stine Dulong of SkandiHus, who lent me tablecloths and pottery, respectively, of such beauty. I owe so much to my friend Fiona Golfar, whose wardrobe I ransacked for the photograph on the back cover, and whose kitchen cupboards I laid bare for the photos within the book (as I have, indeed, for all previous books, too).

This has been my first book with my new literary agent, Jonny Geller, and I am so grateful for his optimistic encouragement and kind ministrations. There are others, too, I wish to thank for their support in helping me bring *Cook, Eat, Repeat* into the world: namely (and in alphabetical order) Richard Cable, Gin Dunscombe, Jane Haynes, Gail Rebuck, Łucja and Erik Soläng, Kelly Spuhler, and John Whittington.

I wrote too much to leave room for a dedication page, and it's true that this anyway goes without saying, but this book is dedicated with gratitude and love to Mimi and Bruno, again and always.